To Nelson,
with thanks
for your help —
Cynthia

LIVING APART TOGETHER

# FAMILIES, LAW, AND SOCIETY SERIES

General Editor: Nancy E. Dowd

*Justice for Kids: Keeping Kids Out of the Juvenile Justice System*
Edited by Nancy E. Dowd

*Masculinities and the Law: A Multidimensional Approach*
Edited by Frank Rudy Cooper and Ann C. McGinley

*The New Kinship: Constructing Donor-Conceived Families*
Naomi Cahn

*What is Parenthood? Contemporary Debates about the Family*
Edited by Linda C. McClain and Daniel Cere

*In Our Hands: The Struggle for U.S. Child Care Policy*
Elizabeth Palley and Corey S. Shdaimah

*The Marriage Buyout: The Troubled Trajectory of U.S. Alimony Law*
Cynthia Lee Starnes

*Children, Sexuality, and the Law*
Edited by Sacha Coupet and Ellen Marrus

*A New Juvenile Justice System: Total Reform for a Broken System*
Edited by Nancy E. Dowd

*Divorced from Reality: Rethinking Family Dispute Resolution*
Jane C. Murphy and Jana B. Singer

*The Poverty Industry: The Exploitation of America's Most Vulnerable Citizens*
Daniel L. Hatcher

*Ending Zero Tolerance: Students' Right to Rational Discipline*
Derek W. Black

*The Politicization of Safety: Critical Perspectives on Domestic Violence Responses*
Jane K. Stoever

*Blaming Mothers: American Law and the Risks to Children's Health*
Linda C. Fentiman

*The Ecology of Childhood: How Our Changing World Threatens Children's Rights*
Barbara Bennett Woodhouse

*Living Apart Together: Legal Protections for a New Form of Family*
Cynthia Grant Bowman

# Living Apart Together

*Legal Protections for a New Form of Family*

Cynthia Grant Bowman

NEW YORK UNIVERSITY PRESS

New York

NEW YORK UNIVERSITY PRESS
New York
www.nyupress.org

References to Internet websites (URLs) were accurate at the time of writing. Neither the author nor New York University Press is responsible for URLs that may have expired or changed since the manuscript was prepared.

Library of Congress Cataloging-in-Publication Data
Names: Bowman, Cynthia Grant, 1945–    author.
Title: Living apart together : legal protections for a new form of family /
Cynthia Grant Bowman.
Description: New York : New York University Press, 2020. | Series: Families, law, and society |
Includes bibliographical references and index.
Identifiers: LCCN 2020004759 (print) | LCCN 2020004760 (ebook) |
ISBN 9781479891047 (cloth) | ISBN 9781479874248 (ebook) |
ISBN 9781479814459 (ebook)
Subjects: LCSH: Couples—Legal status, laws, etc.—United States. | Long-distance
relationships—United States. | Commuter marriage—United States. | Separated people—
Legal status, laws, etc.—United States.
Classification: LCC KF510 .B69 2020 (print) | LCC KF510 (ebook) | DDC 346.7301/6—dc23
LC record available at https://lccn.loc.gov/2020004759
LC ebook record available at https://lccn.loc.gov/2020004760

New York University Press books are printed on acid-free paper, and their binding materials are chosen for strength and durability. We strive to use environmentally responsible suppliers and materials to the greatest extent possible in publishing our books.

Manufactured in the United States of America

10 9 8 7 6 5 4 3 2 1

Also available as an ebook

# CONTENTS

*List of Tables*                                                        vii

Introduction                                                              1

1. LATs—Who Are They? An Introduction to Some
   LAT Couples                                                            7

2. What Does Social Science Tell Us about LATs?                          20

3. LATs in the United States: New Empirical Data                         37

4. Gender Difference in Living Apart Together                            52

5. Gay Male Couples and LAT (by David Eichert)                           78

6. LATs in the Third Age                                                 97

7. Commuter Marriage and Cohabitation                                   120

8. LATs and the Law as It Now Stands                                    139

9. How Should the Law Treat LATs?                                       153

Conclusion                                                              165

*Acknowledgments*                                                       167

*Notes*                                                                 169

*Bibliography*                                                          201

*Index*                                                                 217

*About the Authors*                                                     225

# LIST OF TABLES

3.1. Distribution of LATs, by Race, in New York and the United States, Compared with All Respondents    40

3.2. Distribution of Household Income of LATs in New York and the United States, Compared with All Respondents and with Census Data    42

3.3. Level of Education Attained by LATs in New York and the United States, Compared with All Respondents    43

3.4. Social Ideology of LATs in New York and the United States    43

3.5. Age Distribution of LATs in New York and the United States    44

3.6. Primary Reason for Living Apart Given by LATs in New York and the United States    45

3.7. Method of Sharing Joint Costs Employed by LATs in the United States    47

4.1. Distribution of LATs by Age and Gender in New York and the United States    61

4.2. Distribution of LATs by Income and Gender in New York and the United States    62

4.3. Primary Reason Why LATs Live Apart, by Gender, in New York and the United States    63

4.4. Person Most Likely to Care for You if You Are Ill: LATs in New York and the United States    64

4.5 Cost-sharing Methods in LAT couples, by Gender, in the United States    66

# Introduction

I begin by proposing a hypothetical that a law professor might use in class to stimulate discussion about the legal situation of two committed life partners, whom I call "Susie" and "Larry":

> Assume that Susie and Larry are a monogamous, sexually involved couple who are not married. They have been committed to one another in this way for 10 years and are recognized as such by their families and friends. They socialize together, take vacations together, celebrate birthdays and holidays together, and participate in each other's family events. However, they do not live together. Although in the same city, each has their own living space and maintains their own independent household budget. They spend time with one another every weekend and one night in between, splitting the cost of joint events. They are in constant contact by phone, email, and text message every day. Each is the other's closest emotional confidante. When sick, they take care of one another, even moving in if their partners cannot take care of themselves after major surgery. How should the law treat Susie and Larry—as single persons? cohabitants? married?

In this hypothetical, Susie and Larry represent a newly recognized phenomenon in family formation: committed couples who do not live in the same residence. Throughout the remainder of this book I discuss questions that are even more basic than those posed above: What should we call a couple like Susie and Larry? What does their lifestyle look like? How do they handle finances and caretaking, both physical and emotional? Do men and women, same- and different-sex couples, and couples of different ages experience this lifestyle in different ways? How do these couples differ from those who cohabit or from commuter marriages? What are the consequences of their unmarried and non-coresidential status? Answering the question about the appropriate legal treatment of couples like Susie and Larry is the ultimate goal of this book, but to do so requires first knowing a good deal about how they—and many other couples like them—live their intertwined lives.

The naming question is easy because there are terms already in use in other countries. A Dutch journalist seeking a term to describe his own relationship came up with the concept "living apart together," abbreviated as "LAT." Disseminated through international scholarly meetings in Europe beginning in 1980, this term caught on in English-speaking countries.[1] The Swedes coined a similar term: *särbo*, a compound word made up of *sär*, which means "apart," and *bo*, which is "to live," and by 1986 it was being used for official statistics.[2] Naming a phenomenon is important because when a term enters everyday usage, the conduct becomes available as an alternative lifestyle.[3] It is noticed by social scientists as well and perhaps eventually studied as a social trend. This has not happened in the United States, although there is a sizeable social science literature about LATs in Europe, the United Kingdom, Scandinavia, Australia, and Canada, which estimates that about 10 percent of the adult population falls into this category.[4] This book is an attempt to bring this family structure to greater attention in the United States.

LAT describes committed (though by and large unmarried) couples who maintain coequal and independent residences, not one home plus a second home that they both use. My own research indicates that LATs are present in the adult population in the United States in at least the same numbers as in Europe, although the lack of statistics in the United States has made it difficult to study them. The group is invisible in the census categories, classified simply as "single persons." Research in other countries shows that LAT couples are very committed to one another and provide both emotional support and physical caretaking for each other, while each partner maintains financial independence. They socialize, celebrate special occasions, and travel together but split joint expenses roughly equally or according to ability to pay, and most do not own any joint assets. The vast majority live geographically close to one another and are in daily contact, either in person, by telephone (voice and text), or by other electronic means (such as email and video conferencing).

This mode of maintaining intimate relationships has become more common relatively recently and is particularly suited to many couples in the modern world, who are responding to changed social and economic circumstances. Women now seek equality with men in both the workplace and the home; but the economy demands full-time dedication from workers, and the population is increasingly mobile. These characteristics are associated with what is referred to as the "Second Demographic Transition."[5] Although couples' reasons for living separately vary, the variations correlate primarily with the age and life stage of the partners. Younger persons who are not yet economically independent of their parents live separately because of schools or jobs in different locations, to test a relationship before cohabiting or marrying, or because they live with their family of origin and cannot afford a place of their own. Persons in midlife may do so because of constraints, such as children from previous relationships who live with them, or out of an affirmative preference for keeping their own homes and maintaining the independence that affords. Persons beyond the age of child-rearing, including those who are retired, may be unwilling to give up their autonomy and familiar surroundings, to sacrifice the financial security their own home embodies, to adapt to the living style of another person, or to alter their relationships with and inheritance plans for their children and grandchildren.

Family law in the United States (generally promulgated through state legislation, although federal statutes can be important as well) is based on a model of the traditional nuclear family and largely fails to address alternative ways of living. Currently about half of all American adults are not married.[6] Many are partnered, however, either as cohabitants or as LATs. When they separate or one partner dies, there are no legal provisions to protect them. Should there be? In my previous work on cohabitation, I argued that cohabitants who had certain qualifying characteristics should be treated as though they were married.[7] The appropriate legal treatment of LATs presents a more complicated question, which I explore in the final chapters of this book. Drawing upon the goals of family law, the legal reforms I propose would support LATs as a form of family in the functions they provide for society as a whole.

In chapter 1, I describe some of the LAT couples I have interviewed (all of whom will remain anonymous) in order to give the reader a lively sense of how they live, their concerns, and their lifestyles, introducing some themes that will recur throughout the book. Chapter 2 surveys what we know about LATs from the social science literature available from studies in the United Kingdom, Europe, Scandinavia, Australia, Canada, and Israel, along with a handful of articles about this phenomenon in the United States. I do this to mine what has been discovered about the numbers of LATs and their characteristics, how they live, the economic relationships between the partners, and the mutual caregiving they offer one another. This is followed, in chapter 3, with findings gleaned from my surveys of LATs in New York State and the United States more generally, which support many of the findings and hypotheses in the literature from other countries but diverge from them in certain respects. Although American couples display arrangements and interactions similar to their counterparts in other countries, my data about their economic relationships and mutual caregiving differ somewhat from those reported in previous studies.

In chapter 4, I begin to explore the functions of LAT for particular subgroups. First, I discuss gender differences. LAT appears to have a particular attraction for women because it allows them to maintain their independence and to avoid a gendered division of labor while still having the benefits of an intimate relationship. For some who are intensely involved in their work, raising children from a previous relationship, or both, LAT offers a way to have a physically and emotionally supportive relationship when cohabitation or marriage is undesirable. Chapter 5, written by David Eichert, describes the somewhat different way in which LAT functions for gay couples. While lesbian LAT interviewees varied little from female different-sex LATs and are thus included in chapter 4, gay males differ starkly in a number of ways, including the sexual openness of their relationships and their recent tendency to marry although continuing to live apart. In chapter 6 I summarize ways in which LAT is proving to be an attractive lifestyle for couples in what has come to be known as the "Third Age," when couples are past the age of child-rearing and typically retired from full-time work. LAT is attractive to this group because it allows them to combine independence with intimate connection, to keep their own familiar spaces, to preserve their inheritance for their children, and, in the case of women, to protect themselves against gendered divisions of domestic labor.

In chapter 7 I discuss both commuter marriage and cohabitation in order to compare and contrast those two living arrangements with

LAT and to prepare the ground for the legal analysis that follows. In chapter 8 I address how LATs are treated under the law in the United States today. Although they exist without any legal recognition or standing, LATs have in fact appeared in case law resulting from litigation in court, particularly when judges are asked to determine whether alimony previously awarded to a former spouse should be terminated based on that person's subsequent cohabitation with someone else. Many of these cases present couples who are LATs, forcing the judiciary to devise tests for determining whether a couple is in fact cohabiting or not. These cases reveal some obvious injustices in LATs' treatment by the law, such as termination of alimony decreed after a long marriage because the former wife has become involved with a new partner, despite the lack of co-residence or any financial interdependence between them. In chapter 9 I address the ultimate question: How should the law treat LATs? After outlining factors that should be considered in determining what the appropriate family law treatment of any individual should be, I argue that the law should support and facilitate LATs' mutual caretaking in a variety of ways while remaining neutral—and therefore nonpunitive—about the lifestyle that a particular couple elects.

At the end of this examination, I propose some ideas about how the law should be reformed to address this new style of coupling. My goal is also to explore our evolving concept of what constitutes the "family" that family law is meant to address.

# 1

## LATs—Who Are They?

*An Introduction to Some LAT Couples*

Before plunging into social science and statistics, let's look at some of the couples who live apart. I introduce you to them now in order to show the variety of their ages, reasons for a non-coresidential relationship, and the differing ways they make their relationships work. In contrast to the composite hypothetical I introduced at the beginning of the book, these descriptions are of real people whom I interviewed in 2016 and 2017 in the United States and England. (Their anonymity is preserved by the use of pseudonyms and the nondisclosure of identifying information.) Their stories introduce themes that will continue throughout the book.

### Jackie and Kevin: Younger LATs

Jackie was in her thirties when she met her partner, Kevin, who is 10 years older.[1] Neither had been married, although both had been in years-long relationships before, including living together with partners. The two think of themselves as a couple, and so do their families. Jackie expressed her long-term commitment to Kevin as follows: "He is the man of my life; I would like to spend the rest of my life with him." Their reasons for living apart are both practical and psychological, at least on Jackie's part. Jackie's parents bought her a studio apartment, and Kevin has government-provided accommodation linked to his job, a shared flat; neither place is big enough for two people. Yet both are such good deals economically that neither partner would want to give them up. Jackie also works from home, which would be difficult in such a small space with a cohabitant.

Jackie's reasons for living separately are more than simply practical, however. After an unhappy experience in her previous cohabiting relationship, she wants to guard her space and be able to get away from Kevin when she feels the need. This makes her feel safe, and she likes the independence of being able to make her own decisions. She is also determined to avoid a gendered division of domestic labor, which she experienced in her previous relationship. Even when Kevin wants to do "masculine" tasks around the house, she resists out of a sense of caution about the loss of her independence in this respect. Neither of them has any desire to have children, and Jackie is opposed to marriage in principle as well.

This LAT couple sees one another four or five times a week, always at Jackie's house because of Kevin's shared accommodation. They text one another about every two hours and phone once a day. They spend every other weekend together and also go away on holidays together, splitting the cost. They divide the expenses of other joint activities roughly 50/50 by alternating payment, but Kevin pays for dining out in a restaurant after the meal and Jackie reimburses him later because he doesn't like to split the bill at the table. Jackie makes less money than Kevin but feels very strongly about maintaining her financial independence. She knows he would want to help her if she encountered trouble but would resist receiving help from a man, always keeping an eye on the balance of expenditures in order to avoid an "economy of gratitude."[2]

Jackie and Kevin are young and healthy enough not to have encountered occasions when one or the other needs physical caretaking, although when Kevin had the flu Jackie went every day to his place with shopping and dinner and to change his bed. They are one another's main emotional supports. Indeed, Jackie thinks of them as being "family": "He is the closest person I can relate to, feel comfortable with, feel myself with. Just be me." Yet when asked if the law should treat them as a family, she says she doesn't want the law to intervene in her relationship—at least not now. She confesses that if they were older and in need, then perhaps this would change. Yet she fears the lack of social recognition of their relationship. "If something were to happen to one of us, there would be no social recognition of the other." And she resents that on job applications she must check the box denoting single status, saying "I am classed as single, and this bothers me, because I am not!"

This sketch of Jackie and Kevin's relationship introduces a number of themes that will recur in this book: the high level of commitment, close contact, and emotional interdependence between LAT partners; practical reasons for living apart, such as real estate incentives for LATs who live, as they do, in major metropolitan areas; financial independence from one another; and the determination of many (if not most) women LATs to avoid a gendered division of labor. Kevin also has some gendered responses: he does not want to be seen splitting the tab with a woman in a restaurant, and he aspires to do tasks that are gendered male in Jackie's home.

## Mike and Nancy: Midlife LATs

Mike and Nancy met in their forties through a dating website; both had been previously married and had children. They live 87 miles apart, and each has a good, and demanding, job in their separate locales. Thus living apart was part of the package from the beginning of their relationship. The primary reason both cite, however, is sensitivity to their children's welfare. Each lives close to their children's other parent, and several of Nancy's sons still live at home. She does not want to move them from their schools, sports, father, and friends; she also has aging family members in the area where she lives. Although her children love Mike, blended families are too complicated, she thinks. Thus, she and Mike see one another every other weekend, when she drives the 87 miles to the village where he lives; and they spend the weekend just enjoying one another, away from the strains of everyday life. At other times, they chat by phone or instant message several times a day. They have taken vacations together when Nancy can get away from her family responsibilities and split expenses roughly equally by alternating payment for joint costs.

Friends, colleagues, and Nancy's extended family all regard Mike and Nancy as a couple and invite them to events together. Mike, however, is distant both geographically and emotionally from his family of origin. This perhaps explains his response to the question whether he thinks of himself and Nancy as "family." A family, in his opinion, has children, looks after them together, and shares all the day-to-day chores of domestic life, which they do not. However, Nancy responds that they *are* family because "he is just always there for me. I could turn to him in any situation. He helps me look after the boys from a distance. I share everything about my life with him." They are clearly the main emotional supports in one another's lives, although they have not done any physical caretaking of one another, in part because they have been healthy but primarily because they live too far apart to provide assistance.

The attitudes of both Mike and Nancy toward intimate relationships are heavily influenced by their previous marriages. Mike's wife left him for another man, and this appears to have shaken his confidence about his ability to be in a residential relationship. Nancy's marriage was emotionally and psychologically abusive, and she was expected to do all the domestic labor for a family of five. Living apart avoids that. They do help out one another with tasks at which each is particularly good. Mike describes himself as "mechanically savvy" and thus will fix Nancy's car or do repairs in her house on the rare occasions when he is there. This might be thought of as gendered, but he also does the cooking for the two of them. Nancy, he says, is better about money, finances, banks, and the like, so he relies on her advice for how to handle those affairs.

Mike and Nancy both voice a desire to live together at some point, even to get married, and think they will one day end up together. Even when their children are grown, however, their jobs would still prevent living in the same place. Given their unhappy experiences with marriage, each appreciates the ability to compartmentalize their relationship from everyday life. To do so prevents conflicts ("when together, we don't have the general crap of life, putting bins out, matching socks, etc. We make nice food and pay attention to each other."). Nancy reports: "It's all about us, our relationship, not about keeping a home, family, kids, just us. We have never had an argument because we don't have the other stuff that complicates relationships." After six years, they have each gotten used to the LAT arrangement and enjoy having their own time and space. Still, at the end of a long day of work, each often thinks they "could do with a hug."

This LAT couple is in a different life stage compared to Jackie and Kevin; their reasons for living apart also differ. They might be categorized as involuntary LATs because they are separated primarily by children and jobs. Unlike the first couple, they express the desire to marry if they could. (Despite the passage of considerable time and settlement of all marital issues, one of them is still not officially divorced because of the cost of hiring an attorney to do so.) Jackie is very committed to her work and puts in long hours while also balancing the work of caring for her home and children alone. She is not interested in sharing these burdens with another person and is determined to succeed in her job. Her consequent inability to move reflects the ambitions of women today in addition to her determination never to enter a relationship that is gendered in its division of labor at home or in the market. Both Mike's and Nancy's attitudes about their relationship are heavily influenced by their past experiences in unhappy marriages and painful separations. Another point to notice about this couple—a recurrent theme—is that their relationships to their families of origin appear to affect their concept of what a family is and does for its members. Mike voices a common perception that unless there are children, a couple is not a family, whereas Nancy bases her answer on the underlying functions that families provide.

## Olivia and Patricia: A Lesbian Couple

Olivia and Patricia, now in their fifties, have been a LAT couple for more than 15 years. Each had relationships before; Patricia was in fact married twice to men, experiences she says "tainted" her attitude toward marriage. Olivia doesn't see what marriage—only recently available to same-sex couples—would add to their relationship, which is already very committed. When they met, Patricia had just purchased her house, which is tucked away in a very private location. Olivia's longtime residence, by contrast, is on a street with other houses. Both are very attached to their homes. Olivia loves her street, backyard, and house, which is filled with plants; indeed, part of it is a greenhouse. Patricia likes a more minimal interior design. But the primary reason they live apart is that they each like the independence that having one's own space affords. Olivia describes her home as her "oasis," which "feeds my soul" and allows her to be herself. Patricia says that her house is not important as a particular house per se but as her own space, which no one can take away; it obviously gives her a deep sense of security.

The women's houses are a bit more than two miles apart, a distance that can be covered in five minutes by car. Each woman feels that she would have to give up what she had worked to achieve in order to cohabit and sees no need to do so. They spend each weekend and one night during the week together, phoning or texting multiple times during the days apart. While having two houses means two lawns to mow and duplication of other tasks, the two residences also allow them to avoid conflicts that might occur when two rather different personalities struggle to work out all the "daily stuff." When conflicts do occur, one partner can simply leave, regroup, and then deal with the issues after coming back together. Like Mike and Nancy (our second couple), they also believe that time apart makes their time together more meaningful. As Olivia describes it: "Having space allows you to be able to see the other person better and appreciate them in important ways that you might lose sight of if they were always there."

Unlike the other couples discussed so far, Olivia and Patricia had at some point to deal with their more conservative families' reactions to their sexual orientation. Olivia says that her elderly parents "love [Patricia], welcome her at every family gathering and, if not there, ask where she is" but never use the word "lesbian" to describe them. All of her siblings regard them as a couple without reservation and invite them both to every family event. Patricia had a harder time coming out to her parents but negotiated that in a previous cohabiting relationship. By now, Olivia says she feels totally a part of Patricia's family.

Although childcare has never been an issue because neither has children, the two women have shared some of the burdens of eldercare, though primarily as a source of backup, emotional support, and advice in medical crises. Olivia visits her out-of-state family numerous times a year, and Patricia accompanies her once a year. Olivia sees Patricia's nearby family frequently. Each of the women considers their relationship to constitute a family, and Olivia is particularly articulate in describing what that means: "Unconditional love. Being there for each other. Support. These are the heart of what family is."

Like the other two couples discussed above, Olivia and Patricia split the expenses of dinners out, entertainment, and vacations, including a big vacation every year or every other year, except in special circumstances. For Patricia's fiftieth birthday, Olivia treated her to a trip to Italy as a gift. Unlike the other couples, the two own property together—a vacation cottage purchased together toward the beginning of their relationship and owned in joint tenancy, and they have also loaned money to one another when needed. Olivia has a will, leaving her house and retirement funds to Patricia, and Patricia intends to do the same. Olivia has also drawn up health care proxies, power of attorney documents, and the like, although Patricia has not yet done so (a common omission among people in general). In this respect, Olivia complains about one aspect of living as they do: if she dies, her retirement savings would be taxed to Patricia, whereas a spouse would receive them tax-free. With respect to legal issues, Patricia suggests that it would be good to have a partnership system for which the two could register and which would allow her to obtain health insurance coverage under Olivia's better employer-provided policy.

Perhaps because they are a same-sex couple, issues of gender division of labor do not seem to come up between Olivia and Patricia. Both cook and enjoy doing so. Both are quite handy and have undertaken big construction projects together. Fortunately, neither has suffered from any major illnesses or disabilities. When Olivia had the flu, Patricia took her soup, and Olivia has delivered supplies to Patricia when she wasn't feeling well. Both are thinking of the long run, though, and know that they will eventually both need care; they also realize that living separately might be impossible for economic reasons after they retire. Olivia assumes that they would live together at that point and would look after each other.

What new themes are introduced by this third couple? First, they are financially more intertwined than the previous couples in their co-ownership of a vacation cottage and provision for disposition of their assets upon death; perhaps this is because they have been together longer. Older than the other couples, they have also been dealing with the problems of aging parents, which they have managed with mutual support and help as necessary or desired. Unlike Mike and Nancy, they could simply move in together; nothing prevents them from doing so. But we hear from them the very strong theme of a drive for independence as the motivation to live apart and the relationship of a place of one's own to a woman's identity. Far from differentiating lesbians from other LATs, this theme proves central in interviews with female LATs in general, as will be described in chapter 4.

## Rachel and Sam: An Unconventional Couple in Their Sixties

Rachel and Sam have been together for about 15 years. Sam is in his late sixties and retired, while Rachel, who is 62, works part-time. They live not far apart in the same village, each in their own house. Sam is fiercely attached to his small cottage and garden. Rachel has only recently moved into her place, in the past having lived in a caravan during the warm months and moving in with Sam in the winter. But Sam's place is small and cluttered with his stuff, so she never felt as though it was hers. In addition, he receives various benefits from the state—pension and housing benefits—some of which he would lose if he cohabited. Neither has much money.

Both Rachel and Sam are fiercely independent and want their own space. Their personalities are quite different. Rachel is sociable and wants to be able to entertain women friends, which she could not easily do when living with Sam; he sees himself as more private and is something of a hoarder. A LAT arrangement has allowed each of them to live life on their own terms. They see one another on Wednesdays and over the weekends but rarely spend the night at each other's places any more. Everyone thinks of them as a couple. They go out to eat, attend social events, and occasionally take vacations together, for which Rachel pays because Sam has no money to spend on holidays. One could describe the financial arrangement between them as based on ability to pay, although Sam contributes labor (especially on construction tasks at Rachel's new house) as a means of repayment. Rachel has made substantial provision for Sam in her will; he has none.

As a couple, Rachel and Sam are unconventional, even for LATs. Having discussed living together and having tried it part-time, both decided it would not work because of their different lifestyles and personalities. Rachel misses the close companionship of a live-in relationship, so for her this is "second best." Yet she is quick to say that she and Sam are family because they look out for one another, are there in a crisis, giving both practical (for example, going quickly in the case of an auto breakdown or accident) and emotional support (physical comfort in the case of a family death). They rely on one another. They have also offered significant physical caregiving in the case of illness: Rachel moved in with Sam to be cared for over a period of months at one point, and she also moved in to look after him after surgery on two occasions. Sam grew up in a foster home and never knew his father, and his answer to my question about whether they are a family is evasive: "Our relatives think of us that way," he says. "[But] I've always been self-sufficient because my family was so odd."

The LAT arrangement of Sam and Rachel raises what proves to be a surprisingly common theme among LAT couples: an inability to live together because of different levels of tolerance of messiness and clutter. It also challenges the common assumption that LAT is a type of relationship that is possible only for people with money because it requires the capacity to afford two households. Two is not always cheaper than one. Finally, at this point their arrangement might be characterized, alternatively, as based on the reliability and companionship of old friends, raising questions about what the borderline between LATs and close friends may be.

## Tracy and Victor: LATs in the Third Age

Tracy is in her late seventies and Victor is in his late sixties; both are retired.[3] Each has been married and divorced, and Victor has several adult children. Although Tracy and Victor have been together for more than 30 years, they provide an example of the ways in which LAT can be an attractive lifestyle for couples in the latter stage of life. Their relationship is also remarkable for the amount of financial intermingling and physical caregiving between the two.

When their relationship began, Tracy lived and worked in London, and Victor was in a town in the north of England where Tracy had also lived earlier. Tracy commuted for 13 years—about 230 miles, or four hours by train—to spend every third weekend with Victor, but subsequently she rented a place near where he lived and spent all but 10 days a month there. Upon retiring, she sold her flat in London and moved entirely to the north, where she owns a house less than half a mile from Victor's. Although their LAT relationship began as a matter of historic necessity, it continues very much as a matter of preference. It suits both the partners to have their separate lives, friends, and interests; they value their own space and time, as well as the freedom to come and go without coordinating with anyone. Moreover, Victor is a hoarder; Tracy says that Victor's house "is so full of stuff; I couldn't live in a place with that kind of clutter." Also, if they spend too much time together, they get on one another's nerves, she says, and need to spend time alone. So they spend weekends together at her house and see one another perhaps three times during the week as well, either overnight if they go out to dinner or a movie or meeting up for coffee in the morning. On days when they don't see each other, they talk by phone in the evening. This arrangement, says Tracy, prevents the relationship from going stale and keeps the romance alive.

Tracy has many more assets than does Victor, who lives on a state pension. Indeed, he would lose various state benefits if he cohabited, but this is not a major consideration in their determination to live separately. As a result of the disparity in their means, Tracy pays for all major expenditures, which have included local holidays and numerous trips abroad, a camper van, and an art studio. Although she paid for the studio, it is titled in joint name and Victor uses it more; she also paid for the camper, but it is registered in Victor's name for insurance purposes. He pays for the maintenance and utility bills on the studio and performs a lot of manual labor at Tracy's house, which serves as partial repayment for her financial help. Although Victor once got into a difficult financial situation and had to borrow money from Tracy, they try to avoid this happening again, although she acknowledges that she would help him in case of need. Otherwise, they keep all their everyday finances separate. Victor is the main beneficiary of Tracy's will and of her pension fund. Their families all think of them as a couple, though Tracy does not categorize their relationship as family because they have no children. (She describes herself as a kind of "step-grandma" to Victor's young granddaughter, though.) Tracy is adamantly opposed to marriage. She wants to avoid a state-sanctioned relationship, particularly one with a patriarchal history. She says that she got married earlier under duress and felt that people treated her differently afterward, but might consider a civil partnership if it were available to different-sex couples and had advantages.[4]

Already at an age when health issues become a central concern, this couple has served as caregivers for one another in the face of major illnesses. Tracy had an illness for much of a year that prevented her from driving and threatened her eyesight, during which Victor came in every day, cooked, shopped, and took her to appointments. Having subsequently developed heart problems, Victor's care (he is 10 years younger than she) may prove critical to her ability to live independently in the years to come, although, unlike other couples, she does not contemplate ever cohabiting if that occurs. Victor has been facing a possible cancer diagnosis, and Tracy is helping to figure out and execute various medical options and accompanying him to medical appointments. Tracy says that, if Victor became disabled, she would look after him; that is "part of commitment as a couple."

In short, this LAT arrangement provides major emotional, physical, and financial support to the partners. Unlike others, however, their finances are intermingled in major ways, both by co-ownership of the studio and van as well as by loans and economic dependence of one partner on the other for joint expenses. They have also displayed major caretaking behavior such as one might expect of spouses, showing the depth of their commitment to one another. Tolerance for messy surroundings figures, once again, in their decision to live apart, but Tracy also appears to be a person who requires a certain amount of solitude. Although she lived with her husband for about 15 years in the past, one has a sense that she would find it difficult to deal with living with someone on a full-time basis at this point in her life. When one sees Victor and Tracy together, however, they present as a very closely entwined couple.

## Some Common Themes

Interviews with these five couples tell us a great deal about LATs and their motivations, lifestyles, and intertwined lives. The institution clearly varies by the ages and life stages of the individuals. The first two couples described, in their thirties and forties, might eventually live together—perhaps even marry—at some future time. The second couple, constrained by children and jobs, could at some point work it out to be in the same place. In response to an inquiry about the status of their relationship two years after our initial interview, Jackie, in the first couple, told me that she is wearing Kevin's ring but that they still don't expect to live together or marry, at least not in the foreseeable future. Yet clearly neither couple can be described as just dating or sampling the market for mates; they are fiercely committed to one another. And they have been together as LATs for five and six years—too long to be categorized as simply transitional LATs.

The older couples I interviewed have not only lived together for a longer time—decades in some cases—but also encountered many of the issues of long life. They have assisted in planning for aged parents. They have taken care of one another in sickness and accompanied their partners to medical appointments. Those without children have made provisions for their partners in their wills and/or as beneficiaries of their insurance policies or pensions. Whatever their concept of family may be, they display many of the behaviors we associate with being members of a family: sharing experiences on a daily basis, providing emotional and practical support for one another, participating together in family events such as holidays, birthday celebrations, and get-togethers with relatives, and planning and sharing vacations with each other. Although they are largely independent of one another financially, no strict accounting is required. Whether a couple aspires to a rough 50/50 split (and in all instances the split is very roughly calculated) or operates so as to allow one partner to take part in joint experiences they could not otherwise afford by dividing joint expenses based on ability to pay, their interactions are characterized by a generosity of sharing.

LATs avoid many of the conflicts that drive other couples crazy, such as those arising from differing expectations of neatness and cleanliness of their surroundings, personal styles, habits or hobbies, and having to nag one another to perform household chores. Whether these struggles make one a better person—or one's union somehow better—is an open question. LATs can simply duck out of these and other quarrels by going home and returning to debate persistent issues on another day. They also avoid the tedium of the everyday and staleness of the relationship that may result from constant togetherness.

I have noted the influence of past experiences of marriage or cohabitation and of a partner's family of origin on their behavior. Unlike some other scholars,[5] I do not interpret these as constraints. LATs who have been divorced have learned from past difficulties and appear to be motivated to seek something else, something better. The gendered division of labor that accompanies many marriages does not seem to operate in any of these relationships, although inclinations in that direction may pop up from time to time—and meet resistance.

One key characteristic of LAT partners—especially women, whether lesbian or not—is their strong drive for independence and a sense of their own identity, which they fear might be stifled in a more conventional relationship. Yet in no sense does this appear to result in selfishness or withholding of the self from their partners. Indeed, many LATs seem emotionally closer than many married couples. Their deep sense of commitment to one another is perhaps the most striking thing about them.

2

# What Does Social Science Tell Us about LATs?

In this chapter, we leave the real-life situations presented by interviews and enter the somewhat drier territory of social science. LATs have attracted a good deal of attention in Europe, where scholars debate whether they represent a new family form. Studies have been carried out mostly by sociologists and demographers, not by legal scholars. Topics they have explored include: the numbers of LATs and their demographic characteristics; age groups and reasons for living apart; the level of commitment between LATs; the economic arrangements between the two partners; and the types of caretaking LAT partners offer one another.

## Evidence about LATs in the Social Science Literature

I describe the information gleaned from the literature in the sections below, under the following rubrics: (1) numbers of LATs; (2) income groups and educational level among LATs; (3) age groups and their reasons to live apart; (4) the duration and commitment of LAT unions; and (5) economic arrangements and caregiving between LAT partners. I also describe the debate over whether LATs constitute a new family form.

### How Many LATs Are There?

A word of caution is in order before considering statistics gathered about LATs in various countries: the numbers and percentages that emerge are often not comparable, either between countries or between studies within the same country. Some studies include married couples; others do not. Some focus on specialized subgroups, such as women or people over the age of 60; others include all adults over the age of 18. Many studies exclude young people who still live at home with their parents and are not financially independent; others include them. A few study only couples that have achieved a certain duration as LATs, such as two or three years in the relationship. Yet despite this lack of comparability, there is a great deal to learn about these couples from the studies that have been published.

Scandinavia appears always to be the pioneer in new family forms; certainly that was true of cohabitation.[1] Early studies of LATs also emerged from that part of Europe. Several large surveys in Sweden during the 1990s reported that 2 percent to 4 percent of respondents were LATs.[2] Another study showed a dramatic increase in the number of LATs, from 6 percent of unmarried, non-cohabiting adults in Sweden in 1993, to 12 percent in 1998, and to 14 percent in 2001.[3] In Norway, LATs made up 8 percent of all those aged from 18 to 74 in 2002.[4] Surveys in Australia and Canada reported that 7 percent to 9 percent of the adult population were LATs,[5] and the one study estimating numbers in the United States reported similar percentages.[6]

Studies from the Continent confirm the prevalence of this phenomenon. Arnoud Régnier-Loilier et al. reported on surveys of people between the ages of 18 and 79 in France, which showed that, in both 1994 and 2005, 10 percent of French men and 11 percent of French women were LATs, a total of 3.8 million individuals.[7] A German study published in 1996 reported that one in 11 individuals between the ages of 18 and 61 were LATs, with 60 percent of them under the age of 30; the arrangement was more frequent in the former East Germany than in the West.[8] This conclusion appears to conflict with the disparity reflected between countries in Western and in Eastern Europe. Studies drawing upon newly available comparative statistics from the Generations and Gender Survey show that roughly 10 percent of adults were LATs in Northern and Western Europe but only about 5 percent in Eastern European countries.[9] The explanation for this seeming contradiction may lie in differing motivations to live apart in different areas of Europe, specifically, the religious and socially conservative nature of societies in most Eastern European countries versus that in Western Europe. A later study, published in 2008, concluded that 29 percent of the single population of Germany were LATs,[10] and official statistics in the Netherlands found that 22 percent of all adults were LATs in 2015.[11]

The increase in the number of LATs over a relatively brief period is notable. Some scholars surmise that a mélange of causes is responsible for this increase.[12] For example, the age of first marriage has risen, and the rate of marriage overall has gone down. Moreover, high divorce rates and low mortality rates mean that the potential population of LATs is larger. Increases in gender equality mean that women both participate in the paid labor market and resist the gendered divisions of labor at home such as marriage has traditionally entailed. Increased travel, as well as increased globalization of the job market, mean that couples fall in love even though they live and work in different places. Finally, advances in communication, ranging from internet dating to email, texting, Skype, and other technologies that facilitate contact across distance make this living arrangement more possible than it was in the past. All of these causative factors appear likely to continue, and thus the incidence of LAT is likely to continue to increase.

More specialized studies emerged from Belgium and the Netherlands. A 2014 study reported that 9.6 percent of all people aged 18 and over in Belgium were LATs; however, excluding students and young people living with their parents reduced that percentage to 4.8 percent.[13] One Dutch scholar focused instead on older persons, reporting that 32 percent of those entering relationships at the age of 50 or above were LATs[14] and that 2.6 percent of all adults aged 75 to 79 were LATs in 2003; their numbers had increased to 4.3 percent by 2013.[15] These studies reveal that age is a very important factor to consider when studying LATs; what the arrangement may mean to a young person can be very different from its meaning to those who are older.

The largest number of studies of LATs has been carried out in the United Kingdom, in part due to the availability of statistics about LATs in the Omnibus Survey, the British Household Panel Survey, and the British Social Attitudes Survey. Based on the 2002 and 2003 Omnibus Survey, John Haskey reported that about two million individuals between the ages of 16 and 59 were LAT, excluding students and those living with the household head, which would have doubled the number.[16] (The British thought that questions about this living arrangement were too sensitive to ask of respondents aged 60 and older.[17]) On the 2004 Omnibus Survey, 19 percent of single men and 21 percent of single women said they had a partner with whom they did not live, compared to 23 percent of men and 27 percent of women who reported cohabiting.[18] These surveys led Simon Duncan and Miranda Phillips, who have published (with a variety of co-authors) a large number of articles exploring the LAT phenomenon, to conclude that 10 percent of adults in Great Britain are LATs, more than 25 percent of all those not married or cohabiting; as a result, identifying individuals as single is inaccurate 25 percent of the time.[19]

Although there are some studies of long-distance LATs,[20] the majority appear to live fairly close to one another. Martin Turcotte reported that 45 percent of LATs in Canada lived in the same neighborhood and 34 percent lived within a 30- to 60-minute drive of one another.[21] In Britain, according to Duncan et al., 18 percent of LATs live within one mile of one another, 29 percent from one to five miles apart, 17 percent five to 10 miles, 19 percent 10 to 50 miles apart, and 9 percent more than 50 miles apart but both still within the United Kingdom (leaving about 8 percent commuting outside those boundaries).[22] In most of these situations, therefore, the decision to live apart was not a matter of geographic constraint. Couples who live separately meet very often, with many seeing each other every day or several times a week, and have repeated and frequent contact by telephone, text, or email in between.[23]

To summarize, surveys show that the numbers of people involved in living as LATs in all these countries are not inconsiderable and that their numbers are increasing. In most countries, these couples are hidden from the census statistics, and their relationships are excluded from social scientific analysis and public policy.

*Demographic Characteristics of LATs: Income and Education*

The few studies that discuss the income groups into which LATs fall suggest that they are comfortable economically. Certain economic assumptions may be drawn about LATs simply from their living arrangements. By definition, each has their own residence. If one excludes younger LATs who are still living with their families of origin and/or still dependent on them, LATs also tend to be self-sufficient economically. A certain income level is necessary to support these two conditions.[24]

One large-scale study in Canada reported that LATs fell into the following income groups:[25]

| | |
|---|---|
| <$20,000 | 40% |
| $20,000–40,000 | 34% |
| $40,000–60,000 | 16% |
| >$60,000 | 10% |

These results were clearly skewed by the inclusion of LATs between the ages of 15 and 25.[26] By contrast, a smaller-scale study of Canadian LATs over the age of 25, ones who identified themselves as voluntary LATs (that is, their choice was based on preference rather than constraint) and who had been in the relationship at least three years, gives what I believe to be a more accurate picture:[27]

| | |
|---|---|
| <$40,000 | 17% |
| $40,000–79,999 | 59% |
| $80,000 and above | 24% |

In this study, 83 percent of the LATs made in excess of $40,000 per year, compared with the study that included younger LATs, which reported that 26 percent had incomes above $40,000. In short, if one defines LATs as including only those people who are financially independent, they appear to be a group that is fairly well off. However, my interviews of LATs in the United States and England, to be discussed in chapter 3, call this generalization into question to some extent.

This same small-scale study of financially independent LATs' income in Canada also reported that they had high levels of formal education; 41 percent of those interviewed had a university or postgraduate degree.[28] Studies can sometimes be skewed by the manner in which subjects are recruited by scholars, who often begin with subjects on their own campus or recruit subjects through university media, as the Canadian scholars appear to have done.[29] However, a study based on randomized statistics about LATs in the United States found that they were almost twice as likely as cohabitants to have a college degree (33 percent for women LATs versus 18 percent for women cohabitants, and 29 percent for male LATs versus 16 percent for male cohabitants) and to be college graduates at about the same rate as married couples.[30] Yet a study of LATs in Scotland reported that not all of those interviewed were highly educated or economically advantaged.[31] And as I discuss in chapter 3, LATs in the United States also appear to come from across the socioeconomic spectrum and to be relatively but not highly educated.

How to explain this inconsistency? The authors of one study, noting the differential effect of education in Eastern Europe, where it is positively associated with LAT, and Western Europe, where it is not, hypothesized that "[t]he highly educated may be a cultural elite resisting traditional norms and perhaps becoming the first to embrace LAT relationships as a new relationship type."[32] This hypothesis suggests that LAT first arises among well-off educated elites, after which the lifestyle is disseminated among the general population, as it had already done in Western Europe but not yet in Eastern Europe. If true, as seems likely, this would explain the disparity between the Canadian results based on the responses of older people in a nonrandom university-recruited sample and the early US randomized study, which was based on national statistics from 1996 and 1998, on the one hand, and my own empirical results based on a random sample in 2016, on the other hand. In the United States, the lifestyle probably did begin among educated elites, but by 2016 it had clearly spread to the population at large.

## Age Groups and Reasons to Live Apart

Because the meaning of living apart can differ according to the life stage of the partners, scholars have focused a good deal of attention on the age distribution of LATs. In this section, I divide LATs into three age groups: (1) those who are young and essentially dating; (2) those who are in midlife, the period when people traditionally marry, build their careers, and raise children; and (3) those who are past that stage of life, in what I am calling the Third Age.[33] Making these distinctions goes a long way toward understanding why people choose to couple but not share a residence and how those reasons differ by age group.

### YOUNG LATS

Haskey has said that about half of LATs in Britain are under 25, which is consistent with studies carried out in other countries.[34] However the statistics are reported, it is clear that living apart is an important arrangement for couples who are young. It is not difficult to see why this is so. LATs who are under 25 may still be students, perhaps living at home, and most of them are not yet financially independent.[35] These conditions prevent them from cohabiting. They may also be testing their relationships.[36] Whether due to constraints imposed by family, work, or education or because of uncertainty about the particular partner, their LAT relationships are likely to be temporary or transitional.[37] One German study has called LAT among this group a "stepping stone to cohabitation."[38]

In some countries, moreover, economic and cultural conditions form a special context. In Spain, for example, late marriage is common, and, unlike in other European countries, the rate of cohabitation is low.[39] Current economic conditions, high unemployment, and lack of affordable housing contribute to late departures from the family nest. Additionally, Spain is a country with very strong intergenerational ties, and children, especially women, traditionally live at home until they marry. About 50 percent of Spaniards still live with their parents at age 28, and 35 percent do so at age 30. It is therefore not surprising that 30.9 percent of women aged 20 to 24 and 23 percent of women aged 25 to 29 in Spain are LATs.[40] Presumably this is a temporary, even if relatively lengthy, arrangement.

The situation in Italy is similar to that in Spain; in Italy, 48 percent of those aged 25 to 29 are LATs, as contrasted to 13 percent in France.[41] Ironically, the social unacceptability of cohabitation in countries with high religiosity and traditional views on marriage results in high rates of LAT as it substitutes for, and offsets the low rates of, cohabitation.[42] Cultural factors seem to have a similar effect on the behavior of some British-born ethnic minorities.[43]

In short, younger people choose to be LATs for understandable reasons, ones that would deter them from entering into either cohabitation or marriage. They are not yet self-supporting, for example, or are caught up in lengthy studies and preparing for their life's work. They are not ready for a long-term relationship and may need to test a number of them before settling into a long-term arrangement. One may refer to this group, as Duncan and Phillips do, as "dating LATs."[44] Or simply decide that they are not really LATs at all.

MIDLIFE LATS

The second group of LATs consists of adults roughly in the range of 30 to 55 years old, the years of child-rearing and career-building. Many of them have been previously married or have lived with a partner, and many have children from those relationships.[45] Their reasons for living in a separate residence from a romantic partner run the gamut from the voluntary to the involuntary with varying degrees of volition and constraint in between. Some, for example, have jobs in different locations that prevent their living in the same place.[46] Others may be caring for elderly relatives either in their home or under circumstances that make moving in with a partner impossible or undesirable.[47]

Children may also play a role in this decision. Children may not like their parent's new partner or be adamant about not moving away from the family home, school, and neighborhood.[48] Moreover, some LATs with obligations to children, like Nancy in chapter 1, may simply wish to avoid the stresses associated with blended families.[49] One LAT interviewed for a 2006 *New York Times* article on the subject illustrated this tension. She was part of a couple who had been LATs for three years; both partners were divorced. Although they lived an hour apart, she praised the relationship because she had a five-year-old and did not want competition for her attention; another LAT with two daughters said that "I deal with the parenting issues, and my kids don't feel threatened by him."[50] The author of the *Times* article also interviewed the Stepfamily Foundation's founder, who "advocate[d] living apart, because blended families are so vulnerable to internecine resentments and power struggles." In fact, he said, only one in three such families survive.

Living apart for the group of reasons categorized as constraints may be temporary; when the constraint is removed—a job found in the same place, children grown up or parents deceased, a mutually suitable residence found—the couple is free to cohabit. But other reasons LATs in this age group give for living apart are economic in nature and less tractable. Although it seems a truism that one house is cheaper than two, it can in fact be very expensive to buy a new house that is large enough for two families.[51] New York City, with its exceedingly expensive housing, can present many obstacles to moving in together, for example, if one or the other partner has a lease on an apartment on which the rent is controlled below its market price or owns a property bought so long ago that the capital gains upon sale would be prohibitive and a comparable home is not affordable.[52] Moreover, if one partner gives up his or her home to move in with the other, the security of knowing that one always has a place to live disappears.[53] In some situations, and in some countries, including the United Kingdom, moving in with a partner may also lead to a reduction in social security, pension payments, or welfare benefits.[54] In the United States, as I describe in chapter 8, it can result in the loss of alimony payments from a partner's former spouse.

LATs in this middle group also report reasons for living apart that are more voluntary than constrained. They are attached to their own homes.[55] Their styles clash with their partner's in home décor, tidiness or cleanliness, hobbies, habits of sleeping and waking, and the like.[56] One couple interviewed by the *New York Times*, for example, had been living separately for 16 years (although only 10 minutes apart by car) because he loved his rural, somewhat isolated home and she was devoted to her apartment in town, where she could have quiet time and avoid the mess of a place that was full of his hobbies.[57] Many LATs express their desire, as well, to maintain their own friends and way of life without feeling any sense of constraint, at least during some part of the week.[58] They need both time and space for their own interests.[59]

Women in particular are concerned about loss of their identity and want to avoid risks, both economic and emotional, that they encountered in past relationships.[60] This may include a gendered division of labor or a tendency to defer to the partner's choices, on the one hand, and the economic devastation experienced upon divorce, on the other.[61] For all these reasons, as I discuss in more detail in chapter 4, autonomy and independence have become centrally important to these women.[62] Finally, some LATs fear that stressing the current relationship with the daily struggles inevitable upon living with another person will destroy it.[63] Thus living apart is a protective measure intended to value and preserve an intimate relationship.

In short, many of the persons in the midlife category could live together but prefer not to.[64] One study of some 60 LATs between the ages of 25 and 44 in Scotland estimated that this was the preferred option for about one in six of them, none of whom were under 30 and most of whom—including all the women—were in their forties.[65] These LATs had long-term, socially recognized relationships and did not expect or wish ever to live together; they also had no wish to have children in the future.

## THIRD AGE LATS

A study in the Netherlands found that of all those between the ages of 55 and 89 who had repartnered after the death of or divorce from a former partner, 32 percent were LAT (versus 24 percent cohabiting and 40 percent remarried), with women more likely to make this choice than men.[66] This group of LATs, who are past the age of child-raising and retired or approaching retirement, has attracted particular attention from scholars because their choice appears genuinely voluntary, not constrained by external factors, and because it has implications for caretaking of the elderly.

The reasons older couples give for living apart are quite different from those described in connection with younger LATs. For many, their own home represents a connection to the past and a long-term investment in a particular neighborhood, neither of which they want to lose.[67] It may also be the place where children and grandchildren come to visit and thus is important to relationships with them, as well as being an asset they want to preserve for the younger generation.[68] An older person's home also embodies financial security—in many cases, their largest asset.[69] Or they simply don't want to move and have to fit into someone else's tastes and décor.[70] And again, if the alternative is remarriage, they would risk losing pension rights and other benefits in some countries.[71]

Many older people also see having their own residence as an important aspect of autonomy and independence.[72] Women in particular express this desire,[73] in addition to a determination to avoid an asymmetrical distribution of household labor and unequal demands for caregiving, which they have either experienced in prior unions or assume to be inevitable in relationships with men.[74] Finally, like those in midlife, some older LATs believe that living apart is good for their relationship because it allows them to escape the everyday and preserve the romance.[75]

I discuss LATs in the Third Age in more detail in chapter 6.

## Duration and Commitment

The length of LAT relationships not surprisingly bears a significant correlation to the age of the partners. LATs simply must have lived longer to have relationships that have lasted for long periods. Studies that include LATs aged 18 and up tend to show relationships of relatively short duration. One large-scale study in Australia of all adults 18 and over, for example, reported a mean duration of 2.4 years and a median of 1.5 years.[76] However, 28 percent of the LATs in that same study stayed together as a couple for three years or longer, including almost half of those aged 45 and over.[77]

Studies focused on LATs who were 55 and older showed partnerships of much longer duration: 46 percent of French couples aged 55 and older had been together more than nine years;[78] the average duration for Swedes aged 60 and older was seven years;[79] and the average duration for Canadian LATs between the ages of 39 and 92 was 10 years.[80] This variance in duration between younger and older LATs makes sense in light of the fact that, for the youngest group, living apart is likely to be a transitional phenomenon, whereas for older groups it may be either a choice constrained by external factors or a long-term preference. One study of LATs of all ages in Germany suggested that the overall four-year duration was a result of "45 per cent dissolving, 35 per cent being converted into a cohabiting union and 10 per cent converting into a marriage within 10 years" (with 10 percent presumably continuing).[81] Thus the four-year average included unions that were quite brief and others that were transformed into cohabitation or marriage after a fairly long period of time, as well as ones that were semipermanent.

The duration of LAT unions can be seen as one indication of the commitment between the partners. Commitment in relationships of various types has attracted a good deal of scholarly attention recently. A preliminary question, of course, must be what is meant by "commitment." In addition to length of the relationship, one British study includes in its definition of commitment sexual exclusivity, moral and social expectations, and relationship investments, like children and joint property, which LATs may actively seek to avoid.[82] Another group of scholars, this one in the Netherlands, proposes the following dimensions of commitment: psychological attachment to the partner, mutual desire to remain in the relationship, and investments, broadening this category by including intrinsic investments of time, effort, and emotion in addition to material ones like children and co-owned property.[83] They conclude from this study that, if the relationship is satisfactory, then extrinsic investments play little role in the partners' commitment to one another. Yet another study, of LATs in Canada, agrees, finding that the commitment of LATs is rooted less in structural commitments and more on emotional support, intimacy, and satisfaction with the relationship; it also found that sexual monogamy and mutual trust on that score are central.[84]

Many LATs report that they are highly committed to their partners, with some saying that their commitment was as great as if they were married.[85] More specifically, a desire to avoid commitment was not given as a reason for living apart.[86] Some scholarly commentators have pointed out that the level of commitment between LATs is remarkable, given that it does not depend on any structural or legal commitment to one another, such as shared housing, possessions, or the legal obligations attendant upon marriage or, in many countries, obligations attendant upon cohabitation.[87] LATs' commitment is thus solely voluntary, based on their feelings for the other person. Therefore, a stable LAT relationship can be viewed as evidence of a very strong commitment, in that it continues despite not being supported by a formal social or legal framework and the legal and economic consequences of separation are minor.

## Economic Arrangements and Caregiving

With the exception of a few studies, much of what we know about the economics of LAT relationships is largely anecdotal. In the words of one LAT in Australia, "[W]e keep our money completely separate. I don't know about his financial affairs and he doesn't know about mine—although he's better off financially than I am."[88] This seems to be fairly typical of the way LATs handle their finances, though perhaps with greater and lesser amounts of knowledge about one another's situation. It is distinct from the income-sharing methods of married couples and cohabitants, the majority of whom pool their income.[89] A study of 116 LATs aged 60 and older in Sweden revealed that they kept their finances separate, with each being responsible for his or her own expenses while dividing expenses for joint activities; the couples had no joint savings or ownership of any kind.[90] Financial autonomy appears to be particularly important to women, especially ones who have rebuilt their lives after divorce, a theme that will be explored in more depth in chapter 4.[91]

One study, carried out in Belgium in 2011 and 2012, specifically focused on LATs' handling of money.[92] This study confirmed that LATs' most common arrangement was to keep their money separate and to divide joint expenses—such as food, recreation, vacations, and holidays—on a 50/50 basis regardless of income disparity between the two partners. Its authors found that LATs' attitudes toward monetary sharing were starkly gendered: men were more likely to treat money as a collective resource and viewed sharing as an inherent part of being a couple, whereas women emphasized economic independence and equality. Men's attitudes, of course, may simply be shaped by societal expectations about male roles; a more sinister aspect is that a sharing arrangement provides control over the female partner.

LATs give one another a great deal of support that is not financial, however. Older and long-term LATs in the Netherlands care for their partners when they are in ill health, although they may be ambivalent about accepting such assistance themselves for fear of losing their independence or being a burden on the other.[93] Older LATs in Sweden reported receiving more support in these circumstances from their partner than from children and friends, and the partner provided someone to talk to and to help them get to the doctor if necessary.[94] Asked if they would take care of their partner for some months if he or she were ill, 65 percent of the women and 49 percent of the men said that they would do so.[95]

By contrast, LATs in Britain responding to a large-scale survey of all age groups appeared to count on their families more than their partners for caregiving during an illness.[96] Although some LATs expected practical care from their partners, it was significantly below the level offered in coresidential partnerships (cohabitation or marriage). Most (53 percent) said that they would expect care from their family of origin instead of from their partner (20 percent).[97] However, the difference from Sweden may depend on the fact that many younger LATs were included in the British survey, who are likely still dependent on and close to their families of origin, whereas LATs in their older years typically have lost their parents and could only turn to their children for help from family members.

In a US study based on qualitative interviews of 25 LATs between the ages of 60 and 88, the respondents expressed reluctance to undertake a legal obligation to care for a partner in ill health and gave this as a reason to live apart rather than together.[98] While these older LATs felt highly committed to their partners and expressed a desire to give them both physical and emotional support, they did not want to be required to do so. This reaction is understandable in light of the functions considered to be private responsibilities in the United States. Whereas social welfare programs in Europe and elsewhere provide universal health care, pensions, and other types of support in old age, in the United States these welfare functions are privatized; families must provide their own insurance, savings, and caretaking services. As a result, the authors of the US study thought it was not surprising that "avoidance of obligatory commitments among older LAT partners may be stronger in the United States compared to European countries."[99] Regardless of their desire to avoid legal obligations, however, the LATs interviewed cared deeply for one another and were "seeking the same level of intimacy, trust, and companionship that marriage affords."[100] They clearly were performing many of the functions of a family, although not all of them, and were contributing to an improved quality of life in old age.

## Are LATs a New Family Form?

Discussion of the functions LAT partners provide for one another has led to debate among scholars about whether or not this lifestyle constitutes a new family form. This hypothesis was raised in a 2004 article about LATs in Scandinavia in which the author posited that LAT relationships were a new family form that had become visible only after cohabitation had been widely accepted as a social institution.[101] So perhaps the issue should be rephrased as whether LATs are a new-to-us family form, one recently discovered and subjected to analysis by scholars.

The debate over whether LAT is a new family form has been liveliest in the United Kingdom, occasioned by Sasha Roseneil and Shelley Budgeon's 2004 assertion that LATs represented a postmodern living arrangement that was distinctly different, decentering sex and love re-lationships and placing more importance on friendship.[102] Some have speculated whether the increase in LAT relationships confirms sociolo-gist Anthony Giddens's thesis about increasing individualization in in-timate relations, illustrated by his concept of "pure relationships," which are dependent only on individual satisfaction and endure only as long as that lasts.[103] The evidence of commitment and caregiving between LATs described above suggests the contrary.

Social scientists in the United Kingdom have attempted to put the vary-ing hypotheses to the test of empirical study. John Haskey and Jane Lewis concluded, based on responses in 12 follow-up interviews to the 2004 Omnibus survey,[104] that LAT relationships did seem to attract highly indi-vidualistic people keen on maintaining their independence but that LATs did not understand their lifestyle as "a new and radical form of relation-ship."[105] Rather, they argued, "LAT represents a particular kind of sharing and is characterized more by caution and conservatism than radicalism and individualism."[106] Indeed, Haskey and Lewis quarreled with the terms of the debate in general, contending that "caution and conservatism [do not] necessarily signal selfish individualism and a 'flight from commit-ment.'"[107] They also suggested that, for some older LATs, the relationship may simply be seen as more discreet than cohabitation.[108]

Duncan and Phillips took on the debate based on data from a large-scale, statistically representative 2006 British survey that included 320 LATs.[109] The question they posed for investigation was whether being a LAT was merely a "stage" as opposed to a "more permanent end-state"—that is, a new family form.[110] Based on LATs' responses to this survey, they concluded that LATs were both, depending on the group— especially the age group—studied, which they divided into "dating LATs" and "partner LATs."[111] In this and a subsequent article, Duncan and Phillips characterized partner LATs based in part on the types of ac-tivities they shared; although all LATs socialized together, partner LATs also saw relatives together, went on vacations together, and celebrated holidays together, all of these being activities associated with long-term partners and families.[112] For these LATs, living apart represented a new and chosen way of living, but for others it was primarily a life stage.[113] Duncan and Phillips also raised the important question whether tran-sitional LATs represent a life course transition or a cohort effect shared by individuals born in the same historical period; if the latter, one might expect the phenomenon to spread as an age cohort grows older and thus increasingly to become an accepted family form.[114]

If LATs are asked directly whether they are "family" to one another, as my own and one other study did, they often hesitate, clearly challenged to come up with a definition of what qualifies as "family." Mariya Stoilova and colleagues think this is because they "lacked words to label various shades of family attachment in detraditionalized configurations."[115] Yet in their study, fully two-thirds of the respondents identified their LAT partner as family, whereas some of those who did not floundered because they held a traditional notion of family associated with marriage or cohabitation. By contrast, the authors concluded that "family" was more generally understood as based on "a feeling of belonging, being together, and exchanging care and support."[116] Given the high level of care and support exchanged by their subjects, the failure to identify a partner as family did not necessarily qualify as an indication of lack of commitment.

Still other scholars have concluded that LAT has in fact become a new family form for those later in life, for whom a steady, long-term relationship—but not marriage—was the goal.[117] Eighty percent of those interviewed in one US study said they saw LAT as a legitimate family form—a family of choice rather than of duty—and the majority saw it as a superior form of relationship.[118] One study by a PhD student in the United States found that this was especially the case for women later in life; she surmised that "LAT may be developing as an alternative to marriage *because* marriage has remained essentially a highly gendered, interdependent and integrated relationship in the U.S.," rather than keeping pace with cultural changes.[119]

In short, some LATs may be, although not consciously, pioneers in a new form of family. Whether this is so depends, at least in part, on their age and stage of life. One's conclusion as to whether their new way of "doing family" constitutes a new and lasting family form may be a matter of semantics.

* * *

In sum, a good deal of research has been done about LATs, mostly in countries other than the United States, where they are only starting to be noticed by social scientists. It is clear from these studies that a substantial number of people in the adult population officially classified as single are in fact LATs. These couples are, by and large, extremely committed to one another and perform many of the functions we associate with families for each other, providing emotional support on a daily basis, care during illness, companionship in social activities, close daily communication, and an intimate physical relationship. Although their reasons for living apart may differ by stage of life, many LAT unions are of long duration and constitute a clear, and intentional, substitute for marriage or cohabitation.

In chapter 3, I describe my attempts to make up for the neglect of LATs as an object of study in the United States.

# 3

# LATs in the United States

*New Empirical Data*

LATs have not attracted the attention of social scientists in the United States, at least in part because statistics have been unavailable. Until recently, only two US studies asked whether respondents had a partner with whom they did not live: the 1996 and 1998 General Social Surveys and the 2004–2005 California Quality of Life Survey.[1] In 2016, I therefore set out to collect my own data. I submitted a series of questions about LATs to both the Empire State Poll (ESP), which surveys respondents in New York State, and the Cornell National Social Survey (CNSS), which surveys respondents in the continental United States; both are administered by the Survey Research Institute at Cornell University (SRI) and randomly sample adults aged 18 and over.[2] SRI personnel also cross-tabulated the results with various demographic items in the broader survey for me. Although the sample size in both these surveys was small—800 respondents to the ESP and 1,000 to the CNSS—they are the only polls specifically eliciting detailed information from people living as LATs in the United States to date.

I also undertook a series of qualitative interviews with LATs in Ithaca, New York, and New York City during 2016 and in England in 2017. Interviewees were recruited by word of mouth, by asking friends and colleagues whether they knew any couples who lived in separate residences. I carried out a total of 21 semistructured interviews of an hour or more in length, 15 with women LATs (four of whom were in two lesbian couples) and six male LATs, one of whom was gay. All were White, with the exception of one Black male. The total included, in all but three cases, interviews with both partners.

My interest in the qualitative research was neither to interview a representative sample nor to contrast the experience of LATs in the United States and England, and in fact I noted no differences between the two settings. Rather, I wanted to obtain a thicker description of living as a LAT and of people who found it an attractive lifestyle, as well as an in-depth understanding of their motivations and manner of interaction. I was particularly interested in people who had lengthy experience of living as a LAT, and thus the group of interviewees were older than those in the survey sample. Their ages ranged from 36 to 83, with an average of 64 for the women and 69 for the men. Thus they excluded younger "dating" LATs.

I began by assuming that LATs would almost universally be unmarried. Interviews disabused me of this notion. Although most were unmarried, for a variety of reasons some LATs were still legally married to a previous partner from whom they were never divorced. Moreover, results of the New York survey and also the interviews with gay male LATs revealed that some LATs were married to their LAT partners yet continued to live apart, that is, that marriage and LAT were not mutually exclusive. As explained in chapter 5, this was particularly common among gay male LATs.

This chapter describes and discusses what I found out from my surveys and interviews.

## 2016 Survey Results

The results of the New York and national surveys appear here roughly in order of the topics discussed in chapter 2: (1) the incidence and demography of LAT unions; (2) the age distribution of LATs and their reasons for living apart; and (3) economic relationships and caregiving between the partners.

### Numbers and Demography

Of the 1,000 respondents to the national survey, 93 reported that they were currently in a committed unmarried relationship with someone with whom they did not live. On the earlier New York survey, I failed to limit the responses to couples who were unmarried. Of the 800 respondents to the New York–based poll—half of them from upstate New York (more rural and conservative) and half from downstate (the more liberal New York City metropolitan region)—103 reported that they were currently in a committed couple relationship with someone with whom they did not live, but 10 of the New York LATs were in fact married to their partner.[3] In sum, LATs amounted to about 9 percent of the overall respondents to the national survey and 12 percent in New York;[4] when generalized to the population aged 18 or over, these percentages are comparable to those obtained in Britain and other studies discussed above and higher than those reported by Charles Strohm et al. in the one statistically based US study.[5]

Another question inquired how long a couple had been together, offering alternatives that ranged from less than six months to more than 10 years. Defining a couple as "long-term" if they had been together more than two years, a little less than 50 percent of the respondents nationally were long-term LATs compared to 60 percent in New York. The higher percentage of long-term LATs in New York may indicate that there were more LATs by choice among them. Alternatively, the length of the unions in New York may have been increased by the inclusion of married persons living separately from their spouses. Shorter relationships made up a little more than 50 percent nationally and around 40 percent in New York. Many of the short-term LATs may be "dating LATs," to borrow Duncan and Phillips's term. These percentages were heavily influenced by the inclusion of respondents as young as 18 years of age in both surveys.

Similar to those studied in Europe, the majority of LATs in the United States live quite close to one another: 52 percent to 54 percent on both surveys lived less than 10 miles apart, and 76 percent lived within 50 miles of one another. Yet about 24 percent of the respondents to both surveys were long-distance LATs, living more than 50 miles apart, with 10 percent (CNSS) and 18 percent (ESP) more than 100 miles apart. Indeed, seven of the LATs on the national survey reported that they lived more than 1,000 miles apart, thus at airplane rather than automobile distance from one another.

Although it obviously depended on distance, the vast majority of LATs saw one another in person daily (about 25 percent) or several times a week (an additional 40 percent). And they had frequent contact by phone, text, or email when they were apart, 91 percent to 95 percent of them on a daily basis. Thus, while maintaining separate residences, these LATs saw their partners very often and kept in touch typically on a daily basis.

The gender ratio among overall respondents (not just LATs) to both the New York and national surveys was virtually 50/50: 51 percent male and 49 percent female. Similarly, LATs among the New York respondents divided 50/50 into female and male. However, LATs in the CNSS database were 55 percent male and 45 percent female, which is probably an artifact of random sampling; but the result was that there were more men than women in the national group of LATs surveyed than in the overall sample.

The ratio of same-sex- to different-sex couples also varied on the two polls, with same-sex LAT respondents making up 4 percent of all LATs on the national poll and 11 percent in New York, which may reflect the more liberal and gay-friendly atmosphere of parts of New York State. On the national survey, the percentage of LATs in same-sex relationships in California alone, a state with a very high percentage of same-sex couples,[6] was 14 percent. One author who has studied LATs in California has suggested that living apart can provide a more discreet, and thus safer, lifestyle for gay males.[7]

The distribution of LATs among racial groups in the United States, as set forth in table 3.1, yielded some results that were surprising when compared to the percentages of those groups in the overall samples. Readers should note that totals for each column in table 3.1 in fact exceed 100 percent because Hispanic, Black, and White are not mutually exclusive categories, and the survey asked about race in separate questions for each category. A considerable number of respondents obviously replied that they were in more than one category, and each of those responses has been counted separately, resulting in totals exceeding 100.

TABLE 3.1: Distribution of LATs, by Race, in New York and the United States, Compared with All Respondents

| Race | % of LATs: New York | % of all respondents: New York | % of LATs: United States | % of all respondents: United States |
|---|---|---|---|---|
| Hispanic | 19.35 | 13.1 | 19.35 | 9.2 |
| White | 76.34 | 69.5 | 76.34 | 83.1 |
| Black | 12.90 | 21.5 | 12.90 | 10.1 |
| Native American | 6.45 | 2.4 | 6.45 | 6.4 |
| Asian | 7.53 | 5.9 | 7.53 | 4.7 |
| Other | 2.15 | 5.6 | 2.15 | 1.9 |

The majority of LATs on both surveys were White (76 percent), but Hispanics were overrepresented compared to their numbers in the survey population overall. Hispanics were prominent among LATs both in New York State and nationally (19 percent in each). Nationally, they lived apart at double the percentage they represented within the sample population as a whole (19 percent versus 9 percent). Some of the disparity regarding Hispanics disappears when compared to official national census statistics on race, which report that in 2015 (just before the surveys were carried out) Hispanic individuals made up 18 percent of the population as a whole—close to the 19 percent reported as LATs in my national survey.[8] Nonetheless, I was somewhat surprised by the prominence of Hispanics among LATs given the frequent assumption in the literature that LATs were to be found primarily among the more economically well-off individuals in the population, whereas Hispanics and persons of color are among the most vulnerable groups in this respect.

One survey of older adults in the United States reported that a higher percentage of African Americans were LATs than of all other groups, a statistically significant difference.[9] My results did not confirm this. Although Black LATs made up slightly more than their percentage in the national survey (13 percent versus 10 percent), Black respondents in New York constituted only about half of all Blacks on that survey (13 percent versus 22 percent). These results may be ambiguous, particularly because Black women reported LAT status almost twice as often as Black male respondents did. The sexual behavior of poor African American men has been the subject of a good deal of study, which tends to show that because of the legacy of slavery, their profound distrust of women, and their own traumatic family histories, Black men have more partners than White men and Black women, of shorter duration, and sometimes simultaneously.[10] They come in and out of their children's lives without a strong relationship to their children's mothers and may thus have several residences they visit and perhaps none of their own.[11] This pattern of intimate relationship does not fit within the definitions of either cohabitation or LAT, so the survey questions may have not seemed relevant to them at all.

The majority of LAT respondents to my surveys were employed: 68 percent in New York State and 65 percent nationally; 73 percent of those employed nationally had full-time work, and 68 percent of those employed in New York also worked full-time (the remainder would presumably have been working part-time, unemployed, or retired). Retirees made up only 4 percent of LATs in New York compared to 10 percent nationally. Their prominence nationally may indicate, as discussed above and in the developing literature, that LAT is an increasingly attractive living arrangement for older adults.

Table 3.2 shows the distribution of household incomes among LATs in New York and nationally compared to the household income distribution in the national sample and to contemporaneous statistics obtained from the Census Bureau.[12]

These statistics show that a majority of LATs lived in middle- to high-income households: 55 percent to 60 percent at or above a $50,000 annual household income. For purposes of comparison, the national median household income in 2015, as calculated by the Census Bureau, was $55,775.[13] What is remarkable is that LATs seem to distribute across the income spectrum, indicating that they are a broad-based, cross-class phenomenon.

LATs appear to be relatively, although not highly, educated. Nationally and in New York, about 35 percent of LATs had a college degree or higher; this was in fact lower than the percent in the national sample overall, in which 46 percent of respondents had higher education. But, as shown in table 3.3, more than two-thirds of the LAT respondents had at least some college education, with less than 30 percent having only a high school education or less.[14] LATs thus seem to be somewhat less educated or at best typical in educational achievement compared with the

TABLE 3.2: Distribution of Household Income of LATs in New York and the United States, Compared with All Respondents and with Census Data

| Income | % of LATs: New York | % of all respondents: New York | % of LATs: United States | % of all respondents: United States | Census statistics |
|---|---|---|---|---|---|
| < $10,000 | 9.09 | 3.60 | 4.40 | 2.40 | 6.9 |
| $10–$49,999 | 35.35 | 32.80 | 36.26 | 29.30 | 38.2 |
| $50–$74,999 | 20.20 | 23.40 | 29.67 | 29.60 | 17.8 |
| $75–$99,999 | 16.16 | 12.90 | 12.09 | 12.10 | 12.2 |
| $100–$149,999 | 17.17 | 15.80 | 8.79 | 13.20 | 13.6 |
| $150,000 and over | 2.02 | 11.50 | 8.79 | 13.40 | 11.3 |
| All income | 100.00 | 100.00 | 100.00 | 100.00 | 100.00 |

sample of all respondents. This does not confirm the positive correlation postulated in studies from other countries between level of education and LAT. Yet overall, LATs are a fairly educated group.

Nearly a quarter of all LATs responding to the national survey lived in New York State (9 percent of LATs) and California (14 percent of LATs), indicating perhaps that the lifestyle thrives in more liberal environments. All respondents to the ESP and CNSS were asked to characterize their social ideology. The LATs responded as in table 3.4, as compared with the overall national sample.[15]

TABLE 3.3: Level of Education Attained by LATs in New York and the United States, Compared with All Respondents

| Level of education | % of LATs: New York | % of all respondents: New York | % of LATs: United States | % of all respondents: United States |
|---|---|---|---|---|
| Grades 1–8 only | 0.97 | 1.40 | 1.08 | 0.80 |
| Grades 9–11 | 6.80 | 7.00 | 4.30 | 3.30 |
| High school or GED | 21.36 | 23.20 | 21.51 | 21.90 |
| Tech/trade/ vocational school | 3.88 | 2.50 | 2.15 | 2.00 |
| Some college | 33.01 | 23.20 | 35.48 | 26.60 |
| College graduate | 20.39 | 24.10 | 26.88 | 25.60 |
| Postgraduate or professional | 13.59 | 18.70 | 8.60 | 19.90 |
| All education levels | 100.00 | 100.00 | 100.00 | 100.00 |

TABLE 3.4: Social Ideology of LATs in New York and the United States

| Social ideology | % of LATs: New York | % of all respondents: New York | % of LATs: United States | % of all respondents: United States |
|---|---|---|---|---|
| Extremely liberal | 7.07 | 7.10 | 4.30 | 6.00 |
| Liberal | 15.15 | 15.70 | 21.51 | 17.30 |
| Slightly liberal | 11.11 | 9.70 | 7.53 | 6.40 |
| Moderate/middle of the road | 38.38 | 37.00 | 36.56 | 33.90 |
| Slightly conservative | 12.12 | 8.90 | 8.60 | 11.50 |
| Conservative | 8.08 | 14.50 | 13.98 | 16.80 |
| Extremely conservative | 8.08 | 7.00 | 6.45 | 8.20 |
| All ideologies | 100.00 | 100.00 | 100.00 | 100.00 |

Although the LATs were somewhat more liberal and somewhat less conservative than the national sample, the group basically divided into thirds across the spectrum, with most falling solidly in the middle of the road. Thus, most LATs do not seem to see themselves as radical in any way, even though they may be developing a radically new lifestyle. This finding is consistent with the conclusion reached in the study of LATs in Scotland (see chapter 2) who typically had no name for their status and were not aware that they were setting a new trend. "Yet," the study's authors commented, "at the same time they were accumulating a particular practical knowledge of being a couple that is likely to contribute to ultimately shifting meanings."[16]

## Age Distribution and Reasons for Living Apart

The age distribution of LAT respondents to my surveys is shown in table 3.5.

Classifying the group aged 18 to 24 as "young," less than a quarter of the total LATs sampled in New York State and less than 30 percent nationally fall into that bracket, lower than estimates from Britain and Europe. These are the LATs who might be expected still to be students and dependent on their parents. If age 55 and up is taken as "older," then only about 16 percent of the LATs fell into that group both in New York and nationally. There were fewer (6 percent to 9 percent) than I expected of retirement age. In short, the vast majority of LAT respondents in the US surveys fell into the midlife group.

TABLE 3.5: Age Distribution of LATs in New York and the United States

| Age | % of LATs: New York | % of all respondents: New York | % of LATs: United States | % of all respondents: United States |
|---|---|---|---|---|
| 18–24 | 23.30 | 11.00 | 29.03 | 10.50 |
| 25–34 | 21.36 | 15.50 | 26.88 | 12.80 |
| 35–44 | 15.53 | 16.88 | 11.83 | 12.70 |
| 45–54 | 23.30 | 21.25 | 16.13 | 19.40 |
| 55–64 | 10.68 | 17.38 | 7.53 | 21.60 |
| 65 and older | 5.83 | 18.00 | 8.60 | 23.00 |
| Total | 100.00 | 100.00 | 100.00 | 100.00 |

TABLE 3.6: Primary Reason for Living Apart Given by LATs in New York and the United States

| Primary reason | % of LATs: New York | % of LATs: United States |
|---|---|---|
| Constraints | | |
| Too early | 18.8 | 22.6 |
| Job-related reasons | 14.9 | 14.0 |
| Study-related reasons | 11.9 | 7.5 |
| Because of my or my partner's children | 6.9 | 4.2 |
| Because of other responsibilities | 10.9 | 6.5 |
| Preferences | | |
| Want to keep own home for other reasons | 9.9 | 7.5 |
| Live apart by preference | 26.7 | 15.1 |
| "Other reasons"* | N/A[1] | 22.6 |
| All reasons | 100.0 | 100.0 |

* The option "other reasons" was not given on the New York State survey. However, two LAT respondents answered that they did not know.

When asked for the primary reason they lived apart, the LATs gave a variety of responses to the options they were given, as set forth in table 3.6.

When categorized into reasons reflecting constraints (the first five reasons given) and those that were voluntary, 23 percent of the national sample (who also had the "other reasons" option not available to the New York respondents) indicated that they were LATs by preference. But almost 37 percent of the group from New York did so. This disparity is consistent with the finding reported above that LAT relationships in New York were longer in duration, which is characteristic of older LAT couples who have voluntarily chosen to live apart.

The reasons for living apart given by respondents varied by age group. As one might expect, those who reported that it was too early to live together clustered in the age group from 18 to 34, and those citing their studies fell exclusively within the category from 18 to 24. Those who were particularly influenced by the desire to stay in their own homes were older, the majority aged 45 and above. Motivation relating to children was cited as a primary reason by only four respondents, all of them over 35; this response could relate to the presence of children in the respondent's home or in the partner's home; it might also reflect a sensitivity on the part of older respondents to leaving the home where their children had been raised and still regarded as home. "Other responsibilities," with elder care suggested in the question as one possible response, was cited by more of the LATs than was "children." Without knowing more about the respondent's reasons, this result is ambiguous.

What is remarkable about the distribution of responses is that "preference" unrelated to any of the other options was cited by so many respondents (27 percent in New York) and that they were arrayed across the age groups, with a substantial proportion among the young and midlife groups. A minority were 55 and up, the group in which I expected to find most LATs by preference. The biggest lesson for further research, however, is that the largest total group of respondents (23 percent nationally), arrayed across all ages, answered "other," indicating that the categories I borrowed from the British Social Attitudes Survey need to be expanded. My qualitative interviews suggest that matters of personal style, and, in particular, messiness or clutter versus a preference for a tidy environment and/or minimalist décor, play a large role in individuals' decisions to live apart.

*Economics and Caretaking*

When asked if they shared costs for joint activities, 85 percent of the LATs sampled in New York and 77 percent nationally said that they did. Because the answer to this question was ambiguous (not sharing could mean one partner always paid), questions about the method of cost-sharing were added to the CNSS; responses are displayed in table 3.7 for the 72 out of 93 national survey respondents who answered this more detailed question; all answered the basic question on whether costs were shared.

Only a very small proportion of the LATs relied on methods typical of married or cohabiting couples, such as contributions to a common pot or payment by the only wage earner.[17] (The four respondents who chose "other," when asked to specify, did indicate that one of the two always paid; the sole payor in each instance was a male.) The vast majority of respondents said either that they alternated paying for items (54 percent) or kept strict 50/50 accounts (17 percent). Although some adjusted this for ability to pay, the underlying assumption of each partner's

TABLE 3.7: Method of Sharing Joint Costs Employed by LATs in the United States

| Method | # of respondents | % of LATs |
|---|---|---|
| Strictly 50/50 | 12 | 16.7 |
| According to ability to pay | 13 | 18.1 |
| Alternating payment | 39 | 54.2 |
| Each contributed to a common pot | 4 | 5.5 |
| Other | 4 | 5.5 |
| All methods | 72 | 100.0 |

economic independence is inescapable. This appearance of economic independence is reinforced by the fact that the overwhelming majority—89 percent—held no property of any kind in common.

Consistent with their lack of economic interdependence, only 19 percent of the LATs responding to the national survey had made any provision for their partner in case of death, for example, by drafting wills; the largest single age group to have done so was made up of those between 45 and 55. Yet the vast majority of LATs seemed certain that their partner would help them financially if they were in difficulty: 80 percent said that their partners would be likely to help with a gift or loan, and only 20 percent said that they would not help at all.

The next set of questions sought to uncover various levels of commitment and caretaking, both physical and emotional, between the partners. When asked "If you had an illness and had to stay in bed, who would be most likely to care for you?," 24 percent of the LAT respondents nationally (27 percent in New York) said their partner would; 54 percent nationally (50 percent in New York) said a family member would; and 10 percent nationally (8 percent in New York) said "someone who lives with me." The remaining responses were scattered among "a friend" and "other." The percentage who would rely on family constituted the majority across all age groups, although it was higher among the younger age groups (63 percent among the 18 to 24 group), which is understandable given their youth and likely dependence on their families of origin. In this respect, the Americans were like their British counterparts and unlike the Swedes in expecting more in the way of physical caretaking from members of their biological families than from their LAT partners. In the case of LATs who were elderly or lived quite a distance apart, they may also have perceived their partners as unable to offer physical care if they were disabled.

Yet when asked whom they would talk to if they were upset, almost half of the national sample prioritized their partner. In short, these LATs expected emotional support from their partners even when they did not expect physical care.

## Findings from Interviewing LATs

In this section I describe my general findings from the qualitative interviews and present some conclusions that are at odds with the survey results in some respects, largely as a result of the ages of the interviewees.

The 21 subjects I interviewed (including both members of nine couples, with each partner interviewed separately) differed substantially from those surveyed, most notably by age and duration of relationship, in part perhaps because they were recruited by an older academic asking her friends for names. The LATs' ages ranged from 36 to 83, with an average of 65, and the average duration of their relationships was 18 years (ranging from 1.5 to 39 years), so these interviews capture the experience of a distinctive subset of the total LAT population. Everyone I interviewed was very committed to their partners and to their current lifestyle as LATs, and most did not contemplate living together in the future unless constrained to do so by poverty or illness in old age. When I contacted them two years after the initial interview, all the couples were still together, though one was now cohabiting.

In all but two couples, the LAT partners lived in the same town. Yet one couple was 87 miles apart and another 2,000 miles apart. Except for the two long-distance couples, who were constrained by work and family in different locations, all of the LATs interviewed could have moved in together but chose not to. This common front may have had something to do with their age and the longevity of most of their relationships; some had discussed living together early in their relationship but rejected the idea and were pleased with how it had worked out.[18] One couple had lived together in the past, then moved apart, and were happier as LATs. Eight were divorced; two were widowed; seven had never married; and four were still married to their previous spouses at the time of the interview (one subsequently obtained a divorce). The last is apparently not unusual, but it surprised me.[19] This initially surprising result can be attributed to a variety of economically rational reasons. For example, two midlife LATs had separated from their spouses and resolved all economic issues but could not afford the legal costs necessary to get divorced. The other two were not divorced despite decades of separation for peculiarly American reasons—the necessity of keeping an ex-spouse on a health insurance policy, for example, or a desire to avoid payment of the capital gains that would come due upon sale of a jointly owned building.

All of the LATs interviewed were economically self-sufficient, and most split joint costs either by alternating or sharing 50/50 but described themselves as being very relaxed about it. Contrary to assumptions in the secondary literature that LATs must be relatively well-off economically to afford this lifestyle,[20] my interviews, like my survey results, showed that this lifestyle spanned various income groups, with some LATs barely getting by (albeit with social assistance available in England).

Several other results contrast with the findings from the surveys described above as well as in the secondary literature. In three of the nine couples in which there was an income disparity between the partners, the female partner was better off than the male partner; as a result, in three of the four different-sex couples in which one partner paid all the costs of joint activities, that partner was the woman. Moreover, some of them co-owned property together—a vacation home, a camper van, a building used as an artist's workshop, an Airbnb in which one partner lived—and short-term financial assistance between partners was relatively common. Any jointly owned assets were acquired during the LAT relationship and, for most, did not represent a large portion of the partners' assets.

Ten of the LATs interviewed had made wills providing for their partners, and two more intended to do so; those who did not leave money to their partners either had few assets or had children and grandchildren and a partner well able to take care of himself or herself. The older age of the interviewees does not explain this difference from the surveys. Providing for one's partner in case of death did not correlate with age on the national survey; indeed, those in midlife were the most likely to have done so. In short, there were more indices of economic interdependence than I expected from reading the social science literature, although each LAT interviewed remained economically self-sufficient.

Finally, there was a stark difference between what the LATs surveyed expected in terms of caretaking if they were ill—that is, that family members would be more likely to look after them than their partners—and the actual caretaking experience of the LATs interviewed, who had given major physical care to one another in such situations.[21] Physical caretaking had occurred in eight couples. In five of those couples, each partner had rendered major caregiving services to the other, such as moving in to provide several weeks of postoperative care. In three couples, contrary to the stereotypical expectation, the male partner was the caretaker. The difference between my survey and interview results may reflect the more advanced age of the interviewees, many of whom had already encountered the health problems common later in life and, if their parents were still alive, were more likely to be taking care of them than vice versa. By contrast, the survey data included respondents as young as 18 years old and others who could still look to their families of origin for physical caretaking.

All the interviewees relied first on their partners for emotional support, would talk to them about problems about which they were upset, and went to them for physical comfort and solace. In short, they were providing for each other many of the functions we associate with family.

* * *

In sum, the LATs who responded to my 2016 surveys were similar to those discussed in the social science literature from other countries in several respects. Their numbers, measured by percentage of the adult population, were consistent (about 10 percent), as were the distances they lived apart and the frequency of contact. They also appeared to be similar to the LATs studied abroad in their approach to cost-sharing, and the US survey respondents resembled the British in their expectation that their LAT partners would not be their primary caretakers in case of illness or disability. The age distribution of the US LATs in my sample was somewhat different from those in other studies, however, with the vast majority in their middle years and somewhat fewer in the younger group (only 44 percent were aged 18 to 34). They were also scattered across the spectrum of income and education more evenly than one would expect from the literature, which posits that LATs are primarily well-off and highly educated. Finally, the surprising results about race—the disproportionate numbers of Hispanic and African American LATs—have no corollary among studies in other countries.

By contrast, the LATs I interviewed were older, had been together longer, and were more heavily female than those surveyed. They related to one another similarly to the survey respondents, except for two major areas: First, they reported a good deal of economic interdependence, including co-ownership of various assets, primarily real property, and periodic financial assistance; and second, they had provided major physical caretaking to one another. These are significant findings, but they may apply only to a specialized subgroup of LATs given the peculiarities of my sample. Nonetheless, the interviews yielded a great deal of information, in particular about how women and people now in their older years live apart and why. Chapters 4, 5, and 6 will focus specifically on subgroups in the LAT population: women, gay males, and persons in the Third Age.

4

# Gender Difference in Living Apart Together

Some scholars argue that LAT has particular attraction for women, allowing them to maintain their own identities rather than becoming submerged in coupledom, whether married or unmarried.[1] This chapter explores that argument in light of the literature already produced on this issue in non-American contexts as well as my own empirical evidence, both quantitative and qualitative. The issue for examination is whether LAT provides a way to maintain an intimate adult affiliation that is particularly attractive to women today, especially to women in different-sex relationships, when their lives have diverged substantially from the assumptions underlying traditional family law. Does LAT respond to a preference to maintain their independence, for example, and to avoid an inequitable division of domestic labor?

The impact of LAT on women and the gendered nature of responses to it have attracted a good deal of attention by social scientists in the United Kingdom, Sweden, the Netherlands, Belgium, Canada, Australia, and Israel, and I describe their findings and conclusions below. I then present the results of my own research, reanalyzed as they pertain to gender. Finally, I discuss the conclusions I draw from this research and compare them with the debate over women and LAT that has been prominent in the social science literature.

## The Debate over Women and LAT in the Social Science Literature from Abroad

A gender difference with respect to LAT first attracted the attention of social scientists in other countries who were studying adults in midlife and old age. The large-scale 2002 study of individuals between the ages of 55 and 89 in the Netherlands who had repartnered (by marriage, cohabitation, or LAT) after being divorced or widowed reported that the majority of both men and women repartnering after 1985 chose LAT over remarriage, but women were more heavily represented among the LATs.[2] Its author noted that the responses of women in her follow-up interviews were consistent with another scholar's finding that "a relatively high percentage of women move away from a male-dominated first marriage toward a power-sharing type of repartnering."[3] The most recent statistics from the Dutch statistical agency show that four in 10 women living alone, especially those over 40, prefer LAT to cohabitation—a rate twice that of men.[4]

Moreover, a Swedish study of persons aged between 60 and 90 years old, the vast majority (90 percent) of whom were divorced or widowed and had children and grandchildren, reported a gender disparity in the motives LATs gave for living apart.[5] More women than men mentioned the importance of having a home of one's own and the importance of being freed from duties that would arise if one were married.[6] Based on their data from this and subsequent interviews, Sofie Ghazanfareeon Karlsson and Klas Borell theorized that having a separate home allowed women to construct boundaries, both in space and time, to protect themselves against an inequitable division of domestic labor and to enable them to maintain networks of family and friends that might otherwise cause conflicts with their partner.[7]

The idealized view of home, Karlsson and Borell astutely noted, "is not gender-neutral; it presupposes the care and service [of a woman]" and thus had been a place of work, not rest, for women.[8] All the divorced respondents cited their divorces as a turning point, when they attained a freedom they were not willing to give up. Maintaining a separate residence from a new partner allowed these older women to control how much domestic service and care-related work they gave and to protect their social relationships. Ironically, the Swedish LATs tended to meet in the woman's home, and she did the cooking; but she undertook these chores only during the periods the couple spent together and took no responsibility for her partner's home at all.[9]

The Swedish LATs also gave gendered responses to questions about caring for their partners if they were ill or disabled. Although all said they would give some care, albeit a limited amount, significantly more men than women expressed themselves willing to look after their partners, even full-time.[10] The authors noted that women were well aware that care of the elderly was heavily gendered female and knew what it involved; they surmised that the female respondents were more cautious in their answers as a result. A later article specifically about caregiving based on the same Swedish study reported that the women LATs had fewer expectations of care than the men did. The male LATs claimed to be more willing than the women to provide such care but in fact reported receiving more services in this respect from their partners than the women did.[11] So perhaps the older women responding to Karlsson and Borell's questions were simply more realistic than the men.

In 2012, an Australian social scientist, Karen Upton-Davis, published an article based entirely on the European secondary literature, with a heavy emphasis on Karlsson and Borell's findings described above.[12] On that foundation, she proposed that women who choose LAT relationships were "resisting the social injustices and systems of oppression that so often accompany living together" and thereby engaging in "a form of political resistance against powerful, patriarchal structures."[13] She proceeded to test this hypothesis with a pilot study in which she interviewed 20 women over the age of 45 who said they had affirmatively chosen to live apart.[14] Although the study was both small in scale and unrepresentative, she concluded that it supported her previous hypothesis that for women "LAT relationships protect against both the erosion of autonomy and the erosion of resources and that because of the freedom that results . . . offer more scope for intimacy and emotional connectedness than either marriage or cohabitation."[15] It is difficult to discern the exact support for this hypothesis in her article because Upton-Davis presented only a composite story constructed from the separate responses of the 20 women she interviewed. Nevertheless, she reported that the women, some of whom felt they had previously lost their identities in marriage, were enjoying their independence as LATs, including financial independence, having been liberated "from the bond of economic subservience and domestic service to the men with whom they share an intimate relationship."[16]

A 2013 article came to similar conclusions, based on the responses of 11 Israeli Jewish women aged 51 to 61 who had previously been married but were now LATs.[17] As in the Australian study, the sample was recruited by posting appeals in an academic setting, asking friends, and snowball sampling.[18] The Israeli women described themselves as having established their own identities in a process of growth following divorce.[19] Their choice of LAT, the author said, was driven by opposition to traditional gender roles. Nonetheless, during the several days each week the couple was together, typically at the woman's home, she performed traditional gender roles, while otherwise avoiding them during the remainder of the week. The women also tended to "mother" their partner's children and extended family. In short, the Israeli LATs, like those in Sweden described above, objected to the traditional division of domestic labor but could not seem to escape it in their new relationships, although they managed to reduce it to part-time or weekend work. They also reported that LAT allowed them to escape daily friction and to keep the romance in their relationships alive.

The Israeli findings were particularly interesting for what they revealed about the women's attitudes toward economic gender roles. The women LATs in Israel found financial independence to be central to their autonomy, so much so that it was difficult for them to accept any money from a LAT partner at all. Their reactions appeared to reflect trauma experienced upon the breakdown of previous marriages and a determination to protect themselves against any similar economic catastrophe by maintaining total financial independence. Based on this small and unrepresentative sample, the author of the Israeli article concluded that "[t]he release from shared property and the separation of economic and geographic domains create[d] a new cultural institution," comparing it to Giddens's notion of the pure relationship referred to in chapter 2—an intimate sexual and emotional relationship based on equality, trust, and self-disclosure, entered into and maintained for its own sake and not dependent on external factors, such as marriage, children, or economic reasons, to be continued only so long as both parties were satisfied with the personal benefits each derived from it.[20]

The Israeli findings about the financial relationships between LAT partners were replicated by a larger-scale study in Belgium about the economics of LAT relationships.[21] Its authors interviewed 54 LATs and concluded that gender was the most important factor in how they assigned meaning to money. The LATs in this study maintained separate finances and typically shared costs for food and recreation equally. For some of the women, who saw the dangers of financial inequality and wanted to avoid an economy of gratitude, economic independence appeared to be an unconditional requirement of the relationship. When they accepted any help at all from their LAT partners—which would occur only because of income disparity or financial difficulty—they were very ambivalent about doing so and placed strict conditions on the exchange. The male LAT respondents, by contrast, saw financial sharing as a central part of being a couple, with money as a collective resource, and were uncomfortable with the women's insistence on full economic independence and equality.

What are we to make of this? For those who have experienced the breakdown of coresidential relationships and the subsequent financial consequences for women and their children, that experience appears to account for an allergy to economic dependence of any sort on the part of LAT women. The goal of standing on one's own feet economically, however, is a goal that is often impossible to reach, especially for women with children, in an environment where women's work is paid less than men's and childcare is expensive. The male respondents to the Belgian survey, by contrast, seemed to embrace a more traditional attitude that may reflect their assumption that they would be the principal providers for any family unit. This might be more realistic in some ways, but their uneasiness with women's drive for economic independence and equality may also confirm the dangers the LAT women perceived and the costs of accepting financial support.

Another recent article examined the gender question in the context of midlife or older LATs in Canada.[22] The interviewees were 56 LATs between 39 and 92 years old recruited through university and social media channels, all heterosexual, with an average age of 59 and with three or more years' duration in the relationship. The authors noted that the women LATs' accounts reflected a desire for control over both finances and household labor because of previous experiences of inequity. Decisional control, in particular, was important to these women—to be able, for example, to spend money on purchases without asking their partners' permission. Living apart also helped them "avoid conflict or resentment related to having to fight or 'beg' their partner to complete tasks."[23] They emphasized the ability to avoid risks to their sense of self by maintaining boundaries of all sorts—spatial, financial, and legal. These women wanted to protect the freedom to schedule their days and their pursuits, whether they were social, recreational, or work-related, while still enjoying an intimate relationship with a man. Living apart allowed them not to lose their identities in the relationship, they said, and also had a positive effect on the quality of the relationship by allowing them to avoid sources of everyday conflict and to focus intensely on one another when they were together. The authors commented that LAT thus provided "an individual solution that detracts attention from the broader issue of gender inequalities in cohabiting relationships" while allowing older women to experience the potential of Giddens's pure relationship.[24] In other words, the women were able to live relatively autonomous lives in a relatively equitable relationship so long as it was confined in time and space.

A study carried out for a 2015 PhD dissertation in the United States confirmed many of the gendered aspects of LAT. Its author, Denise Brothers, found that women between the ages of 64 and 94, who had lived through the women's movement of the 1960s and 1970s and had experienced a period when marriage was compulsory in their own lives, openly resisted gendered patterns in their relationships.[25] For this reason, she concluded, "women choose to partner in a LAT way because it allows them to circumvent traditional gendered roles which would likely be 'triggered' within the context of marriage."[26] Her subjects chose to live apart for this and other reasons that were similarly gendered. For example, she found that the women she interviewed had fuller lives than the men, with hobbies, work, volunteering, and networks of family and friends, all of which they wanted to protect; and LAT allowed them to do this. It enabled them to "redo gender," as Brothers called it, by performing gender in a new type of intimate relationship that was neither institutionalized nor bound by normative expectations.

Simon Duncan, a British scholar who has participated in many studies of LATs, has challenged this developing opinion that women were using LAT as a way to undo gender and introduce democracy in their intimate lives.[27] He criticized the small and selective samples on which these conclusions were based and pointed out that responses to a large-scale, statistically representative 2011 survey of LATs in Britain showed very little variance by gender.[28] Interviews of individuals drawn from the statistical survey gave similar results, with men's and women's attitudes to LAT being almost identical.[29] Focusing solely on the women selected for further interviews revealed that only a minority of them (seven out of 25) fell into a group whose reasons for LAT Duncan classified as genuinely purposeful or chosen. He excluded from this group all who cited any negative reasons for living apart, including not only responsibility for children, other obligations, and external constraints such as lack of money, location of jobs, and incarceration but also finances, doubts about the current partner, experiences from prior marriages, violence, and the like.[30] The majority of LATs interviewed, he found, would live together if they could or did not feel vulnerable doing so, even though they enjoyed the incidental benefits and freedom of living apart.[31] In other words, "LAT was seen as second best."[32] Duncan concluded that "women, at least in Britain, seldom use LAT to purposefully or reflexively subvert or undo gender."[33]

Duncan's analysis was clearly more rigorous scientifically than earlier studies and at the same time more nuanced. He interrogated the concept of autonomy, perceived in terms of agency, as much more complex than a clear on/off capacity to decide for oneself. No one is fully autonomous; even LATs by voluntary choice are constrained by emotional bonds with their partners.[34] Moreover, he pointed out, new forms of living do not simply appear one day, fully formed; rather, they grow within and by adaptation from previous lifestyles.[35] This more evolutionary perspective may explain, for example, the tendency of the Swedish and Israeli LATs described above to live apart to avoid a traditional domestic division of labor yet to perform tasks that have traditionally been gendered female when the couple is together.

At the same time, Duncan's interviews as well as those in the nonrepresentative samples studied by others do show that a solid percentage of women appear consciously to choose LAT because of their desire for a more egalitarian relationship combined with ample (though never complete) freedom. Moreover, the majority of women LATs who might prefer to cohabit nonetheless enjoy the freedom they have in their current nonresidential relationships. Perhaps this is the way social change begins—with a minority opting out of traditional institutions and others thus being exposed to the attractions of new living arrangements.

## Gender and LATs in the United States

This section discusses information available about LATs and gender in the United States based on the few social scientific studies available and then turns to information gleaned from my own surveys and interviews in 2016 and 2017.

## Information from Social Science and Popular Press Articles

Prior to the empirical research I undertook in 2016, very little information about LATs in the United States was available. However, a couple of surveys, by now dated and/or limited to a single state, had included a question about whether the respondent lived separately from a partner.[36] This allowed a modicum of information to be gleaned by cross-tabulating responses to that question with demographic data, including gender. The result was two articles by social scientists.[37] The first focused more on sexual orientation than on gender but pointed to a series of gender differences in its findings:

1. While 45 percent of women LATs live with children, only 9 percent of male LATs do.
2. For women, but not men, having a college degree increases the odds of being a LAT rather than married.
3. As compared to married couples, heterosexual LATs have more individualistic attitudes, are more work-oriented, and are more likely to prefer that men and women share market and nonmarket work.
4. These attitudinal differences are similar for women and men, except that women LATs are more likely than married women to agree that work is a person's most important activity.
5. Lesbians and heterosexual women do not differ significantly in the prevalence of LAT relationships, although the percent of lesbians is marginally higher.[38]

In short, many women LATs, unlike men, were still raising children from previous relationships; they tended to be more highly educated than married women; and they were more individualistic, work-oriented, and gender-egalitarian in their attitudes than women in coresidential relationships.

The other US study, by Jacquelyn Benson and Marilyn Coleman, included interviews with 25 self-identified LATs (10 men and 15 women) between the ages of 60 and 88 who said they were part of a committed couple; they were recruited through an email listserv at a Midwestern university and were clearly nonrepresentative in terms of race, education, and other factors.[39] The authors concluded that the older women's reasons for living apart differed from the men's: the women wanted to avoid the demands of caregiving and an inequitable balance in domestic labor, whereas the men wanted to protect their leisure time. Three men reported that they missed the instrumental benefits of marriage or cohabitation, specifically having a wife to perform domestic chores. One woman proclaimed that she wanted to prove that she did not need to rely on a man to take care of her again. Although this was a small and nonrepresentative sample, it did offer some evidence that, at least for women in their older years, a desire to avoid gender-based inequality in an intimate relationship was a motivating factor in their decision to live apart.

Beyond these sources, one must search the popular press for any information about LATs in the United States. One lengthy article in the *New York Times* in 2006 included interviews with several female LATs.[40] Three of the women interviewed, aged 39, 46, and 47, mentioned responsibilities to children from previous marriages as one of the reasons they lived apart; none of the men did. Two of the women were also very direct about wanting to avoid demands they had experienced in their previous marriages, one whose husband had expected to be waited on and another who told of a suffocating marriage with a demanding husband; each of them positively enjoyed the distance and freedom of their current LAT relationships.

## Gender in My 2016 Surveys

In this section I reexamine the data produced by my 2016 surveys through the lens of gender, asking whether women and men are attracted to LAT for different reasons, whether their reasons relate to inequitable division of domestic labor between men and women, whether financial independence is a significant factor to them, and the like. What, if any, are the gendered dimensions of the data produced by the two surveys? And how, if at all, do my results differ from the theses about gender propounded in the secondary literature?

TABLE 4.1: Distribution of LATs by Age and Gender in New York and the
United States

| | New York | | | | United States | | | |
|---|---|---|---|---|---|---|---|---|
| | LATs # | | Percent by gender | | LATs # | | Percent by gender | |
| Age | M | F | M | F | M | F | M | F |
| 18–24 | 10 | 14 | 20 | 26 | 18 | 9 | 35 | 21 |
| 25–34 | 14 | 8 | 28 | 15 | 14 | 11 | 27 | 26 |
| 35–44 | 4 | 12 | 8 | 23 | 5 | 6 | 10 | 14 |
| 45–54 | 13 | 11 | 26 | 21 | 6 | 9 | 12 | 21 |
| 55–64 | 6 | 5 | 12 | 9 | 4 | 3 | 8 | 7 |
| 65+ | 3 | 3 | 6 | 6 | 4 | 4 | 8 | 10 |

The LATs responding to the New York State survey consisted of
50 men and 53 women (49 percent/51 percent); those responding to the
national survey were more lopsidedly male (51 men and 42 women, or
55 percent/45 percent), perhaps because of the nature of a random survey or perhaps because the lifestyle appeals more to gay males. Total
respondents to the two surveys, not just LATs, were 51 percent male and
49 percent female, so it is difficult to conclude from the numbers alone
whether LAT appeals more to men or to women.

The duration of the surveyed LATs' relationships showed no difference by gender. Their age distribution by gender is shown in table 4.1.[41]

As noted in chapter 3, most of the LATs, male or female, were between the ages of 25 and 55. Table 4.1 shows that there were more males
than females aged 18 to 24 in the national sample and more females
in the New York sample, with the situation reversed in the age group
25 to 34, with more women in New York and slightly more men in the
national sample. However, in the midlife group—those from 35 to 55—
women seemed to predominate. If one defines "older" LATs as those
aged 55 and above, the proportion of males to females was roughly equal
in this group, constituting about 17 percent of all those in New York State
(17 of the 103 total) and 16 percent of those nationally (15 of the 93 total).

There were no significant correlations between gender and race, with
one exception: Black women LATs outnumbered Black men LATs by almost two-to-one. A plausible explanation for this disparity may be the

low rates of marriage among the Black population in general, combined with the very high rates of incarceration of Black men; this would account for both the unusually high rates of living apart (involuntarily due to imprisonment) and the gender imbalance, as men vastly outnumber women in the prison population, and incarcerated men cannot be surveyed by telephone. Additionally, as I discuss in chapter 3, inner-city Black men may have difficulties relating to the concept of LAT, given their patterns of intimate relationships of short duration and with multiple partners.

Cross-tabulating household income of LATs with gender showed that the women in these relationships tended to be poorer than the men, as shown in table 4.2; this is not surprising given that men still make more, on average, than women.[42]

As noted in chapter 3, LATs are found across the income spectrum. Nationally, however, there were substantially more males (35) than females (19) in the higher income groups. Thus women were likely to be the poorer partner in these relationships, with all the implications about possible power differentials that were seen as important by women in some of the studies described above.

The data available in these surveys of most relevance to gender issues is that about LATs' reasons for living apart, their expectations for

TABLE 4.2: Distribution of LATs by Income and Gender in New York and the United States

|  | New York | | | | United States | | | |
|  | LATs # | | Percent by gender | | LATs # | | Percent by gender | |
| Income | M | F | M | F | M | F | M | F |
|---|---|---|---|---|---|---|---|---|
| < $10,000 | 2 | 7 | 4 | 13 | 0 | 4 | 0 | 10 |
| $10,000–19,999 | 3 | 2 | 6 | 4 | 3 | 5 | 6 | 13 |
| $20,000–29,999 | 2 | 7 | 4 | 13 | 5 | 3 | 10 | 8 |
| $30,000–39,999 | 7 | 2 | 15 | 4 | 2 | 6 | 4 | 15 |
| $40,000–49,000 | 7 | 5 | 15 | 10 | 6 | 3 | 12 | 8 |
| $50,000–74,900 | 9 | 11 | 19 | 21 | 16 | 11 | 31 | 28 |
| $75,000–99,999 | 6 | 10 | 13 | 19 | 8 | 3 | 16 | 8 |
| $100,000–149,999 | 10 | 7 | 21 | 13 | 5 | 3 | 10 | 8 |
| $150,000+ | 1 | 1 | 2 | 2 | 6 | 2 | 12 | 5 |

TABLE 4.3: Primary Reason Why LATs Live Apart, by Gender, in New York and the United States

| | New York | | | | United States | | | |
|---|---|---|---|---|---|---|---|---|
| | LATS # | | Percent by gender | | LATs # | | Percent by gender | |
| Primary Reason | M | F | M | F | M | F | M | F |
| Too early | 11 | 8 | 22 | 16 | 12 | 9 | 24 | 21 |
| Job-related | 11 | 4 | 22 | 8 | 7 | 6 | 14 | 14 |
| Study-related | 2 | 10 | 4 | 20 | 3 | 4 | 6 | 10 |
| Children | 3 | 4 | 6 | 8 | 4 | 0 | 8 | 0 |
| Other responsibilities | 4 | 7 | 8 | 14 | 4 | 2 | 8 | 5 |
| Keep own home | 5 | 5 | 10 | 10 | 5 | 2 | 10 | 5 |
| Prefer to live apart | 14 | 13 | 28 | 25 | 6 | 8 | 12 | 19 |
| Other reasons[43] | | | | | 10 | 11 | 20 | 26 |

physical caretaking, and methods of cost-sharing; these are all central to the nature and meaning of LAT as a family-like institution. Duncan placed particular importance on the fact that men and women did not appear to differ in their reasons for LAT; and my survey results, set out in table 4.3, give no grounds to refute his conclusion, especially because our research subject populations differed and my sample was comparatively small. My questions may also not have been adequately designed to bring out gender differences.

A few observations about this data are in order. First, it is surprising that not a single woman on the national survey cited children as a primary reason for living separately, but four men did. Questions about reasons related to work, study, and children referred to either the respondent or the respondent's partner, so the men citing children as a reason might be referring to the presence of their partner's children in her home as a reason to maintain separate residences. Nonetheless, the failure of a single woman to refer to children on the national survey and the 8 percent who did so in New York both seem low, particularly in light of Charles Strohm et al.'s finding that 45 percent of women LATs live with children.[44]

The option "other responsibilities" included a parenthetical giving "caring for an elderly relative" as a possible reason, and women on the New York survey were more likely than men to select that option. Certainly, caring for the elderly is a task that is gendered female in the United States. But "other responsibilities" could also include other responsibilities not contemplated.

One can nonetheless reach several conclusions concerning gender based on the data concerning the reasons LATs gave for living apart. First, their reasons did not differ markedly by gender overall. Instead, reasons given by both groups correlated with age, with those saying it was "too early" clustered in the age group from 18 to 34, for example, and those citing "study" only in the 18 to 24 group. Those giving reasons based on preference were arrayed across all age groups. Second, men and women fell in roughly equal numbers into the two categories of response that can clearly be deemed unconstrained by external causes: LATs who "want to keep own home for other reasons" (other than children and other responsibilities) and "by preference." This group, which can be classified as "LATs by choice," amounted to a relatively significant number, constituting 36 percent of the total LATs in New York State and 23 percent nationally. But there were no more women than men in the group of LATs by choice.

One question on the survey did elicit some interesting gendered responses, however: who the respondents thought was most likely to care for them if they were ill; the results are set out in table 4.4.

Most LATs looked either to their partners or to family for care during an illness. However, although both women and men on both surveys

TABLE 4.4: Person Most Likely to Care for You if You Are Ill: LATs in New York and the United States

| | New York | | | | United States | | | |
|---|---|---|---|---|---|---|---|---|
| | LATs # | | Percent by gender | | LATs # | | Percent by gender | |
| Person | M | F | M | F | M | F | M | F |
| Someone live with | 3 | 5 | 6 | 9 | 7 | 2 | 14 | 5 |
| Partner | 17 | 11 | 34 | 21 | 12 | 10 | 24 | 24 |
| Family member | 19 | 32 | 38 | 60 | 25 | 25 | 49 | 60 |
| Friend | 1 | 0 | 2 | 0 | 3 | 3 | 6 | 7 |
| Other | 2 | 2 | 4 | 4 | 4 | 2 | 8 | 5 |
| Not know | 8 | 3 | 16 | 6 | 0 | 0 | 0 | 0 |

predicted that a family member was more likely than a partner to care for them in case of physical illness, women more, and more consistently, expected that they would need to turn to family rather than to their partner for caretaking; the gender difference was greatest on the New York State survey.

What are the possible explanations for this difference by gender in expectations about future caretaking? First, women know that caretaking is an activity typically carried out by women; they are likely to have undertaken it themselves or seen their mothers do so; and they know what a heavy burden it involves. This may explain their diminished expectations of care from their partners as compared to the male LATs. Second, men and women may be referring to different people when they say a member of their family would look after them; this could mean either parents or children. Responses likely differ by age as well. Younger LATs may assume that their family of origin (or more specifically their mothers) will take care of them in case of illness, whereas older LATs may have lost the members of the previous generation able to care for them and thus look only to their children for care. Because women remain the primary caretakers of children, they may also feel closer to them and more confident about their children's feelings of obligation toward them.

Another gender difference in response, at least in New York State, was that men were more likely than women to say that they did not know who would look after them in case of disability. There are several possible explanations for this difference. First, men may simply be less likely to think about caretaking tasks in advance of need, whereas women are typically socialized to do so. Second, many men may not like to think about being vulnerable at all and thus not look ahead to that inevitability, whereas most women have multiple experiences of vulnerability during their lives (for example, surrounding childbirth). Third, some men may simply not be sure who would come through for them during a crisis, whereas women are more confident in this respect.

Turning to economic issues, the vast majority of LATs—76 percent of men and 83 percent of women—said that their partner would help them out with a gift or loan if they were in financial difficulty. Statistically, based on my survey, the partner in financial difficulty is likelier to be the woman than the man. Additionally, there is some support in my data for gender differences in the ways male and female LATs share

TABLE 4.5: Cost-sharing Methods in LAT couples, by Gender, in the United States

| | # of LATs | | Percent by gender | |
| Method | M | F | M | F |
| --- | --- | --- | --- | --- |
| Strict 50/50 | 8 | 4 | 21 | 12 |
| Ability to pay | 7 | 6 | 18 | 18 |
| Alternate paying | 18 | 21 | 46 | 64 |
| Common pot | 3 | 1 | 8 | 3 |
| Other | 3 | 1 | 8 | 3 |

costs. As set out in table 4.5, the genders differed somewhat in how they described, and presumably perceived, the methods by which they shared the expense of activities such as eating out, entertainment, vacations, and other expenses undertaken as a couple.[45]

A common pot was the rarest method of sharing costs. The most common method was to alternate paying for joint expenses, which presumably yields rough equality over time but involves much more trust than a strict accounting. Women were more likely than men to say that alternating was their method of cost-sharing, whereas twice as many men as women (though significantly fewer of both) said they adhered to a strict 50/50 division. However, some may have assumed that alternating was tantamount to sharing costs 50/50.

Moreover, all four of the respondents who said they used an "other" method of sharing costs, when pressed to explain, responded that the male partner paid for everything. In short, although both LAT partners were self-sufficient economically, when they were together the man paid for all their activities, whether hot dogs at the ballpark or a Caribbean cruise. This may, of course, also reflect ability to pay, that is, the couple's activities were beyond the financial ability of the partner whose income was lower (typically the woman).

To summarize, this section of the chapter illuminates what we know from the two Cornell surveys about how male and female LATs differ and how they do not. There are no significant differences in the duration of men's and women's LAT unions. Men and women do not differ overall in their reasons for living apart, and equal numbers do so by preference. Male and female LATs do not differ in any significant way in their age distribution except that there are more men in the 18-to-24-year-old group nationally. Black women substantially outnumber Black men among the LATs surveyed. Women LATs have lower income on average than men LATs and are thus presumably the more economically vulnerable member of most LAT couples. Women LATs are more likely than men LATs to look to a family member rather than to their partner for care during an illness and to have thought about what they would do in advance. Finally, fewer women LATs than men report a strict 50/50 method of cost-sharing, and in a small number of different-sex couples, the man pays 100 percent of the costs of joint activities.

## Gender in My Qualitative Interviews

I turn now to the results of the interviews of LATs I carried out in the United States in 2016 and in England in early 2017 to glean what they say about gender. The women I interviewed were very well educated, including four PhDs, and work had been a high priority in their lives. Given the lengthy duration of most of their unions (from 1.5 to 39 years, with an average of 20 years for women), the majority of the LATs interviewed had entered their current living arrangement when they were in their forties or younger. Of those who had been in a LAT relationship for less than five years, two women entered the relationship at ages 65 and 67, one at age 44, and one at 36.

One lesbian couple had in fact lived together in the past but moved apart by agreement, with one partner establishing a separate residence. This had reduced conflict, and both partners remained very committed to one another and were satisfied with the arrangement. None of the persons I interviewed said that they were dissatisfied with LAT.[46] The vast majority of the women did not express any sentiment, such as Duncan described, that living apart was "second best." Most of the women were adamant that they would never marry; indeed, many expressed open hostility to marriage as an institution. In short, my results conflicted with Duncan's conclusion that only a minority of women choose LAT for genuinely unconstrained reasons. The vast majority of the women I interviewed either selected LAT as a first choice initially or, after experimenting with it, found that it was the option they preferred above all others.

A number of themes recurred in the interviews, especially in response to questions about why the couple lived apart. The most common one mentioned by women was "independence" (or "freedom"). A total of six women and two males spontaneously used these terms. The following quotations from three women illustrate this issue:

> For me, it has to do with having my own identity and independence. (72, heterosexual, United States)

> Our independent natures. Having our own spaces as we want them and are comfortable with them is important to our daily comfort. (56, lesbian, United States)

> Having distance . . . meant I could have my independence, my home, my own routine for me and the boys, and time with him is special. (44, heterosexual, England)

By contrast, none of the men interviewed who were in different-sex relationships referred to independence as their primary reason for living apart. This is interesting, given the traditional wisdom about men being more inclined to independence than women. Various scholars have argued that women are in general more oriented than men to relationships and see life as a web of interdependence rather than a quest for autonomy.[47] I would argue that the spontaneous use of the term "independence" by women is thus unusual and as a result more meaningful. What is it they are touting their independence from?

The answer to this question has much to do with both societal expectations and experiences in prior relationships. Eight of the women were divorced, and one was a widow. Their experience in previous marriages was key to their choice to live separately from their partners now:

> I felt hemmed in psychologically when I was married. (73, heterosexual, United States)

> It was an outgrowth of having been married to someone with a very dominant personality, as did his family. I took a back seat . . . , felt like I lost my identity, or didn't assert it. (72, heterosexual, United States)

When I get into a relationship, I end up doing what the man wants, even though I'm a strong independent woman. So it's been fun to be in a committed relationship but have freedom. . . . I had a very gendered division of labor with my husband. . . . He was very male, and he took care of male stuff and I did inside stuff. He made decisions, controlled the money. (65, heterosexual, United States)

By contrast, only one man mentioned his prior relationship as having an impact on his choice to LAT. But his experience was not one that led him to avoid cohabitation because of fear of the consequences for himself; rather, he described a painful divorce that had shaken his sense of himself as having the capacity to live with someone successfully.

Duncan classified experience in a prior relationship as a kind of constraint or vulnerability; that is, he characterized a woman's decision to live apart as not a voluntary choice if motivated by a negative experience in a previous relationship.[48] I disagree. As other scholars have remarked, making decisions under constraint does not negate the voluntariness of choosing the best available alternative; we enter into all kinds of relationships, including marriage, based on similar motivations.[49] The women in my study had chosen a new living arrangement so as to maximize their ability to be and do what they pleased, and some did so to avoid past divisions of domestic labor. This was a positive choice on their parts, not a reflection on their new partners or the current division of labor between them. The male partners I interviewed were as likely, if not more likely, to do the cooking than the women when these couples ate together. Among the different-sex couples, there was only one in which the woman always did the cooking and three in which the man cooked; in the remainder, both cooked, usually together. The lesbian couples split between one in which one partner cooked and another in which they both did. And the women avoided having to pick up after a messier partner or do their laundry and cleaning by simply having separate quarters, even though this meant the duplication of many chores at two different residences.

Interestingly, the messiness/neatness divide did not fall along gender lines. Almost equal numbers of male and female LATs (three women and two men) said they could not tolerate their partner's clutter or messiness; two women always went to the man's home, and two other couples always spent their time together in the woman's place as a result. For a variety of reasons, it was extremely rare for any couple to alternate between the two partners' residences on an equal basis. In the case of two couples, this had to do with the presence of dogs or cats in the home.

In response to the question "What do you like about it [LAT]?," one woman summarized sentiments expressed by many:

> Not having to accommodate someone else in terms of how I live, how I put things away, load the dishwasher. A feeling of freedom; I can have friends over with no one there, clean when I want or not. Silence when I want, feeling like I'm not dependent on anybody, can support myself and my home. (67, heterosexual, United States)

These themes—having time for oneself, for friends of one's own, for one's own interests—figured in virtually every woman's account. All of this is possible, of course, in a coresidential relationship as well but is more difficult to arrange, especially in areas, such as New York City, where homes are small. Having separate homes and limiting the relationship in terms of time and geography make it much easier.

Another common theme was that it was more possible to keep the romance alive in the relationship when partners don't see one another 24/7 and share all the details of everyday life.

> It's very romantic. . . . Long distance fuels the romance; we can't wait to see each other again versus being there every morning and talking about what we are having for dinner. (65, heterosexual, United States)

> It stops the sexual relationship from getting stale, routine. (75, heterosexual, England)

> Having space allows you to be able to see the other person better and appreciate them in important ways that you might lose sight of if they were always there. (56, lesbian, United States)

Turning to economics, all of the women LATs interviewed were financially self-sufficient, and none paid for their partner's living expenses. Many couples were relatively equal in economic circumstances.

In couples where one partner was better off than the other, three out of five involved a woman who had more income and/or assets than her male partner. Several co-owned various assets with their partners. Each of the lesbian couples and one of the different-sex couples co-owned real estate of some sort together, in one case a home bought in the name of one partner with contribution from the other, where one lived and the couple ran an Airbnb out of it together.

Methods of sharing costs for joint activities, such as dining out and vacations, varied. In four couples, one partner paid all the costs of any major items (airfares, hotels, restaurant meals, and the like); all of these were different-sex couples. However, unlike the survey respondents and contrary to expectation, in three of the four the partner bearing the full expense of joint activities was the woman. In each of these cases, the woman had superior assets and her partner might not, or could not, have undertaken such expenses on his own. However, all the women interviewed described a fairly relaxed style of cost-sharing, a loose 50/50 or simple alternation:

One or the other picks up the tab; we don't keep track. (56, lesbian, United States)

We alternate with expenses so over time it works out. Just spontaneous, never kept track of it; neither feels cheated. (67, heterosexual, United States)

We keep our money separate though we are very generous with one another. No joint account; it balances out, one person buys groceries, or if out to eat, conscious turn taking. On vacations, we alternate days of paying for everything. Dinners out? We don't keep tabs but try to alternate. We have a kind of generosity of spirit around money. (68, lesbian, United States)

In a few couples, the man, according to his partner, always paid for dinners out (or for "date nights"), and they split more major expenses such as airfares and vacations; but the male partner in one of those couples described the arrangement to me as 50/50. This difference in perception may help explain the gender disparity in the responses to the survey described above; that is, the male partner may in fact perceive any type of sharing as being 50/50. In more than one couple, moreover, the male partner paid in public, and the partners settled up afterward—a way, as one scholar points out, of "doing gender."[50]

Fully 10 of the 21 LATs interviewed—seven women and three men— had made provision for their partners in their wills; for most of the women, her partner was the primary beneficiary. Two more women indicated that they knew they needed to make wills but hadn't yet done so; they said they intended to leave everything to their partner when they did. If the testator had no children from a prior marriage or other obligations, she left as much as all her assets to the partner and, in other cases, at least a substantial portion. The number of women who had made wills leaving substantial amounts to their partners, or who intended to do so, was high—nine out of 14 women interviewees, or 64 percent—higher proportionally than the male LATs who had done so (three out of seven, or 43 percent). It is unclear what might cause this disparity; perhaps it is a continuation of women's tendency to plan ahead and to caretake.

Finally, in contrast to the doubts expressed by survey participants responding to abstract questions about who would care for them in case of illness, the LATs interviewed not only immediately named their partners but also had in fact taken care of each other whenever necessary. Those who were younger or had never encountered ill health had visited, brought meals, and shopped when their partners had the flu. Older ones had seen one another through major illnesses and operations, in some cases moving in with the partner for weeks at a time for caregiving in the aftermath of major surgery. This had occurred in a total of five couples, and in three of those couples the male partner had been the caregiver to the woman (the other two involved either caretaking by the woman or mutual caretaking). Thus caregiving there was, but it was not gendered.

All of the women interviewed relied primarily on their partners for emotional support, would talk to them about problems that upset them, and go to them for physical comfort and solace.

## Differences between My Survey and Interview Results as to Gender

There were a number of differences between the survey responses and the interviews with relevance to gender. It is important to recall that the group of those interviewed differed from the survey sample in various ways: most of them were older and better educated, and most of their unions had lasted longer. Bearing those differences in mind, there remain contrasts between the two groups with respect to the three questions central to conclusions about LAT as a possible new family form: their reasons for living apart; their economic relationships with one another; and inter-partner caretaking.

While a minority of the LATs surveyed lived apart by preference, the vast majority of those I interviewed—including virtually all the women—said that they did so by choice and not as a second-best alternative to some form of coresidential relationship. Only two LATs interviewed cited children as the primary reason for living apart, and they were a man and a woman in the same couple. Each was concerned for his or her own children from a former relationship who still lived at home, so the result was not gendered. Although three other women and one other man also had children, all those children were adults and no longer lived at the family home.

A number of differences between the surveys and interviews appeared with respect to economics. First, most of the women interviewed were either equal to or better off than their male partners, contrary to the statistics produced by the surveys, which predicted that women would be the less well-off partner in LAT couples. In those couples in which there was a disparity involving a man and a woman, in three of five cases the woman interviewed had more money than her partner. Second, cost-sharing described by the women interviewed was very relaxed, with little 50/50 accounting such as described on the survey. Loans were common and co-ownership not unusual, in contrast to the picture of strict financial independence emerging from the surveys. Third, a large proportion (64 percent) of the women LATs interviewed intended to leave all or substantial portions of their assets to their LAT partner upon death—a sharp distinction from the 19 percent of the LATs responding to the national survey who had made any provision at all for their partner in case of their own death. In short, the interviews gave a picture of LATs as more economically interdependent than expected from the survey data. Moreover, there did not appear to be any gender difference in caretaking: male LATs had taken care of their female partners about as often as the reverse.

* * *

Several important conclusions can be drawn from my interviews with women LATs. First, LAT was clearly a lifestyle of preference for those interviewed because it answered their needs for independence and avoided problems that may accompany cohabitation. Second, the interviewees displayed considerable economic interdependence despite each partner remaining financially self-sufficient. Third, these couples in fact relied on one another for substantial physical and emotional caregiving, contrary to the expectations expressed by the subjects responding to the surveys and to the gendered expectations of respondents in other studies. There was no gender difference in the care given and received.

## Conclusions with Respect to the Debate about Gender and LAT

A quick survey of the ways in which my data confirm or disconfirm the findings in the secondary literature about LAT and gender is in order. First, my qualitative research clearly confirms some findings in the literature. A number of my female interviewees, like those studied by Laura Funk and Karen Kobayashi, pointed to a strong desire to protect their own identity, or sense of self, which had been lost in previous relationships. As Karlsson and Borell noted, they also chose LAT in order to maintain their networks of family and friends without interference. My interviewees did so also in the interest of protecting their own pursuits, whether birdwatching, practicing the piano, or keeping pet animals—but so did men (for example, to watch sports on TV). Many women mentioned that LAT allowed them to keep the romance alive in their relationships by avoiding conflicts common in everyday coresidential life. Funk and Kobayashi, writing about Canadians, and Ofra Or, writing about Israeli women, saw LAT as creating Giddens's pure relationship; and one of the women I interviewed gave some evidence of this without being aware of the intellectual underpinnings: "It's all about us, our relationship, not about keeping a home, family, kids. Just me and him." There was none of the contingency of commitment associated with Giddens in this response, however.

Many authors have noted that previous relationships and especially a divorce can play a significant role in attracting someone to LAT. As a motivation to live apart, Karlsson and Borell and also Or emphasized women's desire to avoid an unequal division of labor after a negative experience in past relationships, even though they reported that the women they studied tended to repeat a traditional division of labor when with their LAT partner. Some of the women I interviewed had had bad experiences in this respect in previous relationships, but none of them cited avoiding an unequal division of labor as a reason for choosing LAT. Moreover, the division of domestic labor was not an issue in their current LAT relationships, which appeared by and large to be highly egalitarian. In short, they were not in fact living apart to avoid an unequal division of labor in their current relationship. Perhaps the previous experience influenced their choice of new partners instead of the lifestyle. Their caretaking behavior, moreover, did not display any replication of traditional gender roles, and a drive to avoid taking care of their partners did not figure in their motivation to live apart (contrary to the suggestions of Benson and Coleman). All were willing to do so, and most had.

Many authors have emphasized the desire on the part of women LATs to be independent with respect to money and to control their financial choices. There was some support for this in my interviews. One woman had refused to take money from her partner when he offered to help her pay off substantial debts, explaining that she would prefer to rely either on herself or her family, and one woman stated firmly that she never wanted to support a man again, as she had in her past marriage. But other women LATs were giving substantial support to their partners.

The desire to buy things for oneself without approval by one's partner—reminiscent of a wife needing to ask her husband before making purchases—was voiced by only one woman, and she was a lesbian who had never been married to a man. With the exception of men paying for self-described "date nights," I did not see a gendered relationship to money in my interviews. Instead, inter-partner finances were characterized by an ease and generosity on the part of both men and women.

Moreover, despite the economic self-sufficiency described in the secondary literature and confirmed by my own surveys, my interviews revealed an unexpectedly high level of economic interdependence on the part of women LATs, which may have been the result of the greater length of their relationships. Additionally, living apart appeared from my interviews to appeal to women who were relatively well-off compared to their male partners.

Does this mean that women are not attracted to LAT because of a desire to avoid an unequal division of domestic labor and economic dependence? The important distinction, I would argue, is between how LATs consciously experience what they are doing and how it is characterized. Apart from their opposition to marriage, none of the women I interviewed would have agreed with Upton-Davis that they were engaging in a conscious effort to resist social injustices and systems of oppression that accompany living together and were thus involved in some form of political resistance against patriarchy by way of their living arrangements. Although virtually all the interviewees were fairly reflective, feminist, and politically conscious individuals, this was not the lens through which these women viewed their relationships. At the same time, they did display a desire, as Upton-Davis proposed, to protect themselves against an erosion of their autonomy and to gain more scope for intimacy and emotional connectedness (which is how I interpret their language about focusing on the relationship, avoiding the struggles of the everyday, and keeping the romance alive). Moreover, although none of the women LATs asserted an intent to avoid an unequal division of labor and economic dependency as a primary motivating factor, they were in fact accomplishing both goals. And all were choosing and maintaining a lifestyle that does not conform to societal expectations.

Strohm et al. concluded that women who lived apart from their partners were more individualistic and work-oriented than other women, such as those who marry. This provokes some intriguing ideas. Perhaps LAT provides an ideal relationship for women who are economically secure, who do not need to rely on men to support themselves, and for whom their work is a major and consuming endeavor. This description would characterize most of the women I interviewed. Observing the couples of which they formed one part, what they got out of LAT was an emotionally supportive partner, someone who was there for them but did not place demands on them that would interfere with the woman's other pursuits. In some cases, the woman was the stronger partner economically and supported the joint aspects of their common life, but she had access to physical caretaking and emotional support in return. This is not such a bad bargain for the modern career woman.

Another interesting question is posed by Funk and Kobayashi's assertion that LAT is an individual, personal solution that detracts from dealing with continuing inequalities in coresidential relationships. They presumably meant this as a negative comment. It is true that women LATs, as individuals, have opted out of relationships that are often characterized by unequal divisions of domestic labor, decisional control, and economic power and have gained for themselves both equality and freedom in ways that they may not have been able to achieve in coresidential relationships. It is not so clear, however, that their doing so detracts from dealing with those wider issues as a society. This is not a zero-sum game; one can develop alternative family forms and simultaneously work to democratize traditional forms. As Duncan has noted, "[U]ndoing gender should not be conflated with relationship form."[51] Indeed, some of us are engaged in undoing or redoing gender in the context of marriage as well. Seeing people who live in new and different ways can provide an impetus for change within the older forms; in other words, change can be engendered by the existence of alternative institutions and models. Describing and analyzing the ways in which LAT works for some women may be a step in that direction.

5

# Gay Male Couples and LAT

BY DAVID EICHERT

This chapter examines the unique ways in which same-sex LAT couples, and in particular gay male LAT couples, structure their relationships. While there are many similarities between different- and same-sex couples,[1] same-sex couples must also navigate some different and additional concerns when deciding whether or not to live apart. Very few studies about LAT have focused on same-sex couples, despite evidence suggesting that same-sex couples are significantly more likely to maintain separate residences as compared to different-sex couples.[2]

To better understand how same-sex LAT couples structure their relationships, I conducted a series of interviews with 14 members of 10 different gay male LAT couples in New York City. Given the difficulty in identifying subjects, I recruited interviewees by connecting with personal acquaintances and posting about the study on social media and dating websites aimed at gay and bisexual men. At least one partner in each couple lived in New York City at the time of the interview. Additionally, two couples were referred to me by other LAT couples. Most interviewees were White men born in the United States, although one interviewee was African American and four men were immigrants (one each from Central America, Western Europe, the Middle East, and China). All interviewees were assigned male at birth. Additionally, four of the 10 couples were young (both partners were under the age of 35), which corresponds with research suggesting that gay male couples are more likely than lesbian and different-sex couples to live apart early in life.[3] While this convenience sample is certainly not nationally representative, the data nevertheless demonstrate several important themes around which gay male LAT couples structure their lives and relationships.

I begin this chapter by analyzing the interviews in the context of existing literature about gay male couples, focusing on several themes that will be important for future researchers studying LAT couples. Following that, I focus on two male couples in particular to illustrate the diverse ways in which gay male LAT couples may differ from other LAT couples.

## Gay Male LAT Couples in New York City: An Analysis

Although same-sex LAT couples share many of the same concerns and motivations as different-sex LATs, there are also marked differences between these two groups that should not be ignored. This section focuses on several of these themes, including questions of identity construction, reasons for living apart, debates about the value of marriage, financial concerns and money management, sexual exclusivity and non-monogamy, caregiving and the meaning of family, and daily interactions.

### Identity Construction and Coming Out

When studying non-heterosexual individuals in LAT relationships, it is important for researchers to understand that a person's choice of identity labels ("gay," "queer," "same-sex attracted," and the like) varies significantly depending on the historical moment and social context in which that person lives.[4] An individual may prefer one (or more) terms because of the political or social meanings attached to the word or reject non-heterosexual identities that clash with the person's worldview and politics.

Moreover, sexual identity is about more than the gender of a person's sexual partners. Not all individuals who experience same-sex sexual attraction are sexually active, and heterosexual individuals engage in homosexual sex for a variety of reasons.[5] Some individuals who identify as lesbian or gay also sometimes engage in sexual or romantic relationships with different-sex partners both before and after self-identifying as a sexual minority, further complicating the use of labels.[6]

These nuances can be seen in how the individuals interviewed for this chapter classified their sexual identities. All were in committed relationships with male partners, and all but two of the men interviewed for this study identified as gay. One interviewee identified as "gay or queer"; the other man felt uncomfortable with labels but identified as "toward the bisexual/gay side of the spectrum." Both of these men were under the age of 30.

Location is also a key factor in how same-sex couples interact with their surroundings and their sexual identities. Being openly lesbian, gay, or bisexual in New York City is dramatically different from living as a sexual minority in a small town. Lesbian, gay, and bisexual individuals in rural areas often face high rates of victimization because of their sexuality and lack access to the very visible gay nightlife that is a defining facet of urban gay life.[7] The high concentration of sexual minorities in certain urban centers also makes a person's sexual minority status there commonplace, resulting in an "unmarked," or invisible, identity for urban gays versus a "marked" identity for sexual minorities in rural areas.[8] All those I interviewed enjoyed high levels of societal acceptance that would likely be harder to find in many other parts of the country.

Individuals in same-sex relationships must also decide whether or not to "come out" as gay to their families of origin. This decision, as well as the manner in which a person comes out and the words chosen by the individual to publicly define their relationship, are all informed by the person's cultural perceptions of homosexuality, views about the need to come out, and physical and financial security.[9] Choosing to keep one's relationship a secret has both advantages and disadvantages. Whereas one person may want to preserve family unity by staying in the closet, such a choice also means that the person must censor significant portions of their life when engaging with family members. By contrast, coming out about a same-sex relationship may expose a person to physical insecurity and emotional distress due to rejection by family members, although it is often accompanied by a significant positive effect on the person's mental health and well-being.[10]

Understanding these conflicts is especially important for understanding LAT couples because some same-sex LAT couples choose to live in separate locations in order to conceal the true nature of their relationship from disapproving family or friends.[11] This was true of one interviewee, a college-aged man who chose not to tell his parents about his same-sex marriage for fear of being cut off financially. Other than this one individual, however, all the men interviewed for this chapter were out to everyone in their lives and believed that their friends and family members viewed them as a couple, even though several interviewees had family members who objected to their lifestyle for religious reasons.

## Choosing to Live Apart

Most of the gay couples interviewed lived within 10 to 30 minutes of each other. Some lived much closer, such as one couple with first- and second-floor apartments in the same building in Manhattan; and some lived much farther away, such as one man who hated living in New York City so much that he moved back to Nevada while his partner was finishing graduate school in New York.

Most of these couples see each other multiple times a week. They often have a schedule in place that gives structure to their living arrangements; one couple, for example, is together from Friday to Sunday and apart Monday through Thursday. Other couples see each other less frequently, such as one couple for whom one to two weekends a month was the maximum amount of time they could tolerate togetherness.

Interviewees gave diverse answers as to why they chose to maintain separate residences. For many, differences in opinion and lifestyle (interior decorating, sleep schedules, levels of cleanliness, preference for solitude, and the like) were important reasons for living apart. Some claimed that living apart helped to reduce conflict in the relationship, with one couple claiming that moving into separate apartments had saved their relationship. Others preferred the "excitement" of spending time together and believed that living together seven days a week would make the relationship less meaningful. One interviewee even said that living apart was a safeguard against becoming "allergic" to his partner from overexposure.

The difficulty of living in New York City was also an important factor for many interviewees. Three couples rented apartments that would be too small for two people, so living apart was the best alternative. One interviewee had a rent-controlled studio apartment on the Upper East Side that was too valuable to give up. Another, an artist, could not imagine moving all of his art supplies into his partner's tiny studio apartment in Brooklyn.

Several also expressed the view that living apart provided a way to ensure their independence and freedom. Two couples even explicitly agreed at the beginning of their relationship to live apart in order to avoid becoming too dependent on each other. Another couple never discussed living apart; instead, what began as occasionally spending the night at the other person's apartment simply continued unchallenged and unquestioned for two decades.

Finally, for two young couples, education was a major factor in the decision to maintain separate residences. In addition to the young man described above, who hated New York City so much that he moved to Nevada while his partner finished graduate school, another couple was split between two universities in different cities. While both couples planned to move in together as soon as possible, one partner from the latter couple expressed uncertainty about the tenability of that plan and worried that spending a lot of time together would ruin their relationship.

## Gay Marriage, Gay Liberation, or Both?

Even though different-sex couples sometimes struggle with the decision to marry, the question can be especially difficult for same-sex couples. Until recently, most gay activists in the United States rejected the institution of marriage as oppressive and heterosexist,[12] with some arguing that the state should not play any role in defining a person's intimate relationships.[13] This was and continues to be especially true for many lesbians, who may be more skeptical of marriage than gay men.[14]

Now that marriage is an option for same-sex couples, many gay LAT couples have reconsidered the value of a wedding. Several factors can be determinative of the decision to get married, including the legal and financial benefits of marriage, the value of marriage as a statement of commitment to each other or to family and friends, the importance of marriage as a political statement, the social disapproval of peers, and opinions that marriage is "oppressive," "liberating," or "boring." Moreover, a couple's decision to marry can be informed by other dynamics, such as education, income level, age, and so on.[15]

Research on same-sex marriage suggests that committed couples often experience a "spark" or moment that pushes the couple to rethink

GAY MALE COUPLES | 83

the possibility of marriage.[16] This spark can be romantic, such as attending a wedding and wanting the same public expression of love, or practical, such as realizing the legal and financial benefits of marriage. Some wealthy same-sex couples have even turned to financial planners to determine when and how to marry to maximize the financial and tax benefits of marriage.[17] Social pressure can also spark the decision to marry if a couple's family or friends expect the couple to take advantage of newly won legal options.[18]

Five of the 10 couples interviewed for this study had gotten married by the time of the interview, and one couple was engaged. Their reasons for marrying were diverse. While two couples chose to marry in part because they wanted a romantic ceremony to demonstrate their love to friends and family, all of the couples had practical reasons why they made this choice. Three couples got married because they wanted both partners to have access to one partner's job-related benefits (health insurance, pension, or survivor benefits). One couple chose to marry after buying a house together and realizing that marriage was the easiest way to secure joint ownership over it (a fact that they revealed with some embarrassment). Three couples married to ensure that they would always have hospital access in the event of an accident or medical problem, with one interviewee pointing out that "[m]arriage was never an issue until it became an issue of our physical security." Four interviewees named political reasons why they chose to be married, including one gay LAT who wanted to "say a big 'Fuck You!' to Mike Pence."

The remaining four couples were not married and did not have any plans to get married. All four acknowledged that there were practical benefits to marriage but were apathetic and/or opposed to the idea of marriage. If their situation changed in the face of old age, caregiving needs, or financial problems, all four said that they might consider marriage but that it was not currently a priority in their lives. Two interviewees in particular expressed clear opposition to marriage, with one calling it an "unnatural contract" and arguing that gay marriage had become "the biggest bullshit political pawn" because it failed to resolve major problems of queer marginalization in American society. Another said that attending a friend's same-sex marriage ceremony in 2015 made him briefly reconsider marriage but that his partner's continued opposition to the idea extinguished any interest he had in it.

To summarize, it appears that gay men in LAT relationships approach marriage with different interests and priorities as compared to different-sex or lesbian LAT couples. Marriage was certainly not a priority for the gay interviewees, and some now-married couples had been together for 10 to 30 years before tying the knot. These couples did not marry immediately after same-sex marriage was made available to them; rather, they chose to do so following the 2016 presidential election. This demonstrates how political concerns and worries about physical security have, in some cases, pushed gay LAT couples to marry despite longstanding skepticism about marriage.[19] Moreover, all of the married couples were firm in their continued decision to live apart; marriage was not a dramatically different stage of their lives but rather a formal arrangement with certain legal and emotional benefits. The unmarried couples applied a similar calculus to their decisions not to marry: the benefits of getting married were less than the perceived burdens and obligations of marriage, so they avoided it.

## Financial Concerns and Money Management

Most couples interviewed for this book (gay or otherwise) were in their later years of life and enjoyed a comfortable financial situation that allowed them to own or rent separate living spaces. Because gay men are often childless, they have more expendable income compared to lesbian or different-sex couples on average and are thus better able to afford the costs of maintaining two separate households.[20] Several older gay couples interviewed even owned houses outside New York City where they spend weekends together before returning to their separate apartments in the city.

One of the younger couples was in a very secure financial situation thanks to the support of wealthy parents. The three other young couples had to find ways to make living apart financially feasible because paying twice for housing, internet, and utilities is impossible for many young people. One young gay man moved back in with his parents in New Jersey and spends a significant amount of time traveling to his partner's apartment in Harlem. Another, living in New York while his fiancé lives in Nevada, took advantage of their separation to rent a tiny room with a twin bed in an apartment with five other roommates to cut down on costs.

There was great diversity as to how interviewees managed their finances. Only one couple shared 100 percent of their money in a joint bank account, demonstrating a type of financial interdependence that would be expected of a traditional coresidential different-sex couple. Several other couples maintained separate bank accounts but did not pay attention to how much each partner spent on joint activities, such as vacations or going out to dinner together, because they believed it usually balanced out and did not want to create conflict by meticulously counting every dollar spent. In the case of one couple, as discussed in more detail below, one partner fully supports the other, to the point that the other partner is 100 percent dependent on his husband. Still other couples never discussed finances with each other or kept a close tally of how much each partner spent on joint activities.

Several older gay LATs had a will or marriage arrangement that guaranteed that each partner would receive 100 percent of his deceased partner's wealth. Other couples arranged for the surviving partner to get some but not all of the deceased partner's wealth, with the remaining property going to family members or charitable causes. One interviewee had a will that (unbeknownst to his partner) would leave a sum of money to the partner, even though the two had a strict rule never to discuss one another's finances. Two couples had also executed prenuptial agreements that prevented one partner from receiving certain family-owned properties. None of the younger LATs had a will that provided for the surviving partner, although one young man had a life insurance policy that would pay out a small amount of money to his partner.

To sum up, gay male LAT couples organize their finances along a spectrum from complete interdependence to complete independence, employing a wide array of economic arrangements according to personal preference. For some, maintaining separate bank accounts was part of a conscious effort to preserve each partner's autonomy. Other individuals felt that separate bank accounts would be best during their lifetimes while also choosing to leave everything to their partners after death.

## Sexual Exclusivity and Open Relationships

Justice Anthony Kennedy of the US Supreme Court, in his majority opinion in *Obergefell v. Hodges*, held that same-sex couples deserved access to marriage because marriage "embodies the highest ideals of love, fidelity, devotion, sacrifice, and family."[21] However, for many same-sex couples, Justice Kennedy's inclusion of "fidelity" as a fundamental component of marriage could not be further from reality. Rather, many gay couples choose to structure their relationships or marriages around rules of non-monogamy, choosing to be in "open" relationships or marriages.[22] Such an arrangement is usually made by mutual consent, where the two partners agree to a set of rules or conditions that govern the kind of sexual relations that each may engage in outside the relationship.[23] Other couples choose to leave the terms of the agreement ambiguous.[24]

Gay men engage in sex outside committed relationships at a much higher rate than lesbian or different-sex couples.[25] Research suggests that between 20 percent and 56 percent of gay men in relationships mutually agree to engage in sexual intercourse with individuals outside of the couple; on average, gay men in open relationships also report higher rates of sexual satisfaction than those in monogamous relationships.[26] Many relationships begin with total monogamy and eventually move away from sexual exclusivity.[27]

When choosing to open a relationship, many couples consider the emotional and sexual ramifications of the decision. Individuals in open relationships often compartmentalize their casual sexual encounters from their emotional and sexual relationship with their partner in order to maintain the arrangement.[28] Gay and bisexual men also frequently consider the risk of contracting HIV and other sexually transmitted diseases when opening up a relationship, although recent developments in pre-exposure prophylaxis have changed sexual patterns to a limited degree among men who have sex with men in the United States.[29]

Almost all the gay male couples interviewed for this study were in some kind of open relationship. In fact, only one of the couples strongly believed that sex outside the couple would be wrong, even going so far as to put a five-year prohibition on sex with other people in their prenuptial agreement. By contrast, scholars studying different-sex couples have found that nearly all of the LAT couples they interviewed had an expectation of sexual fidelity and exclusivity.[30] Gay male LAT couples thus differ significantly from their different-sex counterparts in this respect. Indeed, maintaining separate residences may be particularly attractive to gay male couples wishing to maintain an open relationship. Several of the men interviewed pointed out that hosting other men was significantly easier with separate living spaces, both practically (because the other partner was not required to leave the house during the sexual encounter) and emotionally (because the distance helped avoid jealousy).

While many of the interviewees were in open relationships, each couple structured their open relationship to suit their own needs and desires. For some, their relationship was structured around a set of well-defined rules such as no overnight stays, the decision always to use condoms, or a list of certain people with whom sex was forbidden. For others, however, there were no rules because the couple never agreed to be monogamous in the first place. One LAT even told of a time when he accidentally ran into his partner at a gay bathhouse and was forced to leave because the decompartmentalization of his emotional and sexual lives was too uncomfortable for him.

### Caregiving and the Meaning of Family

Many lesbians, gay men, and bisexual individuals in LAT relationships expect their partners to provide caregiving if necessary.[31] Having secure end-of-life plans is important for many same-sex couples, especially given the fact that same-sex couples have fewer children to rely on in old age.[32] Same-sex couples must also sometimes consider the risk that family members may not consider a person's same-sex partner to be legitimate and thus may not offer the same care and support as they would to a heterosexual person's partner.[33] Moreover, some same-sex couples who are not married may experience legal challenges to their decision-making on behalf of a partner if hostile family members refuse to carry out the medical care wishes of a LAT who is sick or the wishes of a deceased partner for disposition of his body and distribution of his assets.[34]

Every gay LAT interviewed said that his partner would be the primary person to whom he would turn for help if necessary, although several emphasized that they had other friends or family members whom they could rely on to maintain a comfortable level of independence. Many shared stories of how their partners had cared for them while sick. One temporarily moved in with his partner when the partner was recovering from surgery; another told of a time when he rushed to his partner's home in the middle of the night to convince him to call an ambulance.

Another couple, described in more detail below, was even in the process of moving into separate apartments in the same building so that they could provide in-home care to each other as they got older.

Studies show that many lesbian, gay, and bisexual individuals in LAT relationships also provide regular caregiving to their families of origin, including elderly parents or other frail relatives, and friends. This includes both direct hands-on care (transportation, meal preparation, housework, bathing) as well as indirect advocacy roles, such as connecting family members to medical and legal services when necessary.[35] Although none of the men interviewed for this chapter was currently providing care to elderly family members, several had done so in the past. They described how their partners had been there for their families-in-law and provided emotional support. At the same time, three interviewees said that they felt no obligation to help their partners with elder care if it was ever necessary. Two interviewees further said that they felt no expectation to help their own parents because they had sisters who would likely be responsible for caring for their aging parents.

The men interviewed also demonstrated a wide understanding of the concept of family. Many had to pause and think about whether "family" described their relationship. Some stated that they were not in a family with their partners because to them the word "family" implied having children and replicating traditional family norms such as living together. None of the interviewees had children, which corresponds to the trend of same-sex couples having fewer children than different-sex couples, with gay men being even less likely in general to have children as compared to lesbian women.[36]

Others interviewed "absolutely" thought of themselves as a family, stating that family describes people who "have each other's backs at all times." One interviewee stated that he was in a family with his partner but that their family also included close friends; another interviewee was unsure, saying, "I don't know if family is the right term. We're definitely a 'couple.' I think of us as 'us,' not as 'me.' 'We' rather than 'I.'" Another interviewee chose to rely on other people's opinions, stating: "Our families consider us family, so I guess that means we're family."

This diversity in how gay male LATs navigate caregiving responsibilities and family dynamics further illustrates how gay men differ from one another in their approaches to traditional family responsibilities. Whereas some individuals structure their relationships around ideas of moderate interdependence, other couples feel no obligation to replicate traditional family roles. Moreover, gay male LATs seem to be less concerned than different-sex female LATs about the gendered meanings of various care-giving practices; whether a gay man's partner was expected to fulfill a certain role did not rely so much on gender norms as on other factors.

## The Gay Day-To-Day

A significant body of research shows that same-sex couples and LAT couples place a higher emphasis on an egalitarian division of labor in the home compared to different-sex coresidential couples.[37] Many of the gay males interviewed told me how they made a conscious effort to divide household chores according to each partner's personal abilities instead of proscribed gender-based roles. Several couples had one partner who was better at cooking than the other, so he would generally prepare meals while the other partner would contribute in other ways (washing dishes, taking out the trash, and the like). Additionally, with the exception of two couples who paid for a maid service, almost all said that they were personally responsible for cleaning their own apartment. Couples with houses outside New York City tried to share the cleaning equally.

When apart, the LATs interviewed used different methods to stay in contact—texting over WhatsApp, phone calls, video calls, email, and the like. Some couples were in frequent contact when apart, with one couple sending each other around 100 texts a day in addition to multiple phone calls. Others were fine communicating only once a day or once a week. One couple even shared a schedule so that they would not accidentally reach out to the other person at an inappropriate time.

* * *

The results described above show that there is tremendous diversity in how gay male LATs choose to structure their relationships, with each couple arranging their lives in a way that is most comfortable for them. The following section focuses on two of these couples to further illustrate this point. These stories demonstrate the many challenges and advantages that living apart offers to interested gay male couples.

## A Closer Look at Two Gay Male LAT Couples

### Couple One: Aaron and Bart

Aaron and Bart are a married gay LAT couple in their sixties living in New York City. They have been together for 33 years, having first met at a gay pornographic bookstore in New York City. Aaron currently lives on the Upper West Side, and Bart lives in Brooklyn, a 30-minute trip by subway. However, at the time of the interview they were finishing work on an apartment in Aaron's building for Bart, which will allow them to live at the same address but on different floors. Aaron and Bart also spend most weekends together at their house in the Hamptons on Long Island and communicate several times a day over WhatsApp.

Even though Aaron and Bart live apart from each other, they share many of the same responsibilities as coresidential partners. When Aaron tore a shoulder muscle, for example, Bart rushed with him to the hospital for surgery. When Bart's father died, Aaron accompanied him to the funeral. Bart even moved in with Aaron for a short time when Aaron was bedridden after an appendectomy.

Aaron and Bart lived together for the first 15 years of their relationship. They moved in together because it was much less expensive than paying for two apartments in New York City. That ended, however, when Aaron began having an affair with one of their close friends. Soon Aaron had fallen in love with the other man and planned to leave Bart, but the other man ended the affair. Heartbroken, Aaron finally confessed to Bart, which sent the couple into months of relationship counseling and soul-searching. After much negotiation, they decided to open their relationship and live in separate apartments, which has been their situation for about two decades.

For Aaron, living apart is primarily about sex. He likes being sexually active with a wide range of men and thinks that it would be impossible for him to maintain that lifestyle if he shared an apartment with Bart. Living apart is thus for him an easy way to avoid jealousy and to facilitate overnight stays with other men. For Bart, the benefits of living apart are more nuanced. Living apart means that he has the freedom to maintain his own schedule and watch whatever he wants on television. Bart has sex with fewer people than Aaron, which makes him feel lonely sometimes. Moreover, Bart spent a lot of time and resources decorating

Aaron's apartment when they lived together, so the thought of other men staying the night in "their" apartment occasionally makes Bart jealous.

Aaron and Bart currently live in their own apartments in New York City from Monday to Thursday every week, then spend the weekend together at their house on Long Island; although that house is solely owned by Aaron and only his name is on the title, both Aaron and Bart consider the house to belong to both of them. During the week they see each other two to three times, often for breakfast or lunch. They frequently meet for meals in Greenwich Village because it is roughly equidistant from both of their apartments.

Three years before their interviews, Aaron and Bart got married. Aaron was long opposed to the idea of marriage, stating that his politics of gay liberation fundamentally rejected both the institution of marriage and the idea that the state should play a role in validating a couple's existence. Bart did not share the same opposition. Although he did not want or need a "big white wedding," he still wanted the emotional and romantic benefits of marriage. Bart also viewed marriage as a way of guaranteeing that Aaron and Bart would stay together, given Aaron's promiscuous past.

In the end, however, the couple's decision to marry was a very practical one. Aaron was about to retire and realized that marriage would give Bart health insurance, survivor benefits, and access to Aaron's sizable pension. Aaron was determined to make the process as unromantic as possible; he didn't even propose, much to Bart's continued annoyance. However, Bart was able to get several concessions from Aaron; for example, after much negotiation Aaron agreed to buy and wear wedding rings.

Financially, Aaron and Bart share everything, but Aaron has much more money than Bart, who was compelled to declare bankruptcy after his small business failed during the financial crisis in 2008–2009. Due to the fact that a person's property can be seized at any time in the seven years following bankruptcy, Aaron and Bart decided to put everything in Aaron's name. Thus, all their possessions (two cars purchased after the bankruptcy, the two apartments on the Upper West Side, and the house in the Hamptons) were titled solely in Aaron's name. Aaron also financially supports Bart; although they maintain separate bank accounts, Bart receives a monthly allowance from Aaron and has a credit card in

Aaron's name. Aaron paid the rent on Bart's apartment. Both men try not to let this economic imbalance affect their relationship, to mixed success.

To make up for the inequality of this arrangement, Bart started to do most of the cooking and interior design for the couple when they were together. This makes Aaron uncomfortable because it seems to replicate traditional gender roles, where the financially insecure member of the couple does more housework. Bart does not see the situation in the same way and argues that he is better at keeping house than Aaron and that Aaron is "awkward in the kitchen." The couple hires a maid service to clean both of their apartments.

Would they ever live together? Both said no. From Aaron's point of view, his sex drive is still as strong today as it was 10 years ago, so he doesn't see any reason why it would die down in the future. For Bart, it is more a question of space. New York City apartments are too small to accommodate their independent needs, and they would never want to live at their house in the Hamptons full-time. The decision to live in separate apartments in the same building is thus the ideal solution for their situation, especially as they get older and might need to provide in-house care to each other.

### Couple Two: Carl and Daniel

Carl and Daniel were referred to me by another couple. Carl works in publishing and is in his late forties; Daniel is a therapist in his sixties. Because of their age difference, Carl and Daniel describe their relationship as having a "little bit of a daddy/boy dynamic" both sexually and emotionally.[38] They met when Carl came to Daniel for counseling. After finishing their sessions together, Carl asked if it would be appropriate to ask Daniel on a date. Daniel suggested letting 90 days go by in case Carl wanted to come back as a client, and on day 91 they went on their first date. They have now been together for 10 years.

Carl lives on his own in Astoria, Queens. When he moved into his apartment six years ago, it was his first time living without roommates in two decades. The thrill of living on his own has still not worn off and was a significant reason why the couple chose to live apart. Carl is also a big fan of Astoria; he excitedly described to me the wonderful cultural and culinary attractions of his neighborhood for several minutes. Carl and Daniel also maintain separate residences because Daniel's studio apartment in Midtown Manhattan doubles as Daniel's therapy office where he receives clients. If Carl lived in Daniel's apartment, he would be forced to leave every morning before the first client arrived.

Both partners were clear that the decision to live apart was not due to conflicts in the relationship or an inability to live with another person. Daniel even explained that he had previously cohabited with another man for almost a decade, so he thought that he could easily live with Carl if they wanted to. Carl similarly emphasized that their living arrangement was not the result of incompatibility or conflict but rather motivated by the many benefits that living apart affords them. Both said that they preferred to "be apart and wish we were together, than to be together and wish we were apart." Similarly, living apart allows Carl, whom Daniel affectionately described as a "big honkin' geek," to stay up playing video games until 2 a.m. without worrying about waking Daniel.

Despite their separate living arrangements, Carl and Daniel spend a good deal of time together. Daniel stays the night at Carl's apartment in Queens most Wednesday nights, and Carl comes to Manhattan on the weekends. If Daniel is scheduled to meet clients on Monday morning, Carl goes home on Sunday night; if not, Carl brings an extra change of work clothes and goes home after work on Monday. When they are apart, Carl and Daniel stay in contact by texting each other over Google Chat (Google's version of instant messaging) and sometimes end the night by calling each other over FaceTime (a video calling service from Apple).

At the time of their interviews, Carl and Daniel had been married for 11 months. Initially Daniel was opposed to the idea of marriage; as "an old-school 1970s feminist," he did not understand why the gay community would want to reproduce an "oppressive" practice like marriage. Carl did not share the same opposition yet did not feel any pressure to hurry up and get married.

Several factors changed their minds. For Daniel, the election of President Donald Trump presented a worrying situation for gay couples. In such a political climate, Daniel came to believe that gay couples had an obligation to get married because, in his view, marriage helps normalize gay relationships in the eyes of straight people. Marriage also has practical benefits. Daniel now has access to Carl's union health insurance, and neither partner has to worry about being turned away by hospital staff for not being an immediate family member if the other is in an accident. Additionally, both Carl and Daniel had a growing desire to celebrate their relationship with their family and friends and to make a visible commitment to each other.

Daniel surprised Carl by proposing on the beach during a vacation to the Caribbean in 2017. Together they designed their entire wedding, discarding any traditional elements they were not interested in replicating. Following a pattern adopted from Orthodox Jewish weddings, the celebration largely revolved around the audience entertaining Carl and Daniel with jokes, songs, and other small performances. Some of their friends were surprised that Daniel and Carl chose to retain their separate apartments after marriage. Carl's mother was especially confused and challenged their decision several times, although after having it explained to her she now jokes about wanting to live apart from her husband.

Even though the decision to maintain separate residences after their marriage was not a problem legally, the couple does occasionally run into minor logistical problems. Because Daniel is on Carl's health insurance, Daniel's prescriptions are sometimes mistakenly sent to Carl's address. Other than that, however, their married status overcomes many of the legal barriers that unmarried LAT couples might experience within the medical system. This was especially the case when Daniel seriously injured his back shortly after their wedding. Daniel said that it was particularly meaningful for him to be able to say that "his husband" was with him; everyone at the hospital immediately understood the nature of their relationship and respected it without question. It was also a relief that Carl was his next of kin. (Before their marriage, Daniel's older sister was listed as his next of kin despite the fact that she was not as closely involved in Daniel's life as Carl.)

Carl and Daniel are both self-supporting. They maintain separate bank accounts and pay for their individual expenses separately. They try to split the cost of a joint dinner or a Broadway show evenly, although neither cares much about ensuring an even 50/50 split. For large joint activities like their honeymoon, Daniel paid for the plane tickets and hotels, and Carl paid for the car rental and all daily expenses, which they estimated to be a more or less equal division. Both say that they would help each other financially if necessary. This in fact happened once at the beginning of their relationship when Daniel gave Carl the money he needed to pay off the remainder of his student debt (around $8,000).

Carl has never written a will but expects that everything will go to his husband if he dies first. Daniel has an old will from before their relationship that lists Daniel's former partner as executor and divides up Daniel's estate among several nonprofit organizations. During our interview Daniel made a mental note that he needed to update his will.

Although Carl and Daniel do not plan to adopt children, they are particularly close to Carl's nieces and nephews, which allows them to redirect their paternal interests into being uncles. Carl's father's health is gradually deteriorating, and Carl and Daniel both expect to eventually travel to Virginia to arrange for his end-of-life care.

Carl and Daniel are in an open relationship with loosely defined rules based around "kindness and respect." They originally had strict rules about safe sex, but now they consider pre-exposure prophylaxis to be adequate enough protection for safe condomless sex. While their separate living arrangements facilitate their open relationship, it is often irrelevant because they frequently engage in sex together with other people.

\* \* \*

These two couples demonstrate many of the details that make gay male LAT couples different from other kinds of LAT relationships. For both of the couples detailed above, for example, non-monogamy was an important feature in the decision to live apart, and separate living quarters made sex with others much less complicated. Both couples also made the decision to marry after years of resistance to the concept, thanks in large part to worries about physical insecurity and political turmoil, while different-sex LATs continue to oppose the institution. These differences and many of the other factors described above mean that future researchers studying LAT couples should take care when studying gay men to distinguish the differing incentives and motivations that drive the decisions of gay male LAT couples from those of other LATs.

## Conclusion

To summarize, while same-sex LAT couples grapple with many of the same questions and considerations as their different-sex counterparts, they also face many unique challenges associated with their identities. Same-sex LAT couples may live apart for different reasons—to hide the nature of their relationship or to facilitate a non-monogamous sexual arrangement, for example—or approach day-to-day life differently than their heterosexual counterparts. Gay male LAT couples in particular seem to be distinct from lesbian and different-sex LAT couples in their more liberal approach to sexual exclusivity and their reduced opposition to marriage. Location also makes a significant difference in how a gay couple structures their living arrangements. In addition to providing a more gay-friendly urban lifestyle, life in New York City influenced the interviewees' choices, with its small rent-controlled apartments, accessible public transportation, and culture of widely available casual gay sex. These findings emphasize the importance of distinguishing same-sex couples from other LAT couples and of understanding the differing political and cultural forces that influence how individuals and couples structure their living arrangements.

# 6

## LATs in the Third Age

As the Baby Boom generation enters retirement age,[1] patterns of living among older persons are beginning to change. Unlike their predecessors, the Baby Boomers lived through the sexual revolution, got divorces more easily and more often, and institutionalized new patterns of coupling, such as cohabitation. As a result, the rate of marriage has declined, and the percent of the population classified as single has gone up.[2] This age cohort has now moved into the 65-plus group and makes up those we think of as the retirement generation, frequently called the "Third Age" group. As longevity has increased and the divorce rate for this age group has risen,[3] growing numbers of older persons are unmarried and for longer periods. Yet they appear to have a continued desire for intimate relationships, along with an interest in more flexible forms of living. Many sociologists and gerontologists have noted that LAT is particularly suited to this stage of life.

This chapter examines LAT among Third Age adults, relying on a number of sources. First, I explore the burgeoning literature on dating and partnership among older persons, as well as that on sexuality and intimate relationships throughout this period of life. Second, I discuss research that has been conducted about LAT and persons in this age group. Third, I describe what my own empirical research has revealed about LAT among persons aged 65 and over.

## New Attention to Sexuality and Intimate Relationships in Later Life

The attention now being given to relationships in later life is not surprising, given that the group of persons over 65 constitutes almost 20 percent of the US population over the age of 18.[4] Slightly more than half of this group (53 percent) are married, but the gender distribution both in actual numbers of men and women in this population and in the percentage who are married is lopsided. About 73 percent of men 65 and older are married versus 43 percent of women, leading some to describe the marriage market in this group as severely biased against women.[5] While some attribute this to the scarcity of men in this age group due to the greater longevity of women and the tendency of men to marry younger women,[6] others contend that this is not the only factor; women also appear to be choosing to remain unmarried after divorce or the death of a spouse, whereas men remarry.[7] Only 5.2 percent of adults 65 and older remarry, with the result that 41 percent of those in this age group were officially unpartnered in 2017.[8] Being single, however, does not mean that persons in this group are uninterested in intimate relationships.

In this respect, it is important to consider who is currently entering the Third Age. Those who reached 65 in 2017 were born in 1952 and turned 20 in 1972. Sociological research on relationship patterns emphasizes the importance of looking at data from a life course perspective, focusing on the common experiences of a particular age cohort, made up of "people who are born into a cultural period marked by distinctive events and beliefs that have particular impact on individuals as they become adolescent and move into adulthood."[9]

What was going on when the Baby Boom generation reached young adulthood? This was the rebellious generation, young people who challenged not only the politics of their elders but also their values and lifestyle, participating in the civil rights, antiwar, and women's movements. This was the generation of the so-called sexual revolution, when sex outside marriage became common and women began to insist on sexual satisfaction for themselves, relying on the availability of the contraceptive pill and abortion. No-fault divorce became available; divorce rates rose; and divorce was no longer exceptional or stigmatized. As of 2015, 14.3 percent of men and 18.1 percent of women in the United States had been divorced at least once, and rates of cohabitation more than doubled for men and more than tripled for women between 1990 and 2015.[10] The Baby Boom generation wrote new rules about intimate relationships and experimented with a plurality of new lifestyles, and those same men and women have continued to do so into their Third Age.

One sign of this is the proliferation of books and articles about sexuality and older persons. A quick check of Amazon.com listings revealed some 25 books with the words "sex after sixty" in their titles. Most of these were popularized and advice volumes, but scholars, especially ger-ontologists, have also turned their attention to this topic. While early social scientific and medical studies of sexuality largely ignored this age group, in 1981 Bernard D. Starr and Marcella Bakur Weiner carried out a survey that elicited responses from 800 people between the ages of 60 and 91, asking them very detailed questions about their sex lives.[11] They reported that the need for physical contact was powerful from infancy throughout life and that "older people indeed [are] interested in sex, they also think about it, desire it, and engage in it when they can, with the same average frequency that Kinsey reported for his 40-year-olds."[12] A more recent study of a large national probability sample reported that 67 percent of men and 40 percent of women between 65 and 74 still engaged in sex (with 65 percent of those having sex two to three times a month or more often) and regarded sexuality as an important part of their lives.[13] Social scientists have long recognized that intimate rela-tionships clearly benefit both the psychological and physical health of older adults.[14] This research has led to concern among nursing homes as to how to accommodate these needs among their residents.[15]

Pharmaceutical aids such as Viagra caused feminist scholars to raise some concerns about this new focus. Due to normal physical changes, sexual intercourse becomes more difficult for both men and women as they age, leading some to propose redefining sex not just as penetration but instead refocusing on touch, caressing, cuddling, and more diffuse, varied, and relational expressions of sexuality between partners.[16] Yet the extensive promotion and use of Viagra and similar products plays into traditional male-oriented notions of sex as a goal-oriented perfor-mance. Older women, however, may find penetrative intercourse pain-ful. Products that prioritize penetrative sex may thus result in sacrificing an opportunity for men and their partners to develop more egalitarian and mutually satisfactory physical relationships in later life.[17]

Whether or not women can successfully challenge the construction of sexuality as male-biased as the Baby Boom generation enters old age, there is evidence that both men and women desire a continuation of their sex lives. Indeed, scholars have pointed out that this period, which is both post-reproductive and post-productive (a time of the "empty nest" and of retirement from full-time work), is a time when, for the first time, life is not reserved for projects determined from the outside and thus allows the development of new and more profound intimate relationships.[18] This new appreciation appears to result both from having more time and from having a sense that the time remaining is limited.[19]

Scholars—of sociology, demography, and gerontology, in particular—have turned their attention to the types and quality of intimate relationships among adults in the Third Age. There is some disagreement about exactly how an intimate relationship should be defined and, specifically, whether a sexual relationship is a necessary part of it. One author, for example, defines an "intimate relationship" as involving "commitment, affection, cognitive intimacy, and mutuality," but she calls it a "romantic relationship" if it includes erotic and sexual intimacy;[20] others use "intimate relationship" as a term that includes all these aspects. But there is general agreement that many older adults are currently involved in a variety of intimate nonmarital relationships, with a primary motivation being their desire for companionship as well as physical affection.[21] Cohabitation among this age group has increased but still is chosen only by a small minority compared to the number of couples in non-coresidential relationships.[22] Research on this phenomenon has commonly been referred to as studies of "dating" among older adults. The earliest scholars in this field found that 90 percent of the daters they studied were sexually active with one another, monogamously for the most part.[23]

One study relied on data from the 2005–2006 National Social Life, Health, and Aging Project (NSHAP, discussed in the next section in more detail). NSHAP surveyed 3,005 Americans between the ages of 57 and 85 and reported that 27 percent of unmarried men and 7 percent of unmarried women aged 65 to 74 and 24 percent of men and 3 percent of women aged 75 to 85 were dating.[24] The resulting statistics and studies about the motivations of these individuals and the quality of their relationships—especially studies comparing widows and widowers—reveal profoundly gendered results. Widowers, who have typically relied on their wives for social connections and as their only emotionally intimate confidante, feel lonely and isolated; they also may not be skilled at domestic tasks and feel depressed being alone.[25] Widows, by contrast, have traditionally been the keepers of kin and social networks; they have relied on these networks during marriage, find them still to be there as support during widowhood, and fear losing them if they remarry.[26] They also enjoy the independence that being single allows.[27]

The health and well-being statistics for older women and men living alone versus those who are married reflect these differing characteristics and capacities, showing that there is little mental or physical advantage to older women from remarriage but a substantial advantage to men.[28] Moreover, 40 percent of older adults' income is from Social Security, so that women's need to rely on husbands for economic support is reduced at this time of life; indeed, they may lose alimony and, in some cases, Social Security drawn on a divorced husband's account if they remarry.[29] Finally, study after study reports that older unmarried women are not eager to take on the tasks of caretaking for another person.[30] In short, Third Age women, most of whom have been married before and are either widowed or divorced, typically revel in their newfound—and in many cases painfully constructed—independence and are reluctant to give it up to cohabit or remarry.[31]

Many of these studies of dating among older adults were in fact studies of LATs. Certainly many of the same motivations seem to be present. However, authors writing since LAT has been noticed as a social phenomenon distinguish it from dating, presumably as a more committed form of relationship.[32] Older LATs interviewed in the United States also reject dating as a description of their relationships, seeing dating instead as describing a temporary relationship.[33] And recent articles note, typically in their conclusions, that LAT may be the ideal relationship for persons in the Third Age.[34]

## What We Know from Previous Studies of LAT and Older Adults

Many of the social scientific studies described briefly in chapter 2 focused on older LATs, typically meaning those who are past the age of childrearing, and subgroups among them, such as those who are retired or approaching retirement. In this section, I describe more fully the results of those studies, focusing on statistics about LATs in this age group, how they live, their reasons for living apart, the gendered nature of their responses, and the implications for caregiving of the aged.

*Statistics*

As noted in chapter 2, one of the earliest studies of LATs was based on a survey in the Netherlands of persons between the ages of 55 and 89. Its author found that, among those who had repartnered after divorce or the death of a previous partner, 55 percent had remarried, 21 percent were cohabiting, and 24 percent were LAT; they were more than three times more likely to be in LAT relationships than persons who were younger than they.[35] In another article, the same author reported that, among those who had started a new partner relationship at the age of 50 or above, 32 percent chose LAT (versus 28 percent who chose cohabitation and 40 percent remarriage).[36] Indeed, a large percent of LAT relationships were entered into at the age of 70 and above. This appeared to denote something of a secular change, because men and women who repartnered before 1984 chose primarily to remarry and those who repartnered thereafter chose LAT.

The other country with similar extensive studies of this group of LATs is Sweden. In Sweden, older LATs made up 5.1 percent of those aged from 60 to 90 in 2014.[37] The author of one recent article speaks of LAT as being "institutionalised in Nordic countries" and reports that the majority of persons he studied who were in new partner relationships after the age of 60 were LATs.[38] In Britain, this group has been less studied, in part because early surveys thought it too sensitive to ask respondents over the age of 60 about their intimate living arrangements,[39] but one study reported that 5 percent of all LATs in Britain were aged 65 to 97.[40] In Canada, scholars found that 2.3 percent of all persons 60 and older were LATs in 2011, an increase from 1.8 percent in 2001.[41] A French demographer reported in 2009 that 4.4 percent of partnered men and 6.8 percent of partnered women in France aged 60 to 69 were LATs; the comparable figures for the 70 to 79 age group were 3 percent of men and 3.1 percent of women.[42] In short, the percentage of all Third Age adults in Europe and Canada who have an intimate partner from whom they live separately ranges between 2 and 5 percent and appears to be increasing, although at different rates in different national environments. It is less common among older adults in Italy, for example, where it is less socially acceptable to enter into a new intimate relationship after separation or widowhood.[43]

A good description of the living arrangements of these couples appears in a study of Swedish LATs between the ages of 60 and 90.[44] The couples studied, about half of whom were divorced and 40 percent widowed, maintained separate residences and, by and large, separate finances; 79 percent had no joint savings of any kind, and more than 85 percent had no shared possessions at all. They lived close to one another, with more than half meeting a couple of times a week and 36 percent almost daily. Moreover, as noted in chapter 2 and confirmed by more recent studies based on European cross-national comparative surveys, LAT relationships last longer among older couples.[45]

Statistical data about this older group of LATs in the United States is largely unavailable, with the exception of one nonrepresentative survey, the National Social Life, Health, and Aging Project mentioned in the previous section.[46] This longitudinal project (with the first wave having taken place in 2005–2006) sampled adults between the ages of 57 and 85, with a deliberate oversampling of African Americans and Hispanics. From the NSHAP data, it is possible to estimate that 14 percent of adults in this age group who are neither married nor cohabiting are LATs.[47]

Additional information about older LATs in the United States is available in the press. An article that appeared in *Newsday* in 2013 spoke of LAT as a growing trend for couples who were older, owned real estate, and had grown children, highlighting an interview with an 89-year-old man who had joined a bereavement group 14 years earlier and who reported that each man in the group now had a LAT partner, with the exception of one who had remarried.[48] Other Third Age LATs described how they enjoyed living close to one another but in separate residences, traveling together, spending holidays together, and being involved in one another's family gatherings but said that marriage would complicate "their retirement funds, real estate and families from past marriages, in addition to intricate inheritance issues."[49] They wanted to keep both their financial and personal independence. One 67-year-old widower thought marriage was for establishing a family, and both he and his partner had already raised their children, some of whom had returned to live at home as adults. Spending one night during the week and weekends together allowed them each to accommodate their different pursuits. "[I]t also," he said, "fuels desire."[50] The *Newsday* article included photos of one LAT couple who were 89 and 77 years old and had been together for 11 years and another who were 77 and 74 and had been together for 16 years. A couples therapist interviewed opined that LAT appealed to older couples with established routines and could work well if the partners communicated well and made adequate time for emotional and physical closeness; acceptance by family and friends was also helpful. The one problem he noted was the possibility of a partner's hospitalization where a strict family-only policy might prevent the other partner from visiting, a subject to which I will return when discussing legal issues confronting LATs in chapter 9.

## Reasons for Living Apart

As one can see from the *Newsday* interviews, the reasons that older couples live apart are particular to this age group. Whereas younger LATs may be constrained to maintain separate residences because of jobs or children in different locations, Third Age couples are largely free of such constraints. Most have retired, and their children no longer live at home. Although they share some motivations with younger LATs, their primary reasons for living apart are unique. The Dutch LATs described in the studies above, for example, spoke of their desire to continue living in a familiar setting, to be able to make independent decisions about daily activities, and to avoid having to make the adjustments that would be required if they shared a residence; repartnering as a LAT was simply less stressful.[51] Swedish women in LAT relationships also mentioned the importance of autonomy, as well as the ability to choose their own daily activities and to avoid the difficulty of adapting to a new partner's ways.[52] LATs interviewed in the United States have expressed similar concerns, along with problems arising from a partner's different habits or from household décor uncongenial to them.[53] The latter concern included not only the desire to avoid mess or clutter but also a reluctance to move into a home decorated by a widower's deceased wife (a concern also voiced by one of the older women I interviewed).[54] Some older LATs, like many of the younger ones, also said that living apart was good for their relationships by allowing them to escape the daily struggles of living together.[55]

Most of the very few articles published about LATs in the United States are about older LATs.[56] The authors of one interviewed 25 LATs

between the ages of 60 and 88 who had been in their current relationships from seven months to 27 years; 92 percent of them had been previously married.[57] The reasons these respondents gave for living apart
were much like those proffered by older LATs in Europe and Britain:

- to seek emotional support while remaining independent;
- to preserve time for their own friendships, rituals, hobbies, and self;
- because marriage is for young people and insignificant at their stage of life;
- because cohabitation exposes one to the partner's bad habits and traits;
- to avoid conflicts because of differences in housekeeping, styles, and the like;
- to avoid past bad experiences of marriage or cohabitation;
- to avoid an inequitable gendered division of labor; and
- to avoid legal obligations to care for an elderly partner.

Eleven of the 25 interviewed said they saw LAT as superior to both
marriage and cohabitation. Although they mentioned their wish to
avoid their partner's negative traits and bad habits, as well as differences
in housekeeping, home decorating, or hobbies, they spoke of wanting an
intimate and committed relationship with the trust and companionship
of marriage but without its negative components.

For many Third Age LATs, their home represents both a connection to the past and a long-term investment in a particular neighborhood.[58] It is the place that children and grandchildren remember and
where they come to visit and thus is important to relationships with
them. Older LATs may also want to preserve this asset as an inheritance
for the younger generation.[59] The home is also an important source of
financial security, often one's largest asset. Many LATs thus want to keep
their own homes for reasons that are both emotional and economic.[60]
A 2013 article in the *New York Times* real estate section included interviews with many LATs in this age group and presented LAT as especially
suited to older New Yorkers who were set in their ways and their neigh-
borhoods.[61] It described, for example, a couple in their seventies who
each lived in rent-stabilized apartments that neither wanted to give up,
although they said they might be willing to move in with one another
if either became seriously ill.[62] Moreover, as noted above, if they were
to remarry, LATs risk losing pension rights and other benefits in some

countries.[63] In the United States, these losses may include alimony from a previous spouse as well.

In addition, many older people strongly associate keeping their own home with autonomy and independence.[64] Women express this reason in particular, arguing that home is a place of one's own where a woman can be her authentic self rather than losing her own identity by becoming half of a couple.[65] Older women are also eager to "avoid an asymmetrical distribution of household labor and unequal demands of caring for a partner," which they may have experienced in prior unions.[66] They emphasize that age has finally given them the opportunity to live without responsibilities for others and to devote time to friends and outside interests of their own.[67] These particularly female reasons for living apart in the Third Age have led some commentators to conclude that the LAT phenomenon represents "the gender revolution continuing into old age," as the women in that age cohort were those "who have been pioneers of the restructuring of family life in the past thirty to forty years."[68] A study of Canadian LATs pointed out, similarly, that the majority of older LATs grew up in the 1960s, when they challenged social norms, but were now more set in their ways; they were also financially independent and did not need to cohabit.[69]

Women born earlier may experience this freedom slightly differently. In a UK study of widows over the age of 65, the LATs who had been born before 1930—that is, who were in age cohorts prior to the Baby Boom—described their lives as "selfish," by which they meant being able to do what they wanted, when they wanted, without having to care for or consider the needs of a partner.[70] The Baby Boomers, by contrast, appear to have seen what the older women described as "selfish" simply as a continuation of rights they had sought throughout their lifetimes.

Describing LAT as a lifestyle that is selfish is clearly gendered, according to two qualitative studies (albeit with small samples) carried out in the United States. The authors of one reported that the women they interviewed had used the term "self-centered" to describe their way of living, a lifestyle they were unwilling to give up after an earlier life of putting others first, but none of the male LATs referred to themselves as being selfish.[71] Another author discussed how her older female subjects' preference for the autonomy of LAT was influenced by their earlier lives, in which they were required to prioritize the needs of family and limit their own autonomy.[72] From the standpoint of their newly achieved independence, many saw themselves as "doing" relationship more authentically than in the past.[73]

## Implications for Care of the Elderly

LAT clearly has policy implications for caretaking of the elderly. This is a theme explored by many of the studies described above. This policy issue has become more salient in light not only of the aging of the population but also of its changing age distribution—changing from a structure described by one author as a pyramid to a beanpole. In other words, the decreasing birthrate has resulted in fewer children and grandchildren at the base upon whom older adults can depend for care in later life.[74] In the face of this problem, some governments, such as in the Netherlands, have even passed legislation imposing responsibilities on partners and children to care for their aging parents.[75]

Some studies have reported that, although LATs support one another in their daily activities, they lag behind coresidential partners in caregiving during illness.[76] One study of 116 LATs between the ages of 60 and 90 found that many LATs expressed themselves as willing to offer care for their partners in old age, but they did so in the context of Sweden, where very high quality state-provided care and services are available for the elderly.[77] Both men and women in the Swedish study reported receiving more care from their LAT partners than from relatives and friends, with women expecting less care than the men and men reporting receiving more care than the women.[78] A study of older LATs in Canada showed good intentions but mixed feelings about expecting care from a partner; the ambivalence was particularly strong about accepting, rather than offering, care.[79] When asked about whether they had actually experienced receiving or giving care from or to a partner, however, more than half the LATs interviewed in one Dutch study reported that they had in fact done so, causing the author to conclude that "[o]lder long-term LAT partners are indeed involved in reciprocal care exchanges."[80] Although need for such care may vary with the national setting, and in particular with the social services that are provided by the state, LAT partners can be an important part of an overall response to the increased needs for care that arise during old age.

Older LATs interviewed in the United States specifically said that they wanted to avoid the physical, financial, and emotional burdens of being the caregiver of an aged partner.[81] Their desire was to avoid any structural or legal commitment, such as the obligations that would accompany marriage. An oft-unspoken fear is of having to care for a partner who develops Alzheimer's disease; another very realistic fear is that a spouse's assets can be reached to reimburse either a nursing home or Medicaid for long-term care. Living separately and unmarried addressed this need for self-protection, which the authors opined might be uniquely American, driven by the lack of social assistance for the aging such as would exist in Europe. Instead, care and support would be offered as a matter of choice rather than of duty.[82] The authors speculated that LAT was a new way of "conceptualizing and operationalizing commitment" that was appropriate to this later stage in life.[83]

How pensions are handled in a particular state system also can have an impact on the choice to live together or apart. In the Netherlands, all retired persons receive state pensions as individuals, and the amount received is adequate to live independently.[84] This system is thus neutral in its impact on individuals' living arrangements, leaving them free to choose to live together or apart without any constraint. In France, by contrast, some pensions may be lost if one remarries and sometimes upon cohabitation, providing an incentive to live apart.[85] In the United States, Social Security benefits derived from a previous spouse may be treated similarly in some cases,[86] and alimony received from a previous spouse may be lost upon cohabitation as well.

Many authors have noted the irony that Third Age LATs, in their rejection of marriage, are less traditional in their social attitudes than younger individuals, speculating that this may result not only from changing ideologies of gender and sexuality but also from their greater experience of life and, perhaps, of having given up on the unrealistic notion that there was any perfect relationship out there.[87] However, even though the desire to marry may decline with age, the need for support and care, as well as the burden of providing it, increase, both driving the LAT phenomenon and also providing an area of difficulty for older LATs.[88]

## Results of My Empirical Research on Third Age LATs

Although the number of respondents to my 2016 surveys who were 65 or older was too small to provide meaningful information about this group, many (15) of my interview subjects did fall into this age group. Only one couple, however, had entered the LAT relationship at 65 or older, and that couple has since moved in together. For all the rest, LAT was a long-term lifestyle. Their lengthy interviews, with each member of the couples interviewed separately, yielded many insights into how LAT works for them in the Third Age. To illustrate, I have selected four couples to discuss below—three of whom consist of different-sex partners plus one lesbian couple.

### Some Representative Older LAT Couples

#### Couple One: Alice and Ben

Alice and Ben had known one another for a long time when they got together as a LAT couple in their fifties. At the time of their interviews, Alice was 74 and Ben was 83. Both were in the theater community in New York City. Each had been married, and Ben had just moved out of the home he shared with his wife when he became seriously involved with Alice. Alice had just bought a co-op apartment about five miles away from the studio Ben moved into. Ben never wanted to get married again; Alice did at first but says she became less insecure as time went on and she realized that their relationship was working well as it was.

The two spend every weekend together, always at Ben's apartment, and often go out to dinner or a show together once during the week. They share their lives by phone when not together—once in the morning, usually sometime in the afternoon, and again at night before going to bed. They take extensive foreign vacations and celebrate birthdays and holidays together. They and all their friends consider them to be a couple; no one would invite one without the other. Yet although they talked about possibly getting a place together at the beginning of their relationship, they never went so far as even to look at real estate. Both owned their apartments, and to find someplace new would be costly; besides, each liked their own home and did not want to give it up for a variety of reasons.

For Alice, LAT allows her to have her own things and to do things her own way when she is at home. Their tastes in furniture and home décor are quite different, and her own apartment is full of things from family and from travels that are personally meaningful to her. In addition, she likes having a space of her own and time to spend alone with her friends; she wouldn't want to see Ben all the time, as would happen if they lived together. For Ben, having his own place is critical to his privacy; he needs time and space alone in order to write and likes to follow what he describes as his own patterns and systems of living. Alice's place is too cluttered for him and seems claustrophobic. And in New York, he says, "you don't give up an apartment."

Alice and Ben are compatible in other ways: They both like music and theater; neither is a sports fan; they enjoy travel; and they keep similar sleeping hours. Although each has a set of friends, they are each other's first confidante, turning to one another to talk about problems and seek comfort. They accompany one another to doctors' visits and are there for each other in case of illness, accident, or surgery. When asked whether they considered their partner "family," Alice said that she did. Ben listed the following family functions they performed for each other: going to the doctor, discussing medical problems, making love, making meals together, entertainment and travel, and emotional support. He was equivocal about calling them "family," however, because of his own problematic history with that institution.

During vacations or when going out together, Alice and Ben share the expenses roughly 50/50, although Ben tends to pick up the tab for dinners out, not only because he has more money but also because, being born in the 1930s, he regards this as part of being a gentleman. Neither pays any of the other's personal living expenses but would help out in financial difficulty; they have in fact done so when facing cash flow problems in the past. Each is the main beneficiary of the other's will and serves as the other's health care proxy as well.

Ben can't remember a time he didn't like being a LAT, and they have been together 25 years. Although sometimes she wishes he were there,

Alice thinks the relationship has worked well for them, even though it is "not a lifestyle I would have ever thought of." She thinks they are closer than other couples she knows and attributes that to not being together all the time.

## Couple Two: Carol and Dan

Carol and Dan, together 29 years, are more typical of the Baby Boom generation, both having been involved in radical politics when they were young. Carol was previously married but felt stifled by that institution; Dan has never been married. They are each in their early seventies. Like Alice and Ben, they live in separate apartments in different parts of New York City, but it takes about an hour to traverse the distance between them by subway. Because Dan is the cook and entertainer of the two and regards Carol's home as somewhat messy, they are always together at his apartment. He is retired but works part-time, while Carol still works full-time, so they get together only on Saturday and Sunday, with occasional dates and phone calls in between, largely because of her schedule and the distance.

The two come from different ethnic groups and have quite different personalities. Dan is outgoing, but Carol is not as social; indeed, she is somewhat reclusive. He likes loud music; she does not. He cooks; she cleans up. Carol gets up very early and has different hobbies than Dan; sometimes he is jealous of the time she spends on them. But they both enjoy going to the theater, dance, movies, and new restaurants together and talk animatedly about politics. They go on at least one vacation (and usually two) together every year, one in the United States and one in Europe, but sometimes they also travel separately. They celebrate Thanksgiving weekend, New Year's Eve, and the Fourth of July as a couple and make a special occasion—a surprise each year—out of one another's birthdays. Because neither is religious, they spend a "Jewish Christmas" together, which Dan describes as Chinese food and a movie. They have many friends together, and invitations are always issued to them both. When the 9/11 attacks on the World Trade Center took place, they immediately sought out one another for comfort.

Yet, as is typical of LATs, Carol and Dan are financially independent of each other with respect to personal living expenses. They split joint expenses 50/50, although he treats on Saturday night, which they regard as date night. They know little about one another's finances. Dan seems to have a bit more money than Carol and helped her with a bridge loan for a deposit on her apartment, but neither has a great deal of money. They own nothing together. Dan has left his apartment and most of what he owns to Carol in his will; she hasn't gotten around to making one yet.

Each partner in this couple has done major caretaking for the other in case of illness. Carol moved in and took care of Dan twice after rotator cuff surgery and a hip replacement operation, and she also moved in— one time for as long as two weeks—so he could take care of her during convalescence from two hip replacements. They are clearly committed to taking care of one another.

At the beginning of their relationship, Dan wanted to live together. Carol was adamantly opposed, based on her feelings of having lost her identity and independence during her previous marriage. Even though they have discussed whether getting married would be financially advantageous, the discussion was premised on the assumption that they would continue to live separately. Only once (when Dan was contemplating moving to another city) did they consider living together, with Carol asking if they could find a place big enough so that they could get away from one another if needed. Sometimes Dan feels lonely and would like to see more of Carol, but they have settled into the arrangement they have, which seems to work for both of them. Given their ease of traveling together, he thinks they could live together if they wanted to.

### Couple Three: Fran and Jeff

The third couple has been together almost 20 years, spanning differences of race, class, and religious backgrounds. Fran and Jeff are in their mid-seventies, and both participated in the anti-racist, anti-imperialist, and feminist struggles of the 1960s and 1970s, causes to which they remain committed. Both are retired now, but Fran in particular is still politically involved. Like many leftists, they often find political questions on which they differ and dispute them.

Each has been married before (Fran twice) and would never do so again. Fran says that she felt hemmed in psychologically when she was married. Jeff felt betrayed by his wife's infidelity but is very attached to the large, rent-stabilized apartment in which they raised their children. If he were to give up this apartment, he would be unable to afford living anywhere in New York City. By comparison, Fran is economically privileged, having inherited a large co-op apartment from her second husband. Their apartments are six blocks apart.

When they first got together, Fran wanted Jeff to move in with her, but he was determined never to live together. Though it took some years to resolve, both are now very satisfied with the arrangement. Although Fran says she is lonely sometimes and wants the comfort of his body there with her, she is happy with being LATs. She likes to have solitude in which to practice her music and to be with her pets, and she gets up earlier and is much more programmed with activities than Jeff is. Having their own space is extremely important to both partners, and their styles are different—his cluttered and hers tidy. They virtually always spend their time together in her apartment, and Fran cooks when they eat in. Even though both are retired, they keep the pattern they established when working, spending weekends together, sometimes getting together during the week, going to concerts, movies, and the like, and talking by phone virtually every night. They regularly vacation together three to four weeks in the summers and have taken international trips together. Both Fran and Jeff have grandchildren who live in the western United States; both are very attached to their children and grandchildren and visit them frequently, often together. Fran's young grandchildren are very attached to Jeff, thinking of him as another grandfather. All the members of their immediate families think of them as a couple.

Although Fran and Jeff split the expenses of their joint entertainment and travels, they do so in proportion to their means, with Fran paying for any expensive travel that Jeff would otherwise not be able to afford. He chips in for dinners and movies, and she pays for two subscriptions for theater or musical events and then takes either Jeff or a friend along with her. They have no joint possessions, and although Fran has made some provision for Jeff in her will (he has no will), her primary beneficiary is her child, who is also her health care proxy. Although both say they would be there for the other in case of the health problems that accompany old age, they have not had occasions to test this so far. Fran has long-term care insurance and says that if worse came to worst, her son would probably insist on bringing her out to live near his family and care for her. They rely on each other to talk about problems.

Unlike the first two couples, Fran and Jeff are very close to their biological kin, but each says they think of the other as immediate family. They speak of their strong emotional bond and support and their fondness for one another's children. They share birthdays and holidays, grandchildren's celebrations, and family photos. They are there for one another if sick or distressed and would provide material support of various sorts if necessary. It is clear that the LAT relationship works for both of them. In fact, Jeff says, their relationship has lasted *because of* living apart and that they never would have made it if they were together 24/7. This, he says, is partly because they met when they were older and set in their ways.

When I asked Fran whether she thought the law should treat them as a couple, she said that it should not. Although she was willing to give support, she did not want to be obligated to do so. Each has medical insurance from prior employers, and they are better off figuring out such issues on their own, in her opinion. On consideration, though, she said that hospital visitation privileges would be one thing she'd like to have.

## Couple Four: Hannah and Isabel

The final couple I have chosen to illustrate the LAT lifestyle in the Third Age is somewhat different from the first three, both because they are of the same sex and because they previously lived together but now choose to live apart. Unlike the other three couples, they don't live in New York City but in a small college town and the rural area surrounding it in upstate New York. They are now in their late sixties and have been together for almost 40 years (with one four-year hiatus early on). This also distinguishes them from the other couples, who all got together in their forties and fifties; by contrast, Hannah and Isabel have been a couple since they were quite young.

Like Fran and Jeff, Hannah and Isabel both come out of a 1960s leftist political background. Hannah is retired, and Isabel is not. They are very committed to one another and appear to have been so ever since their early thirties; they have been through a great deal together over the course of their lifetimes—deaths of family members, Hannah's cancer, eldercare for parents of both, and caring for younger relatives. All the members of both their families regard them as a couple and were surprised, if not fearful, when they decided to move apart.

Their moving to live apart happened gradually and related to differences in habits and lifestyles. Hannah loves living in the country and is very domestic, somewhat reclusive socially, and fond of adopting animals that no one else wants. Isabel is very much a city person, having moved upstate from New York City to be with Hannah, and enjoys socializing, going out in the evenings, attending cultural events, and shopping, unlike Hannah. The two also keep quite different hours, with Hannah going to bed very early and rising before dawn and Isabel liking to stay up and get up later. Isabel is also less domestic, doesn't particularly like animals, and lives with more clutter around her. When they lived together, these differences and their personality differences resulted in a somewhat volatile relationship.

At first, Isabel began to rent a pied-à-terre in town, 10 miles away, during the winter months because she hated driving in the winter, especially after dark. Eventually it came up for sale, and together they decided she should purchase it. Hannah in fact helped Isabel buy the downtown house and retains a one-fourth ownership interest in it; they also run an Airbnb out of it, with Hannah doing the administrative tasks and sharing in the profits. So six years ago Isabel moved all her things out of Hannah's house in the country and into the house in town. They now spend weekends together, always in the country because of the pets' needs to be fed and walked, and they speak by phone multiple times a day—at the beginning and end of each day and several times in between. They also go on lengthy (two-week) vacations together twice a year.

Isabel's move turned out to be very beneficial for their relationship. The tension over living with animals, clutter, and different sleep schedules disappeared, and each could pursue her own lifestyle without feeling guilt or having to tiptoe around the other. Hannah says: "Half the issues went away, and others we could walk away from. We didn't have to fight every fight, we could let it go. And we missed each other and were happy to be together when we were." Isabel agrees, saying they fought less, avoided power struggles, and "felt newer and fresher being together." It seems like the best of both worlds to them, resolving the tensions of living together with each being able to have her own lifestyle and come together when they want to. Establishing a schedule helps avoid making this a constant decision or negotiation.

Hannah and Isabel remain an extremely committed couple. Each brought her elderly parents to the area where they live for care at the end of their lives, and each partner helped and supported the other through that difficult time. Hannah has taken a large role in bringing up a nephew with special needs, and he lived with her for some time. Isabel is fond of him and helps as she is able, sometimes with practical aid like giving him rides home but more frequently with emotional support and advice to Hannah. The two women seem complementary in many respects, with Hannah having practical skills and Isabel being more adept at emotional and psychological issues. They share their respective skills with one another, with Hannah helping Isabel to buy a car, for example, and Isabel advising about care for Hannah's nephew or just listening empathetically. Each is committed to looking after the other in case of illness and has done so in the past. But each also realizes that Hannah is the better caretaker and is also difficult to take care of. As she puts it herself: "I know that [Isabel] can't be my long-term care insurance."

Apart from the Airbnb and joint ownership of the house in which it takes place, Hannah and Isabel maintain separate finances, although they realize that they may need to change this arrangement when Isabel retires. They split joint expenses roughly evenly (although in the past, when Hannah earned substantially more than Isabel, they divided expenses according to ability to pay). Their manner of sharing expenses when on vacation is unusual: airfares and hotels are split 50/50, but they alternate days to pay other expenses. Under this system, only one has to worry about paying bills each day and can also choose to do special things, such as going to a more expensive restaurant, which they might not do if the other had to pay half. Isabel describes their financial arrangement as follows: "We keep our money separate though we are very generous with one another; it balances out. We don't keep tabs but try to alternate. We have a kind of generosity of spirit around money." Sometimes they borrow from one another to address cash flow problems. Their wills leave everything to one another (with the exception of some bequests to relatives), and they are listed as the beneficiaries of one another's bank and brokerage accounts.

Interestingly, this couple has discussed marriage. Hannah is philosophically opposed to marriage, but they investigated whether it had advantages even if they continued to live apart. They concluded that it did not. For example, neither had employer-provided health care that would cover her partner. Yet Isabel is a romantic and, although she realizes it does not suit Hannah's style, sometimes longs for a big community celebration now that marriage has become available to same-sex couples. But, she says, "we already feel married, whether legally or not. We are as committed as any married people are." Hannah describes LAT as a family form that is "a luxury."

## Common Themes and Conclusions about LATs in the Third Age

The four couples I describe above are different in myriad ways, and yet they illustrate many of the points discussed in the social science literature. The interviews revealed some common themes, although with diverse permutations. As one would expect given their ages and backgrounds, all the subjects had experience with previous relationships, including five who had been married at least once and two who were in fact still married though long separated from their spouses, remaining formally married for financial reasons (primarily to protect the former spouse in some fashion). Seven out of eight owned their own homes. The majority were highly educated, and all were clearly intelligent, articulate, and thoughtful about their relationships. All but two were retired.

All four couples are very close and committed; their commitment is indicated by the length of their relationships (ranging from 19 to 39 years), among other things. They interact virtually daily, take long vacations with one another, share holidays and family visits, and spend several nights a week together. They typically spend their time together at the home of one partner—in two cases, the apartment of the male—rather than alternating. Each appears to have gradually lived into the LAT arrangement, with one partner in three of the couples initially wanting to live together but eventually deciding that LAT worked well and one couple experimenting with LAT after living together and finding that it suited them even better.[89] They are all accepted by friends and family as couples.

The reasons they expressed for living apart reflect many of those described in the literature. They want time together but also time to be with their friends and time to spend alone and to engage in their own pursuits, whether it be writing, piano, pets, or birdwatching. Autonomy is important to them. The impact of previous marriages is clearly related to their opposition to marriage and desire for independence. Different personal styles—especially degrees of clutter or mess versus tidiness and a preference for minimalist décor—figured in every couple's desire for individual personal space. Different biorhythms and personalities also played a role. The nature of the New York City real estate market was mentioned by all the LATs who lived there. Interestingly, with the possible exception of Jeff, the need to hold on to apartments they could afford seemed more important to them than long-term attachment to a particular home, as was mentioned by older LATs studied by social scientists in Europe.

The LATs I interviewed differed from those in the literature about older LATs in other ways as well. Obligations to and the preferences of adult children did not seem to play a role in their decisions to live apart. (Only two had children.) Neither did a desire to avoid a gendered division of labor; none mentioned that as part of their reasoning. In one couple, the man always did the cooking; in another, it was the woman; in a third, they shared the tasks of meal preparation. But in each case, the division of labor seemed to reflect genuine individual preferences; for example, one member of the couple really liked to cook, and the other wasn't skilled at cooking. Living apart protected them from other sources of conflict over household work as well.

Moreover, although each LAT interviewed was financially independent, I noted a good deal of economic assistance and interdependence that had taken place among them over the years. Loans were common, all interest-free and sometimes forgotten; sharing expenses according to ability to pay was also common; and it was clear that each LAT was willing to assist the other financially if necessary and possible. Many had made generous provision in their wills for their LAT partner. One couple in fact jointly owned real property and together operated it as an Airbnb. It is interesting to note that two of the older men continued to "do gender" by paying for meals when they went out.

Finally, all the Third Age LATs I interviewed gave each other substantial amounts of emotional support as well as caregiving. Major medical caretaking had taken place in three of the four couples, and all professed themselves willing to give it. Some had also helped partners care for their elderly parents or other family members. In short, they were fulfilling many of the functions of family for one another and thought of their partners as being family to them. Most important, for each couple, the LAT relationship worked, allowing them to live in their own space in the way they liked and to have a deeply committed intimate relationship at the same time. All expressed themselves as being very satisfied with the living arrangement they had worked out.

7

# Commuter Marriage and Cohabitation

Two other relatively new family forms beg for comparison with LAT: commuter marriages and unmarried cohabitation. Commuter marriages resemble LAT in that the spouses live separately, but one home is the primary residence to which the traveling spouse returns. They raise no legal problems because the spouses have all the privileges and obligations of marriage. Cohabitants, by contrast, have very few legal remedies in the United States, leaving the partners extremely vulnerable upon dissolution of their union or if one partner dies, even though they resemble conventional marriages in many respects. Knowing more about each of these institutions gives insight into LAT, by examining how it is similar to and different from each of them. This chapter strives to do this by first describing commuter marriage, based on the scholarly literature and my own interviews with commuters, and comparing and contrasting it with LAT, then doing the same with respect to cohabitation. I also discuss the current legal status of cohabitation and proposals to reform it. This exercise will highlight some of the legal concerns LATs may or may not share with cohabitants, which will be explored in the remaining chapters of this book.

## Commuter Marriage

The Census Bureau calculated that 7,381,154 Americans lived apart from their spouses for reasons other than separation in 2017.[1] This number includes those whose husbands or wives were in the military, incarcerated, or away from home to pursue jobs that have traditionally separated spouses, such as politics, business, sales, immigration, and seasonal work.[2] In commuter marriage the separation is often brought about by valuing the career aspirations of the wife, who was traditionally expected to follow her husband and compromise her own ambitions as necessary.[3] In other words, she was to become either a "trailing spouse" if she followed him or a "captive spouse" if she remained where his job was despite better opportunities for her own career elsewhere.[4] Commuter marriage challenges that assumption as well as the sociological definition of a family as a group that lives under the same roof.[5] The number of married couples who live apart has been increasing rapidly.[6]

## The Genesis of Commuter Marriage and of Scholarship about It

Scholars attribute the growth of commuter marriage to feminism, with its belief in the equality of women to men, occurring in a context where workers are expected to be mobile in order to gain employment congruent with their qualifications.[7] Consistent with this account of its genesis in the women's movement, commuter marriage appeared as a lifestyle in the 1970s and increased dramatically thereafter.[8] It was estimated in 2006 that 3.2 million people were in commuter marriages, a 26 percent increase since 1999.[9] Scholars note that this trend counters the assumptions of traditional economic theory, which has treated the economic interests of husbands and wives as unified and presumes that the national labor market needs a family structure that allows individual workers to move in response to market requirements, presumably taking their families with them.[10] Feminism and commuter marriage challenge these theories.

Journalists began to write about commuter marriage in the mid-1970s, emphasizing how unprecedented it was.[11] They were followed by social scientists, who began to study commuter marriage in the late 1970s and 1980s as an outgrowth of earlier studies of dual-career couples in the 1960s.[12] Research on the topic peaked in the late 1970s to mid-1980s and has declined since.[13] Social scientific studies were followed by stories narrating individual experiences of commuter marriage, often by academics who were themselves engaged in commuting.[14] Commuter marriages are particularly common among academic couples due to the difficulty of finding two jobs at the same institution combined with the scattering of colleges and universities across the country, often in rural areas.[15] Commuting is also easier to manage in such a flexible job setting, with the ability to schedule classes so as to shorten the work week as well as long vacations, including the whole summer, when the couple can be together at their primary home.[16]

The typical pattern of commuter marriage involves one spouse establishing a satellite residence at or near his or her place of work and returning to the primary residence each weekend, although this may not be possible with very long distance commutes.[17] The result is that the spouses compartmentalize their lives into periods of total focus on work, which both seem to appreciate, and a weekend focus on family—at least in theory.[18] In fact, wives often spend weekend time on household work.[19] Nonetheless, studies show that women in commuter marriages are twice as likely as men to increase and intensify their career work involvement; some men actually decrease their work time because of the need to perform tasks for themselves that were previously taken care of by their wives.[20] Whichever spouse remains in the primary residence presumably has continuing responsibility for household work there, although most respond by simplifying and lowering their standards.[21] Ideally, then, the dual-career couple is relieved of the constant burden of balancing market work and household work, meeting these demands in an alternating pattern rather than simultaneously.[22]

These findings lead scholars to question the sociologists' long-time assumption that face-to-face daily interaction is necessary to the viability of a family, and they point out that there are strains that result from long-term daily interactions as well.[23] With the help of modern technology, commuting couples do in fact communicate across distance on a daily basis, although not as spontaneously as if they were in the same house, and the lack of nonverbal cues in media such as email may lead to frustration.[24] There are also indications that the intense focus on work and family may cause broader social networks to suffer, with loneliness as a result.[25] Finally, although more than one study has reported that some percentage of commuters engage in nonmarital affairs, this turns out to be at a lower rate than couples who do not commute.[26]

Social scientists suggest that commuting works differently in different phases of a marriage. For younger people who are childless, it is primarily motivated by a desire to ensure that the wife's career not be diverted at the critical early stage.[27] At the same time, marriages of short duration may face more difficulties with commuting than more established unions because marital roles are still being worked out by the couple and may be experienced as issues of power.[28] Couples who have been married longer have more trust to draw upon in periods of separation and also may have chosen commuting out of a commitment to make up for a previous focus on the career of the husband.[29] These couples are also likelier to have children, however, which complicates the delicate balancing act required by commuter marriage, as the spouse with whom the children reside (the noncommuting spouse) must undertake a disproportionate amount of domestic and child-raising work.[30] There is general agreement that couples who are in midcareer and whose children have left home are best suited to handle commuter marriage.[31] Studies in fact show that length of marriage appears to lower the strain of commuting on the marriage.[32]

## Gender and the Division of Domestic Labor in Commuter Marriages

I have found no reliable data on whether the husband or the wife is more likely to be the commuter. This may differ according to whether the husband leaves to pursue a job opportunity in circumstances where his wife would have given up her own pursuits and followed him in the past or whether the wife is unable to find work she finds fulfilling in the area where the couple has been living for the husband's job. Among the commuting couples I interviewed, about half of those doing the commuting were women and half were men.

Social scientists have been interested in how commuting affects the domestic division of labor, specifically whether it results in a more equitable division of household work between husband and wife. The evidence on this is conflicting. A selection effect (a bias resulting from the selection of subjects to study) may influence study results because research indicates that commuter marriages are undertaken by less traditional and more egalitarian couples in the first place.[33] Clearly the husband's support for the wife's career and the willingness of both to deviate from traditional roles are necessary prerequisites for commuting.[34] Moreover, commuting couples appear to hold increasingly nonconventional views about marital and parenting roles.[35] Given that men did not substantially increase their share of domestic work in single-residence, dual-career marriages, scholars wondered if commuting would have an equalizing effect.[36] In fact, most commuting spouses did develop new competencies, as each had to learn the skills necessary to deal with tasks by themselves during the week. Wives had to develop mechanical skills to perform tasks that they had previously relied on their husbands to do, and husbands had to cook, clean, and take care of their own clothes when they were apart.[37] In short, some tasks were redistributed, with an equalizing effect, but indications were that wives tended to be responsible for more tasks in total than their husbands.[38] And the tasks for which women retained most responsibility were those that were the most time-consuming and typically gendered female, thus preserving a traditional gendered division of domestic labor.[39]

Numerous studies have examined the general satisfaction and quality of life of commuter couples. Unsurprisingly, given that they gain more from the arrangement, women are reported to be more positive about commuter marriage than men.[40] At the same time, women in these marriages appear to receive, or perceive, more messages from their social networks and from the dominant master narrative about marriage that challenge their lifestyle; as a result, they feel compelled repeatedly to explain and defend their decision to commute.[41] Yet studies report that most couples involved in commuter marriages are pleased with the decision to commute; the majority think it has been beneficial to their careers, and almost half think it has been good for their families as well.[42] One study reports no statistical difference on global measures of marital and vocational satisfaction between men and women commuters, between spouses who commute and those who remain in the primary home, or, indeed, between commuting and non-commuting couples, although its authors note differences on selected aspects of the marital relationship, such as women's dissatisfaction with the struggle to integrate their dual roles.[43] Commuters point to the following benefits of their lifestyle: autonomy and mastery of non–gender-linked tasks, a decrease in trivial conflict and increase in romance, an increase in important communications, career mobility, and blocks of uninterrupted time to work. One recent study reports that a substantial minority of the commuters interviewed in fact described commuting marriage as improving communications with their spouses and facilitating their interdependence.[44]

## Insights from Some Commuter Spouses

Because so much of the research on commuter marriage was done several decades ago, I decided to interview a number of currently commuting couples to see if they experienced the same issues as their predecessors. I therefore solicited the views of six married individuals who lived in different places than their spouses because of their work; almost all were involved in academia, whether as professors or students. This allowed me to get a livelier sense of how commuter marriages work, how they serve the couples involved, and their discontents. All of them disliked commuting, and another even refused to answer any questions about his experience for that reason.

Those interviewed included one young couple in their thirties living 800 miles apart so that the wife could pursue a PhD in her field. Previously stuck in the academic town where her husband had a position, she had been relegated to unfulfilling administrative jobs unrelated to her interests. At such a distance, they fly to visit one another every three weeks, alternating the travel, and typically spend up to an hour on Skype or FaceTime every evening, with constant texts during the day. The husband says they "miss the intimacy of sharing daily life together—there are so many mundane but meaningful moments in a day, possibilities for exchange and communion, that you can't recreate in a phone call." But at the same time, his commuter wife appreciates her husband's support for her professional goals. They both hope to end the separation as soon as it becomes possible given the needs of her program and his search for an academic job.

Another, older couple is unusual in the length of time they have been commuting—ten years—and the fact that they see no end in sight until she retires. Their home is almost 500 miles away from the prestigious university where the wife teaches. She is a prominent scholar and would be substantially underplaced and paid much less if she remained at home and taught at the local university. She is also the primary source of the family's income. So she undertakes an eight-hour drive every Monday and returns home on Friday each week during the 13-week semesters and spends all her vacations, summers, and research leaves at the family home. They began this arrangement when their children— two each from each spouse's previous marriage—were young and still living at home. During this period her husband, with assistance from her children's father, undertook day-to-day childcare, and she spent a great deal of time on the phone with her two children helping them with schoolwork and problems. Even though all their children are now away at school, the couple has been rehabbing a colonial-era house and regards it as their home, so the commuting continues. The wife maintains a simple pied-à-terre at her place of work, rented solely for the months she must be in town, and spends a good part of the weekends back home doing housework and pet care. Asked about what she likes about the arrangement, the wife responds: "Not much. It does give me a time to work uninterrupted and also makes seeing each other like a date."

Another commuter interviewed, who has been living 200 miles away from her husband and commuting every weekend for six years, is more positive about the lifestyle. She described it as having provided a nice balance in her life. "I was unpartnered for much of my adult life so I was used to a lot of solo time. So [after getting married and commuting], I had a nice balance of lots of solo time but also some together time." However, once the couple had a child, the arrangement became more difficult, so her husband managed to find a job that allows him to spend about three-quarters of his time with her and to share childcare, which otherwise fell entirely on his wife. This couple is somewhat unusual in that they maintain two primary residences—one in the city where her husband works, and one in the town where she is a university professor. His extended family, including a daughter from a previous marriage, live in the city, so they expect to continue this two-home arrangement.

Yet another commuter, also a university professor, confines himself to the minimum amount of time away from home each week during the 13 teaching weeks of the semester. His wife has a high-powered job 200 miles away, and the couple have extensive social networks and family connections there. They have two children, aged nine and ten. "Sometimes," he says, "I miss my wife and children acutely, but the greatest cost is the burden that my absence puts on my wife, who must assume complete responsibility for childcare while I'm away." Yet, he notes: "Being able to immerse myself in intellectual life while I'm away often feels invigorating."

I asked all these commuters what they thought a couple needed to make a success of commuter marriage. Without exception, they all pointed to the central importance of good communication and the ability to live alone part of the time. Having an end date in mind helped the younger couple. An older commuter with the longest experience of commuter marriage gave a very insightful response that summarizes the necessary circumstances and character to make it work:

> Both partners need to have compelling work that occupies them and provides a good reason for being apart. There need to be social networks at both locations. The individuals involved need to be optimistic and able to function alone; they cannot be people who need a companion every evening. They must be experienced and realistic about the difficulties inherent in all life choices. I think it would be difficult for people who have fantasies about what an "ideal" lifestyle is or who become too lonely while alone.

## Comparing Commuter Marriage with LAT

There are some obvious differences between commuter marriages and LAT. First, commuter marriages are an adaptive response to constraints and/or non-ideal choices, whereas LATs may live apart by choice. Commuter marriage is instead a response to what one book on the subject described as "forced options," a least-cost alternative that allows a couple to adapt to a bad situation, a situation the book's authors attribute, at least in part, to the male model of work and devaluation of other types of work.[45] Second, commuter marriage is almost universally conceived by spouses engaging in it as temporary. Some LATs who face similar constraints related to work or school also aspire to live together at a later date, but some do not; indeed, LAT is a permanent alternative to traditional marriage for some of them. Third, a commuter couple typically has one primary residence to which the commuting spouse returns, whereas LATs each maintain their own primary home, and it is important to them. Unlike commuters, most LATs live quite close to one another and their relationships are more continuous, less truncated, and do not involve the problems of reentry noted in some commuter marriages.[46] Finally—and central to my ultimate questions in this book—commuting spouses are in fact married and thus enjoy all the protections of that status: the duty to support one another, the property and support remedies available upon divorce, inheritance, tax and Social Security benefits, and a host of other benefits vis-à-vis one another, the state, and third parties that depend on marital status. LATs have none of these legal protections.

Yet LATs and commuting spouses also share a number of underlying similarities. Some LATs live apart for reasons similar to commuting spouses, that is, because of jobs in different areas or to pursue an academic degree where the partner does not live. Moreover, LATs respond to motivations comparable to those that lead couples to decide on commuting—most prominently, a desire for autonomy and equality. Gender appears to play a role in the choice of both lifestyles. One author writing about commuter marriage reports that wives who are displaced homemakers are especially reluctant to put themselves in a situation of economic dependence if they remarry, so they commute for that reason, calling to mind previously divorced LATs with similar motivations.[47] Both commuter marriage and LAT are seen by some scholars as instances of the alleged individualization of marriage and family, as the individualist ideology that has long applied to husbands is extended to their wives, thereby transforming marriage from an institution in which one party must be willing to sacrifice herself for the sake of the couple.[48] Finally, the ability to negotiate the separateness required by both LAT and commuter marriage has been immensely improved by the development of communications technologies that allow instant and cost-free access to an absent partner, enabling a couple to speak electronically yet face-to-face on a daily basis via Skype video, WhatsApp messaging, and similar means, thereby increasing their confidence that they can rely on one another despite distance.

## Cohabitation

Cohabitation, like LAT and commuter marriage, is a relatively new way of "doing family." In many ways it resembles traditional marriage, lacking all but the formal status. Its central characteristic—sharing a residence while unmarried—is what distinguishes it from LAT. Unlike LAT, however, there has been a great deal of scholarly interest in cohabitation for decades. In this section I first review what we know about cohabitation from that literature and then compare and contrast it with

LAT. A major similarity between the two, with some exceptions, is the lack of any meaningful legal protection in the United States. I therefore describe the current legal treatment of cohabitation in the remainder of the chapter, contrast it with the treatment of cohabitants in other countries, and discuss some proposals for legal reform as a background to my discussion of how LATs should be treated by the law.

## What We Know about Cohabitation from the Social Science Literature

Unlike LATs, there is official census data about cohabitants in the United States. In 2019, there were approximately 18,477,000 cohabitants, up from about 14 million in 2007 (and 542,000 in 1967).[49] The rate of increase in this lifestyle is astonishing, as it replaces marriage among some groups.[50] Much of the increase has been attributed to the rising age of first marriage and the decline in the rate of marriage overall, although long-term economic trends have also played a role.[51] Over this period, attitudes toward cohabitation—once disfavored, even criminalized—have also changed dramatically, and polls since the late 1990s show that a substantial majority of Americans think living together without being married is acceptable.[52]

A good deal of demographic information is available about cohabitants. This lifestyle is disproportionately common among low-income groups, in part due to a conviction that one should not marry until various prerequisites are met, such as home ownership and the ability to finance a large and expensive wedding, yet both of these are beyond reach for large parts of the population.[53] This has contributed to what has been widely noted as the class and race gap in marriage today: middle-class Whites get married and poorer folks do not.[54] Cohabitation is also more common among Hispanic Americans and African Americans—both groups that tend to be economically disadvantaged—than among the non-Hispanic White population.[55]

Reasons for cohabiting also appear to differ by class. Ideological themes—opposition to marriage as a patriarchal institution, unwillingness to let the state determine one's personal relationships, and, in the past, a marriage boycott until same-sex persons were allowed to marry—are voiced by upper-middle-class and White cohabitants, while others speak of financial incentives and disincentives.[56] If middle-class cohabitants bring up economic reasons, they refer to the economic rationality of the arrangement or voice fears of officially linking their fortunes to someone with a bad credit history and risking being held responsible for that person's debts, whereas working-class cohabitants describe matters of economic necessity, such as the expense of housing.[57]

Other groups likely to cohabit are divorced persons and adults in the Third Age. For some who are divorced, cohabitation is a step to remarriage taken from a position of mistrust of the institution based on bad experiences of it, but for others it provides a long-term alternative to marriage.[58] In 2016, four million adults aged 50 and above were cohabitants (compared with 8.9 million between the ages of 18 and 34), an increase from 2.3 million in 2007. The majority (57 percent) were in their fifties; 30 percent were in their sixties; 10 percent were in their seventies; and 3 percent were 80 or older.[59] For older persons, cohabitation makes sense economically, given both the savings from sharing a home and the ability to avoid both the Medicaid spend-down (a spouse's assets must be drawn upon before Medicaid steps in to pay for a nursing home) and loss of pensions and other benefits that can happen upon remarriage.[60]

Although cohabiting unions overall tend to be brief, with a median duration of less than two years, four in 10 are still together after 10 years (some of these may have married one another).[61] Moreover, the duration of cohabitation appears to be increasing both in the United States and Britain.[62] Among people aged 60 and above, cohabitation is much longer lasting than among younger groups, with a mean duration of eight years in one eight-year study; transitions out of cohabitation are rare among this sector of the population.[63] Among all groups of cohabitants there appears to be a general cynicism about lifelong commitments like marriage in the face of high divorce rates.[64]

Many studies of cohabitation reach conflicting results. Some studies suggest that cohabitants are less likely than married couples to conform to a gender-based division of labor, while others report that cohabitants stick to traditional gendered roles within the household.[65] Some studies report that cohabitants, like LATs, maintain separate finances, perhaps because of the lack of legally enforceable trust between them.[66] Yet there is increasing evidence that the majority of cohabiting couples, unlike LATs, function as an interdependent economic unit.[67] About 55 percent of cohabitants in the United States maintain joint finances, and cohabitants with children behave no differently than married couples in this respect.[68] Moreover, recent studies show that ownership of money in the household is in fact "blurred" among both cohabiting and married couples, whether it is formally in separate accounts or managed by partial pooling.[69] Scholars warn us, therefore, against using a couple's financial arrangements as an indication of the type of relationship they have or their degree of commitment.[70]

Unlike LATs, many cohabitants live in households with children. In 2017, 2,880,000 children lived in such households, 2,426,000 with two biological or adoptive cohabiting parents, and 454,000 with one parent and a cohabiting step-parent.[71] More of these children are African American or Hispanic American than non-Hispanic White; in 2014, 6 percent of non-Hispanic White children, 7 percent of African American children, and 11 percent of Hispanic children lived in cohabiting households.[72]

Studies about the quality of cohabitants' relationships are conflicting. Most studies show that cohabitants are less happy than married people more generally, but some do not.[73] There is disagreement about whether cohabitants are more depressed than married couples if one controls for economic status.[74] Moreover, correlations may reflect that unhappy people are more likely to cohabit than to marry, creating a selection effect, or that their unhappiness results from the greater poverty of cohabitants versus married couples or their lack of legal protection.[75]

## Comparing Cohabitation with LAT

In what ways are cohabitants similar to LATs, and how do they differ? Clearly there are many more cohabitants than LATs. Both lifestyles are particularly popular among Third Age adults and last longer among that group. LATs and cohabitants also share some common motivations for not marrying, including opposition to the institution itself and economic incentives such as fear of losing benefits.

The differences between LATs and cohabitants are starker than the similarities. Although living apart is emerging as an alternative family form, cohabitation has clearly already become an alternative to traditional families. Cohabitants' lifestyle is often indistinguishable from that of traditional married couples.[76] They are much likelier than LATs to have children in the household and do not seem to be motivated by the strong desire for autonomy that LATs express. Cohabitation also bears a strong correlation to class in the United States, whereas LAT is a cross-class phenomenon. The two groups respond to different economic incentives as well; LATs do not live apart because it is cheaper or because they cannot afford to marry. Moreover, cohabitants are economically interdependent in a way LATs are not, sharing a residence, a household budget, and often children.

Regardless of the differences between them, both LATs and cohabitants lack adequate protection by the law. The legal protections each group requires should be tailored to the characteristics and needs of that group. My interest in this book, of course, focuses on LAT. Exploring what protections LATs should receive, I first review both the current legal treatment of cohabitants and proposals for change in order to see what wisdom may be derived from them.

### The Current Legal Treatment of Cohabitants in the United States

Despite the decriminalization of cohabitation, the legal treatment of cohabitants in the United States remains largely negative. In a handful of states they are given no rights at all out of a misbegotten idea that to do so would damage the institution of marriage.[77] This punitive treatment was reaffirmed in 2016 in Illinois, where the state supreme court refused to reverse its policy of denying any rights for cohabitants.[78]

In 1976, in the breakthrough *Marvin v. Marvin* decision, California extended some family law rights to cohabitants under a theory of contract.[79] In that case, one cohabitant alleged that her partner, the actor Lee Marvin, had promised to support her for the rest of her life if she would give up her job and become his homemaker, entertainer, and essentially his unmarried spouse. The California Supreme Court held that promises between cohabitants (except contracts for sex) were as enforceable as any other contracts between two unmarried persons. This included both express contracts (either written or oral agreements) and implied contracts, which could either be inferred from the conduct of the parties or implied as a matter of law to prevent injustice, such as unjust enrichment (where one party confers a benefit on another without receiving appropriate or promised reimbursement). Thus, if cohabitants could prove that they had entered into a contract to share property or to support one another upon dissolution of their relationship, a court would enforce it.

Contracts are notoriously difficult to prove unless they are in writing. Indeed, the plaintiff in *Marvin* ultimately failed to do so. Moreover, where a state requires, as some do, that cohabitants' contracts must be in writing, the contracts signed are likely to be those opting out of *Marvin* rights, that is, where the weaker party waives all their rights.[80] This situation is remedied only by conferring rights by ascription, that is, by extending them to cohabitants who in fact act like married couples in the judgment of the court. This is the law in the state of Washington, but only for property distribution upon dissolution of the relationship or the death of one partner.[81]

In response to the demand for same-sex marriage, a number of states and localities also established a variety of domestic partnership arrangements, some of which were open to different-sex couples. Most of these gave only a limited number of rights, although the California scheme was equivalent to marriage under state law; none could extend the important benefits available under federal law.[82] The climate for legal reform in this area has not been favorable since the US Supreme Court's 2015 *Obergefell* decision legalizing same-sex marriage, as some states simply abolished domestic partnerships once same-sex marriage became available.[83] Even if available, however, domestic partnerships require taking an affirmative action to register, and most cohabitants do not take legal action even when they know it is necessary. In Britain, for example, even after a multiyear national campaign to publicize to cohabitants their lack of rights and the necessity of taking various types of protective legal action, only a small minority did so; and the majority still believed the "common law myth" that they had all the rights of married couples.[84]

Inheritance, moreover, requires that a will have been executed in favor of the cohabitant, and only a minority of the population ever make a will.[85] In addition, a host of government benefits are unavailable to cohabitants, such as Social Security survivors' benefits, favorable tax treatment, and the like. Except in a very few states, cohabitants are also unable to take advantage of tort remedies against third parties, such as lawsuits for wrongful death of a partner or negligent infliction of emotional distress for witnessing negligently inflicted serious injury or death of a partner.[86] Cohabitants may also face discrimination with respect to housing and health care decision-making.[87] In sum, because so many legal consequences depend on marital status in the United States, the nonrecognition of cohabitants' legal status leaves them extremely vulnerable. Experience with their legal treatment, such as the failure of most to register their relationships, make wills, or execute written contracts, will be instructive when considering what legal remedies to grant to LATs.

## Proposals for Legal Reform in the Treatment of Cohabitation

The result of the nonrecognition of cohabitants in the United States is that the law treats functionally similar couples differently based on their possession of a marriage certificate or lack thereof.[88] Some scholars think this is appropriate, reasoning that cohabitants have not assumed any responsibility for one another and that terms should not be imposed on individuals if they have not contracted into them; thus cohabitants should simply be treated as two separate and independent individuals.[89] Scholars embracing this view place autonomy high on the list of their values; they also frequently point to the lack of economic interdependence as a reason to treat cohabitants as separate legal persons.[90] But, as we now know based on empirical studies, the majority of cohabitants in fact maintain joint finances and are economically interdependent in other ways as well.

Other scholars, noting the diversity of cohabitants, argue for a pluralist system of legal rights and obligations. In other words, the state should create a plurality of legal regimes offering different rights to different groups of cohabitants and to married couples.[91] Shahar Lifshitz, for example, proposes that cohabitants be given some of the rights of married couples when their relationships end, differentiated according to factors such as the length of the relationship, the partners' economic interdependence, and the amount of role specialization within the couple.[92] So, for example, cohabitants would generally be entitled to short-term rehabilitative alimony if necessary, but a longer-term cohabitant in a more interdependent relationship would also be compensated for loss-of-career damages resulting from the relationship. This approach to the legal treatment of cohabitants is suggestive of ways to approach legal reforms appropriate to LATs.

The American Law Institute (ALI), a group made up of scholars, judges, and practicing attorneys, has proposed that cohabitants instead be treated according to a status-based model, but only with respect to divorce-style remedies upon dissolution of their relationships; they would thus be entitled to property distribution and alimony as if they were married but have no rights against third parties or the state.[93] The ALI remedies would be presumptively available to individuals who had cohabited for a state-defined period and who act jointly with respect to household management or have a common child; others may establish a similar status by proof of a number of factors having to do with intimacy and interdependence.[94] Another scholar has proposed more comprehensive legal remedies to be effected by passage of a Uniform De Facto Marriage Act that would extend all the rights and obligations of marriage to cohabitants who fall within its terms; this would require them to prove that they "share one another's lives in a long-term and intimate relationship of mutual caring."[95] This standard would cover most LATs within its scope as well.

Not trusting to the discretion of courts to discern who are and who are not cohabitants, I have previously recommended that cohabitants be treated in all respects as though they were married if they have lived together for two years or have a child in common.[96] This suggestion would address the vulnerability and economic interdependence that arise after a substantial period of cohabitation, choosing a duration that excludes a large proportion of those otherwise eligible. The need for remedies after a child has been born should be obvious: not only is the couple then bound by the need to coparent, but the partner bearing the larger share of childcare also requires a subsidy if part of their support is taken away. The needs of lower-income cohabitants are more likely to be satisfied by giving them remedies against the state and third parties (employers or tortfeasors, for example) than by divorce-style remedies. Property and support remedies are effectively unavailable to these groups upon dissolution of their relationships because of their poverty (there is no property to divide, and payment of adequate support is not feasible), so a system limited to divorce-style remedies would not help them a great deal. Again, because LATs are defined by their economic independence from one another and are unlikely to have children in common, extension of similar legal remedies to them is inappropriate.

Unlike the United States, most other developed countries have extended at least some legal rights and benefits to cohabitants. In our close neighbor, Canada, cohabitants—called "common-law partners"—are entitled to support from their partners upon dissolution of their relationships and are recognized as spouses for purposes of federal law, which includes social security and tax law benefits.[97] In Australia, states have passed "de facto relationships acts" granting family law remedies to cohabitants based on status, and cohabitants are also covered by a variety of statutes that treat them as though they were married—with respect to taxation, social security, pensions, immigration, bankruptcy, and workers compensation, for example.[98]

In France, cohabitants may enter into a PACS (Pacte Civile de Solidarité) either specifying the terms of their relationship or simply adopting terms provided by the state, which include some but not all of the rights of marriage.[99] In the Netherlands, cohabitants have a choice between registering as domestic partners and receiving virtually all of the rights of married couples or entering into a contract specifying their rights and obligations. Even if they do neither, they receive many marital benefits under Dutch law anyway, including those related to tenancy, social security, income tax, state pensions, immigration, and death taxes.[100] In short, they are able to select among a plurality of legal regimes to govern their relationships.

The legal provisions governing cohabitants in Sweden were explicitly intended to treat marriage and cohabitation in such a way as to be neutral between them and thus not influence an individual's choice of lifestyle.[101] Thus many typical rules applicable to married couples, such as joint income taxation and joint marital debt liability, were revoked, and other benefits were extended to cohabitants, including pensions, housing allowances, and the right to sue for loss of a breadwinner. Cohabitants are exempt from inheritance taxes and are classified as next of kin for medical and other purposes. There is a presumption that their joint homes and furnishings should be equally divided upon dissolution of the relationship. But neither married couples nor cohabitants receive support from one another upon dissolution, and they do not inherit in the absence of a will. They are adequately protected in both situations by the widespread social supports available to all Swedes as individuals—national health insurance, universal childcare, and various types of income support.

Only England and Wales approach the United States in the inadequacy of legal protections for cohabitants.[102] In England and Wales, cohabitants are entitled to succeed to a leased tenancy (almost 60 percent in fact own their homes, though) and to apply for reasonable maintenance upon the death of a cohabiting partner. Otherwise, they must rely on a theory of constructive trust to recover property at the end of a relationship (a theory that the property is in fact held to benefit the other party even if only one is on the title), which requires a complex and expensive legal proceeding.[103] The Law Commission has recommended adoption of a scheme that would instead apply to all cohabitants with children or to those who had lived together for a state-prescribed period and would provide redress for relationship-generated economic disadvantage, such as loss of earnings or future childcare.[104] No such status-based remedies have been enacted.

Social scientists in Britain have carried out extensive polling to determine what cohabitants and others think the legal rights of cohabiting couples should be. The results show that most think that cohabitants of some years' standing should have legal rights similar to married couples.[105] Many, believing the "common law myth," think they already do. Presented with scenarios depicting cohabitations of differing durations, with and without children, and with differing levels of investment in the relationship, survey responses show that the majority of the population at large clearly believes that cohabitants should have much more extensive legal rights than they do at present, even if they are not identical to those associated with marriage.[106] These results may also be enlightening in the context of LATs, reflecting the assumption that commitment over time is important to legal status, as well as a more general receptivity to extending a limited set of remedies to unmarried couples.

I have several reasons for examining the treatment of cohabitants in other countries and attitudes toward their legal status. A variety of legal models have been developed in the context of cohabitation, some of which may be helpful in determining how the law should treat LATs. Primarily, however, I am interested in the reasoning that has led states and nations to adopt legal schemes applicable to cohabitants, in order to explore the extent to which that reasoning may also apply to LATs in light of the similarities and differences between them.

* * *

In conclusion, commuter marriage, cohabitation, and LAT all are relatively new ways of maintaining an intimate relationship. Both commuter marriage and LAT seem to respond, at least in part, to demands for gender equality. Cohabitation is a much more extensive phenomenon than either of the other two and is, in many ways, a replacement for marriage rather than an alternative to it. Cohabitation is also marked by class, race, and ethnic patterns in different ways than commuter marriage and LAT. But LAT and commuter marriage both seem to be more common among middle-class couples than among lower-income groups.

Both commuter marriage and LAT are new ways to combine independence, equality, and intimacy, but only the first is protected by the law. Most cohabitants must rely either on contracts or enter into domestic partnerships, where available, to protect themselves in their dealings with one another. Benefits from and remedies against third parties and the state are rare. Yet many scholars, as well as the ALI, recommend legal reforms to give cohabitants more adequate protection, as most other major developed nations have done. In chapter 9, I apply what we have learned from cohabiting and commuting couples to consider legal reforms that should be made with respect to LATs. Before that, in chapter 8, I explore the relationship of LATs to the law as it now stands.

## LATs and the Law as It Now Stands

At first blush, it seems that a situation in which two adults in an intimate relationship have separate residences, are financially independent, and spend only a portion of each week together would have absolutely no legal consequences and should not have any. In this chapter I examine the first of these propositions—whether the law in fact visits any legal consequences upon LATs. I turn to the second proposition—whether the law should recognize LATs and for what purposes—in chapter 9.

There are at least two situations in which the law takes account of LATs and imposes consequences as a result of their relationship, almost invariably negative ones. (In the past, LATs might have been caught in the net of the man-in-the-house rules applied to reduce welfare payments to mothers, but this does not appear to be a problem anymore.)[1] The areas in which law encounters LATs today include: (1) cases involving claims for palimony when two unmarried partners separate and one alleges a promise of support; and (2) cases involving the termination of alimony when a recipient former spouse is alleged to cohabit. In each of these situations, courts may be faced with the necessity to decide whether two unmarried persons are cohabiting even if they maintain separate residences and are together only part-time. This case law provides more empirical evidence of the widespread nature of LAT and more insight into the situations in which individuals pursue this lifestyle.

### Claims for Palimony between LATs

The cause of action for what became popularly known as "palimony" originated in the 1976 case against the actor Lee Marvin described in chapter 7; it is a claim based on contract for alimony-like support at the end of a cohabiting relationship. The lawyer who brought the *Marvin* case and succeeded in getting the cause of action recognized in California was Marvin Mitchelson, whom other potential plaintiffs then sought out to represent them in similar cases. Eventually he was consulted by cohabitants who did not live together full-time—in other words, whose situation resembled LAT. The first such case he brought, in 1986, involved a 42-year relationship during which the defendant was in fact married to someone else; although he and the plaintiff were lovers, they had never lived together. She claimed that he had orally promised to provide for her financially for the rest of her life, and he had in fact transferred at least $30,000 to her. Her case failed in the California appellate court on the ground that their relationship did not constitute cohabitation.[2]

Mitchelson tried again in 1993.[3] In this case, the couple had traveled together, and she alleged an oral contract of support; but they had never lived together. The court rejected her palimony claim, but not purely on the grounds that the couple were not cohabitants, saying: "Cohabitation is necessary not in and of itself, but rather, because from cohabitation flows the rendition of domestic services, which services amount to lawful consideration for a contract between the parties."[4] The relationship of the couple in that case did not involve the rendition of domestic services, and so the palimony claim was denied. Nonetheless, this decision seemed to open a path for claims to succeed in cases where cohabitation was not full-time.

Just such a case arose in 2001, involving, like *Marvin*, a famous person—Johnnie Cochran, football star O. J. Simpson's defense lawyer in his televised murder trial.[5] The case involved a 17-year relationship during most of which Cochran was married to someone else but spent two to four nights per week with the plaintiff, eating meals and keeping his clothes there. The two had a son together and bought a house as joint tenants; she had legally changed her last name to Cochran and given up her job based on his promise to support her, and he regularly did so, even after they separated. In response to the question whether palimony claims could be brought when cohabitation was not full-time, the court concluded that "[t]he purpose of *Marvin* was to permit parties to a significant and stable relationship to contract concerning their earnings and property rights" and allowed the claim.[6] Thus, in theory, LATs who cohabit only on a part-time basis could bring claims for palimony based on an express or implied contract in California. But it does not appear that any LAT subsequently succeeded on such a claim, at least not one that reached the appellate court and thus resulted in a written opinion.[7]

The courts in New Jersey, which had adopted *Marvin*, confronted similar palimony claims brought by couples resembling LATs. These claims initially failed in the case of *Levine v. Konvitz*.[8] The *Levine* case involved a romantic relationship of some 70 years standing, which had been a sexual relationship for almost 50 years, including periods when each party was married to someone else. It appears to have been an open secret; everyone knew about it. A wealthy businessman, Konvitz supported the plaintiff to the tune of $6,000 a month (and her daughter as well for some time at $2,000 a month) and bought her a condo close to his own home. When the defendant's wife died, he asked the plaintiff to move in with him, but she refused because of his sons' hostility to her. Instead she spent every weekend from Thursday or Friday to Sunday or Monday with him. This arrangement ceased when his son obtained power of attorney for his aged father and cut off all payments and visits. The plaintiff was 85 years old, and the defendant was 91 when the claim for continued support was filed; he died prior to the decision. The appellate court in *Levine* held that cohabitation was an indispensable element of a palimony claim and denied the claim on this ground. By not allowing her contract claim to be heard, the court visited a substantial injustice upon a woman in a very long-term committed relationship that could be characterized as LAT.

When a similar question reached the New Jersey Supreme Court in another case two years later, however, that court concluded that cohabitation was not required for palimony, although a marital-type relationship was.[9] To define a "marital-type relationship" for these purposes, the court in *Devaney v. L'Esperance* relied on one of its earlier cases in which it had held that an express oral contract of support between cohabitants could be brought against a cohabitant's estate upon his death; that previous court had described a marital-type relationship as follows:

> [one] in which people commit to each other, foregoing other liaisons and opportunities, doing for each other whatever each is capable of doing, providing companionship, and fulfilling each other's needs, financial,

emotional, physical, and social, as best as they are able. And each couple defines its way of life and each partner's expected contribution to it in its own way. Whatever other consideration may be involved, the entry into such a relationship and then conducting oneself in accordance with its unique character is consideration in full measure.[10]

This definition does not rule out palimony claims by LATs, most of whom are monogamous and who render support to one another in a variety of ways. Indeed, the concurring judge noted that any participant in a nonmarital relationship could recover in contract if they could show reliance on an express promise of support, although he found it hard to imagine any situation other than one that was marriage-like that would elicit an implied promise of lifetime support.[11] The decision was to be made on a case-by-case basis.

The LAT's claim in *Devaney* failed not for lack of cohabitation but because the court found that the couple did not have a marital-type relationship like that described in the quotation above. In both *Levine* and *Devaney*, the defendant was married to and lived with (if not full-time) another person and thus presumably did not fulfill the monogamy requirement in the definition, although neither court mentioned that fact. *Devaney* involved a more than 20-year relationship during which the defendant purchased a condo in which the plaintiff lived and where he visited her two to three times a week, often dining there but rarely staying overnight. They went on vacations together, and he gave her money for a variety of purposes. When he ended the relationship and ejected her from the condo, she sued for breach of an alleged promise to support her for life. The New Jersey Supreme Court upheld the lower court's decision to deny the palimony claim. Key to this decision was the court's finding that, in addition to not cohabiting, the nonmarital partners did not spend significant periods of time together, commingle their money, or share expenses (although the court said he had supported her "lavishly").[12] This description is entirely consistent with—indeed, characteristic of—the lifestyle of LATs, but the court found that the couple did not have a marital-type relationship; they had simply engaged in a nonmarital affair of 20-plus years. Thus, once again, a woman in a relationship similar to LAT failed in her palimony claim, albeit on different grounds.

Although the plaintiff in *Devaney* lost, the right of LATs who qualified under the court's description to bring palimony claims was upheld in that New Jersey Supreme Court case, allowing it to be applied in a subsequent case. That case involved a palimony claim after a 17-year more typical LAT relationship ended.[13] The parties maintained their own homes; but she cared for him when he was ill, he helped her with her house, and they spent major holidays, birthdays, and significant events together. Reversing the trial court's dismissal of the claim for lack of cohabitation, the appellate court remanded it for determination in light of *Devaney v. L'Esperance*. Although the record does not reveal what happened in this case on remand (perhaps it was settled), it became clear that a LAT might succeed on a palimony claim in New Jersey provided that the court did not apply too conventional a notion of what activities a marital-type couple do together.

This possibility was foreclosed, however, by New Jersey's subsequent amendment of its statute of frauds in 2010 to require that all contracts between cohabitants be in writing and that each party be represented by an attorney.[14] This legislation presumably makes oral or implied contracts of any sort between cohabitants or LATs unenforceable. Yet as I emphasized in chapter 7, written contracts in such situations are exceedingly rare, even between cohabitants.[15] I have come across no reference, either in my review of the literature or in my interviews, to any written contract between LATs.

The cases involving palimony claims brought by LATs show even more starkly the variety of factual circumstances that surround intimate relationships, requiring courts to scrutinize them for purposes of the particular legal right in question. At least in theory, LATs may succeed in bringing a palimony claim, but it is unclear if any have ever succeeded in obtaining a recovery. Of course, many cases do not reach the appellate court, which involves an expensive process, and those that do may be settled when remanded to the trial court for decision under the applicable law. In neither case would there be a published record of the court's decision, and it would not provide a precedent for future cases.

Of the two situations I discuss in which status as a LAT figures into legal decisions, palimony is the only one in which a LAT could possibly benefit from legal recognition. Termination of alimony cases, to which I now turn, are much more likely to result in taking benefits away.

## Termination of Alimony Based on LAT

Whereas palimony is the product of a contract, alimony is a creature of the law, typically embodied in a state statute governing spousal support upon dissolution of a marriage. In the past, alimony may have been thought of as damages owed upon breach of a lifelong contract of support, but this rationale seems inappropriate in an age when no-fault divorce is universally available. The quid pro quo for support historically was services, sexual and otherwise, but that consideration disappears after divorce.[16] So a contract theory cannot logically underlie the law as it now stands.

To evaluate whether alimony should be terminated when the recipient enters into a relationship with a new sexual partner, it's important to understand what the foundation and purposes of alimony are, a subject scholars have been debating for decades. If, as some argue, alimony is awarded to make up for past contributions of time and labor, along with lost opportunities for income during a marriage,[17] future intimate relationships of the recipient should be irrelevant. Compensation for relationship-generated disadvantage is more in the nature of a debt the spouse who received the advantage owes to the spouse who conferred it. Other types of alimony are intended to reimburse one spouse for specific periods of support in the past, such as when one supported the other during a period spent pursuing a professional degree.[18] This would also be in the nature of a debt, and the recipient's current economic circumstances should be irrelevant. Theories based on business models such as partnership are similar in this respect.[19]

Another theory is that alimony should simply be based on the need of the recipient. Some state statutes calculate alimony by comparing the income of the two parties at the end of the marriage and awarding the lower-earning party an amount equal to the difference multiplied by some percentage (always below 50 percent) that varies by the number of years they have been married.[20] An equalizing impetus seems to underlie this provision, although the income differential is never split in half. The underlying idea is that two persons who have shared a marital enterprise for some period should emerge from it on roughly equal footing; one should not be impoverished while the other walks away rich. Yet other types of alimony are temporary and rehabilitative, designed to allow a partner who has been working at home or not working at capacity to readjust and/or retrain so as to be capable of self-support in the future.[21]

None of these theories can explain why alimony statutes provide that it should cease upon cohabitation and certainly not why such a provision would be stretched to cover a former spouse who is now a LAT; indeed, it can be difficult even to justify cessation upon remarriage. If alimony is a form of compensation for contributions to a past marriage, a new relationship has no relevance to repayment of that debt. If, however, it is meant to address the financial need of a prior spouse, then that need can be evaluated independently rather than using a relationship with a new partner as some kind of proxy. The economics of a former spouse's situation are unlikely to bear much relationship to the amount of time they spend with a new partner or what their relationship is like. Finally, if the new relationship is not a marriage, the new partner has no legal obligation of support at all.

In short, provisions for termination of alimony upon cohabitation appear to rest on considerations other than logic, such as unwillingness to support a prior spouse who is now in a new sexual relationship—out of jealousy or spite or perhaps because the former partner may share some of the money received with their new partner.[22] The fundamental inconsistencies between the theory of alimony and the rules about its termination upon cohabitation have led one prominent scholar of alimony to conclude that the cohabitation rules should simply be abolished, leaving the courts instead to rely on the universal standard for modification—changed circumstances—which includes changed financial circumstances and/or need on the part of the alimony recipient.[23]

In the absence of legal reform, however, statutes in 12 states automatically terminate alimony upon cohabitation, and LATs may be caught in this net.[24] In addition, a settlement agreement incorporated into a divorce judgment may contain language terminating alimony upon cohabitation even without support in state law. Cases are decided by interpreting the governing language in the statute or the divorce agreement or both. Additionally, the theory underlying a state's alimony statute may sometimes prove critical to deciding a case, especially where termination of alimony is premised on a change in the economic needs of the former spouse receiving it.

Several cases decided by California courts illustrate these points. One 1975 case, for example, was decided under a California statute providing that alimony would be terminated if the recipient spouse "is living with a person of the opposite sex and holding himself or herself out as the spouse of the person for a total of 30 days or more, either consecutive or nonconsecutive, although not married to the person."[25] While the partners in this case owned two trailers in the same trailer park, the former spouse receiving alimony had represented herself as her new partner's spouse (to the telephone company); and the two had a joint checking account on which she used his last name. Her alimony was terminated because of those representations alone, based on the "holding out" language of the statute, not on any change in the economic circumstances of the recipient. In fact, her need for alimony was unaffected by the new relationship. The application of the alimony termination law to a woman LAT appears to have been unjust in this case.

By contrast, another California case involved interpretation both of the state's alimony statute and of a marital settlement agreement terminating alimony upon cohabitation.[26] The couple in this case had a classic LAT arrangement, with two separate residences, spending weekends together, taking vacations together, and getting together for holidays; he had keys to her residence and kept some clothes there. Because there was no indication of economic interdependence between the partners, the court concluded that their relationship did not constitute cohabitation within the meaning of the divorce decree. In reaching this conclusion, it considered the language of the statutory provision at that time, which provided for "a rebuttable presumption, affecting the burden of proof, of decreased need for spousal support if the supported party is cohabiting with a person of the opposite sex."[27] In other words, the court interpreted the divorce agreement's stipulation about alimony termination in light of the policy underlying the state's alimony law in general, which looked to the effect of cohabitation on the recipient spouse's need and thus required inspection of the financial arrangements between the LAT partners to see whether they were economically interdependent.

This court's approach seems to be a sensible one, and when properly applied it does not punish a former spouse for entering into a subsequent LAT relationship. It also allows courts to discern cases in which a couple are deliberately styling their relationship as LAT with an intent to evade the law. In a 2014 California case, for example, a couple appeared to be intentionally evading the terms of a divorce judgment that provided that spousal support would end upon the recipient's "cohabitation with an un-related male."[28] In this case, the parties actually shared two residences rather than each living in their own home; she subsidized him; they were engaged and had a joint checking account—and the court did terminate alimony. Taking the law as it stands, this was probably an appropriate result.

New Jersey courts examining whether alimony should be terminated upon cohabitation also consider whether the LAT partners are economically interdependent, but they do so in light of the overall standard about a marriage-like relationship described above in connection with palimony, which requires "mutual interdependence or the undertaking of duties and privileges commonly associated with marriage."[29] Rather than inquiring into the economic needs of the dependent spouse, the court undertakes a larger inquiry into the nature of a couple's relationship. The court in one 2009 New Jersey case interpreting the language of a divorce judgment terminating alimony upon cohabitation emphasized that alimony should be terminated only when the subsequent relationship had shown "stability, permanency, and mutual interdependence."[30] This would, it said, "include, but [was] not limited to, living together, intertwined finances such as joint bank accounts, sharing living expenses and household chores, and recognition of the relationship in the couple's social and family circle."[31] The couple in that case were long-distance LATs. They resided in different states but had jointly purchased a vacation home where they spent time together, in addition to visits back and forth. Not finding a shared residence, financial interdependence, or the undertaking of the duties and privileges associated with marriage, the court declined to terminate the alimony payments. In short, as with their approach to palimony, the New Jersey courts look to how closely a LAT relationship seems like a conventional marriage regardless of its effect on the economic circumstances of the LAT receiving alimony, even though financial interdependence may be a substantial factor in the outcome. In this case at least, unlike in the palimony decisions, the New Jersey approach led to the right result. Yet the court's statement that cohabitation may "include, but [was] not limited to, living together" opens the door to terminating alimony in cases involving LATs under certain circumstances.

The most, and the most elaborately reasoned, cases about termination of alimony upon cohabitation involving LATs come from the state of Illinois. As discussed in chapter 7, Illinois has been an outlier on the issue of cohabitants' rights in general, denying any form of recognition at all, including contracts, to cohabitants.[32] This initially resulted in cohabiting former spouses being treated more favorably than former spouses who remarried, because the law, not recognizing cohabitation, provided only that alimony would terminate upon death or remarriage. The Illinois legislature rushed to amend the statute to add that alimony would also be terminated if the former spouse cohabited "on a resident, continuing conjugal basis."[33]

The cases examined what constituted a relationship that was "resident," "continuing," and "conjugal." Courts in different appellate districts reached inconsistent results. One case held that residence 50 percent of the time was noncontinuous,[34] whereas another found that six weeks' full-time residence (with a married man) was sufficient to terminate alimony.[35] Whether there needed to be a sexual relationship was contested.[36] There was, in short, little logic to the cases. It was also difficult to discern the theory of alimony underlying them.

In the face of this inconsistency in the case law, one Illinois appellate court (*In re Marriage of Herrin*) created a list of factors to distinguish whether a relationship was cohabitation for the purposes of terminating alimony.[37] Courts were directed to look at:

1. the length of the couple's relationship;
2. the amount of time they spent together;
3. the nature of the activities they engaged in;
4. the interrelation of their personal affairs;
5. whether they vacationed together; and
6. whether they spent holidays together.[38]

These factors can be applied to many LAT relationships. In *Herrin*, the couple had two homes, but he spent most evenings at hers; they shared meals, vacationed, and spent holidays together and had been a monogamous committed couple for two and a half years. The former wife argued that her alimony should not be terminated because her new partner did not contribute to her support or affect her need for the $24,000 she had been receiving per year from her former husband. No, said the court, the rationale for alimony was not need but rather the inequity created when a former spouse was involved in a husband-wife relationship without legally formalizing it.[39] In short, the Illinois court was continuing the state's punitive treatment of unmarried cohabitation and concerned about not disadvantaging former spouses who chose to remarry rather than cohabit.

In 2006, a court reaffirmed this position in a case involving a classic LAT relationship: the couple spent several nights every week together, shared several meals every week, spent holidays and attended family events together, and took trips together, but an extensive trial record showed that they were completely independent of one another economically.[40] The wife in this case argued that the factor relating to financial interdependence should be dispositive because alimony was based on need, but the court adamantly rejected this reasoning once again, saying that need was no more a factor in de facto marriages than in de jure ones: "[N]eed is simply irrelevant to the determination whether a *de facto* marriage exists."[41] In short, in both these cases an Illinois court terminated alimony payments to a woman LAT despite evidence that she was financially independent of her LAT partner.

By 2011, however, a series of cases had been decided by Illinois courts in which couples were clearly LATs but the courts did not terminate alimony, rationalizing their decisions by the fact that the activities the couple shared were not marriage-like, giving as one example "household chores."[42] Finally, in 2015, the *Miller* case shifted the conversation by reexamining the *Herrin* factors listed above.[43] Although the LAT relationship in the case *In re Marriage of Miller* was over by the time the matter reached court, the couple had previously spent weekends, vacations, holidays, and other special events together, and the trial court had terminated the former wife's very high alimony that had been awarded on a permanent basis at the end of a 25-year marriage. The appellate court reversed, stating that the six *Herrin* factors were a nonexclusive list aimed at determining whether a new relationship functioned both practically and economically like a marriage. Intimate dating relationships, by contrast, did not have the level of permanence that usually was embodied in a financial and material partnership and commonly included a shared home. Although cohabitation *might* be found, it said, where each partner had a separate residence, that situation was exceptional. Moreover, because termination of alimony is permanent, the new relationship must evince the same quality.

Although it was easy to decide that the LAT relationship in *Miller* was not permanent because it was already over, this reasoning has since been applied in cases that involved ongoing relationships as well. In one 2016 case, a former husband sought to terminate $17,500 per month in spousal support awarded at the end of a 36-year marriage of a very wealthy couple, doing so 10 years after the divorce was final.[44] The wife's new partner had moved into a condominium in her apartment complex after they had dated for four years, five buildings away from hers; they each had keys to each other's apartment and saw each other virtually every day. He regularly slept at her apartment on Friday and Saturday nights but liked to spend time in his own unit alone and to watch sports on television there. They spent holidays together and all kinds of special occasions, including those related to their children and grandchildren. They often vacationed together but always split the cost of joint activities. Their finances and assets were completely separate, and neither was in the other's will or the beneficiary of any annuity. They had no plans to marry or live together and were satisfied with their relationship as it was. In short, they were typical later-life LATs. Following—indeed, quoting—*Miller*, both the trial and appellate courts held that their relationship did not have the level of commitment to transform it into a de facto marriage under the Illinois law requiring termination of alimony.

In short, the courts of Illinois appear to be coming to see LAT relationships as a common and socially accepted form of coupledom. The existence of so many cases confirms that there are many of these couples in the United States, and the courts seem to be learning how to address these cases more appropriately. They are forced to do so in states like Illinois, where the archaic basis of the alimony law requires them to. If the couple just described had married while still maintaining separate condos and thus undertook legal obligations for one another, including spousal support and property remedies upon divorce and a spousal share upon death, and their joint economic situation in fact alleviated the former wife's need for alimony, then her alimony would and perhaps should be terminated. But if it was awarded as a result of her efforts as a wife, homemaker, mother, and supporter of her husband's business over the course of a 36-year marriage, then it should not be terminated because it would constitute compensation earned for services in the past. LATs differ substantially from married couples, however. As long as LAT couples are financially independent of one another, as they typically seem to be, the existence of their relationships should have no impact at all on the continuation or termination of a former spouse's payment of alimony.

I have focused on California, New Jersey, and Illinois in this discussion because those are the states that appear to be developing coherent legal standards to distinguish between cohabitants and LATs for purposes of terminating alimony. Interestingly, two of these states—New Jersey and California—have been among the most generous in their treatment of cohabitants. Illinois—the state that is least generous to cohabitants—nonetheless appears to have developed the standard most likely to treat LATs fairly with respect to terminating alimony.

These are not the only states in which LATs risk punitive treatment under alimony termination rules, however.[45] A Delaware appellate court, for example, reversing a trial court finding to the contrary, terminated alimony in a case where a couple had separate residences and led quite independent lives on the grounds that the male LAT took out the garbage and did yard work at his partner's house.[46] Moreover, in Tennessee, a court terminated alimony payments to a former wife who maintained a residence in a different state from her LAT partner based on a prolonged visit to him, although neither received support from the other.[47] It did so based on its interpretation of "cohabitation" under a divorce settlement agreement that provided, at the end of a 32-year marriage, that the husband pay the wife $52,000 per year plus her health insurance premiums until she qualified for Social Security. These payments were the wife's sole source of support, yet the court ordered that she repay several years of alimony—all that she had received since the date of her prolonged visit. The court based its decision on the definition of "cohabitation" in Black's Law Dictionary, which did not require receipt of financial assistance. In short, there is no lack of alimony termination cases involving LATs, confirming that courts have been ruling on cases in which they were required to distinguish between LATs and cohabitants and also demonstrating the frequent injustices that LATs suffer under the legal system as it stands.

These injustices happen primarily to women, in part because women are the majority of alimony recipients. As scholars point out, the termination-upon-cohabitation rules are gendered in a variety of other ways as well. Courts generally allow male recipients of alimony to retain it even though they enter into new relationships.[48] They are also unlikely to assume support and thus terminate alimony when a former wife's new lover is a woman.[49] In addition, the fact that termination is triggered in most cases only by a relationship involving sex indicates that the rule functions to penalize the choices of relationship made by women who receive alimony and to police their sexuality more generally.[50] What if a woman spent her alimony payments on gambling or drugs? The law would not step in.

To summarize, laws that terminate alimony upon cohabitation—whether the state rule is based on need, financial intermingling, actual support received, or entry into a marriage-like relationship—have caught many LATs in their net, with the result in most cases being to their detriment. Ironically, the rules seem to imply that intimate partners should be responsible for each other's support, even if they are not, either legally or in fact. Indeed, many are LATs precisely because of their wish to avoid financial obligations to one another.

* * *

As this chapter has demonstrated, the law recognizes LATs in at least two contexts: claims for palimony and cases seeking to terminate alimony upon cohabitation. I venture to say that the outcomes in both types of cases more frequently harm LATs than help them. As I will argue in chapter 9, LAT partners should be able to contract with one another about property and support, just as all individuals—whether or not they are intimate partners—are able to do. Moreover, the rules on alimony termination upon cohabitation should either be abolished or applied only in cases of clear economic interdependence that alleviates the need of the alimony recipient. This legal reform would help not only LATs but also cohabitants.

# 9

## How Should the Law Treat LATs?

In chapter 8, I showed that US law does in fact take LATs into account in a number of circumstances. The purpose of this chapter is to discuss whether and, if so, how the law should treat LATs more broadly. I first discuss what the purposes of family law should be in general, because family law's goals should be central to deciding what legal protections LATs should receive. I also discuss evidence about what LATs themselves desire in the way of legal protection. I conclude with some specific recommendations for legal change.

### The Purposes of Family Law

The best way to decide whether LATs should be given more attention by the legal system is to begin with an inquiry into the goals of family law. Depending on one's perspective, there are a variety of public policy goals to aim for. I will outline several general approaches; they are not always mutually exclusive. One's goal may be to use the law to encourage marriage and/or cohabitation, whether for ideological reasons or pragmatic ones, such as encouraging the raising of children in two-parent households. If this is the goal, then law and policy should seek to address constraints on living together, including legal disincentives to doing so and other obstacles, such as a shortage of affordable housing. This is also the way to go if one's aims include the privatization of welfare for political or ideological reasons. US law appears to follow this approach, but only with respect to encouraging marriage; it is generally quite punitive in its treatment of cohabitation and sees marriage as the ideal.[1] Yet it is doubtful whether it is either possible or desirable to shift most unmarried couples into marriage by legal manipulation; some may be unfitted for that status in general, and others may not desire it for a variety of reasons.

Alternatively, one may prioritize individual autonomy and choice, seeking to allow individuals the freedom to choose whatever living arrangements they desire for themselves. Theorists of this persuasion caution against imposing any obligation, contractual or otherwise, on involuntary parties.[2] To foster freedom of choice, law and policy should seek to be neutral in their treatment of marriage, cohabitation, and other forms of adult affiliation; as described in chapter 7, Swedish law provides an example of this approach. The ability of individuals to rely on the state if they are unable to care for themselves appears to be a necessary prerequisite for such neutrality. This is not possible in the United States, which lacks such a social welfare system. Moreover, although freedom with respect to individual choice of relationship status is a desirable goal, autonomy—especially within families—is relational (or illusory). Thus it cannot be the primary or only goal of a system of family law.

Another goal may be to protect vulnerable parties at the end of their relationships regardless of the relationship form they have chosen. If so, the law should address situations in which participation in a committed relationship may leave one of the parties vulnerable at its end and compensate them for relationship-generated disadvantages. Ideally these parties would be protected under a welfare system such as that in Sweden, but this goal can sometimes be accomplished by extending many of the rights and obligations of marriage to persons in marriage-like relationships in countries without social welfare protections, in effect privatizing welfare. This type of protection is imposed on married couples within the current US legal and political systems and should, I think, be extended to the many other couples who share a residence. Legal protections involving rights against the state and third parties are also important and may, as discussed in chapter 7, be the only meaningful rights for persons without property or adequate financial means.

Finally, US law may seek to recognize the many functions that families provide for their members, including economic support, where it forms part of an intimate relationship, and the committed caretaking that is part of most such relationships. We clearly benefit as a society from the caretaking that partners provide for one another, whether they live together or not. Thus family law should seek to encourage and facilitate commitment and caretaking regardless of a couple's living arrangements.

Scholarly discussion relevant to this issue in the United States has almost universally been directed to the question of cohabitants' rights. Views developed in that context based on differing theories about family law yield insights into what the treatment of LATs should be as well, so I begin by describing several approaches advocated by legal scholars. Elizabeth and Robert Scott have argued that the law should recognize an adult affiliation when it fulfills socially valuable functions and thus relieves the state of its obligation to care for dependency.[3] To determine whether an affiliation qualifies, they propose looking to whether it is characterized by:

1. a demonstrated commitment to a long-term emotionally intimate affiliation in which the parties usually live together in a relationship of relative equality;
2. the assumption of responsibility for mutual care (and the care of children and other dependent family members);
3. financial interdependence; and
4. an understanding that the members' welfare is prioritized above that of others.

This approach clearly prioritizes the privatization of welfare in its explicit goal to relieve the state of the obligation to care for dependency. Many, if not most, cohabitants would qualify for legal recognition under the Scotts' theory, but LATs would not qualify, primarily because of their typical lack of financial interdependence and attachment to personal independence.

William Eskridge, by contrast, has argued that family law should provide a "guided choice regime of menus, default rules, and override rules."[4] He therefore suggests creating new regulatory regimes for non-marital relationships that serve the following functions:

1. encouragement of committed relationships;
2. lowering transaction costs for couples to achieve their own goals; and
3. protecting vulnerable persons.

This approach prioritizes both choice and the protection of vulnerable parties. Under this type of inquiry, designed to evaluate cohabitation, there is a powerful argument that some legal recognition of LATs would fulfill the three functions of family law that Eskridge outlines.

Another scholar, Jessica Feinberg, takes a somewhat similar approach. Asking about the role of nonmarital statuses such as domestic partnerships and civil unions in the era of same-sex marriage, Feinberg advocates the creation of a comprehensive system of adult relationship recognition that does not depend on marriage, because a system focused on marriage leaves many couples without necessary protections.[5] To accomplish this, she proposes that states create a nonmarital status with a default regime of separate property and a package of rights that includes certain minimum core protections, including family and medical leave, hospital visitation rights identical to those of a spouse, a preference for designation as health care proxy, power of attorney, and guardianship, conferring a presumption of parentage of any child born during the union, giving rights to stepparents (including standing to seek visitation of the other partner's children), and domestic violence protections. States might also wish to provide rights with respect to inheritance, taxes, testimonial privileges, support, liability for debt, and claims in tort and contract.

This would be an opt-in system requiring registration. The federal government would then decide what federal rights and benefits to provide to those in these state-created statuses but should definitely include those related to the ability of partners to care for each other and exclude those predicated on economic interdependence. Federal benefits extended to unmarried couples who registered for the state-created status would thus include, at a minimum, coverage under the Family and Medical Leave Act, visitation privileges in Veterans Administration hospitals and federal prisons, and the ability to cover one's partner under federal employees' health care plans.

For a variety of reasons—the requirement of registration and the assumption of economic independence, for example—Feinberg's scheme fails to provide adequate legal protection for cohabitants and LATs. However, focusing as it does with specificity on the state-created rights and benefits necessary to be a caring partner, Feinberg's list does suggest a number of legal changes that would benefit LATs and thereby society at large. Their provision should not require registration, however.

Feinberg's approach, like that of Eskridge, rests on a theory of family law that I share: its primary purposes are to allow individuals to choose how they wish to structure their intimate relationships, to support the caregiving functions they provide for one another, and to protect persons who are harmed when relationships end. A growing body of legal scholarship supports these goals in the context of cohabitation, proposing that the law should encourage long-term caretaking relationships and supply benefits tailored to the public goods thereby being fostered.[6] Extending the application of these goals to nontraditional relationships such as LAT would promote both choice and caretaking.

As the next section will demonstrate, LATs are somewhat ambivalent about what legal protections they desire but seem to agree on the need for a number of specific rights they now lack, and many of those rights resemble those outlined by Feinberg.

## What Legal Rights Do LATs Want?

I asked the LATs I interviewed to tell me what legal remedies they thought they needed. For whatever reason, all of the suggestions were made by women. None brought up major legal rights premised on economic dependence and consequent vulnerability, such as Social Security survivors' benefits. Instead, their individual suggestions fall strikingly into the goals I have endorsed above. Based on their own experienced needs, the interviewees suggested:

1. provision of family or compassionate leave to care for a LAT partner;
2. legally specified entitlement to hospital visitation privileges;
3. eligibility for coverage under a partner's health insurance policy;
4. reform of the tax treatment of pension benefits (which are taxed if a LAT or cohabitant is the beneficiary but not if a spouse is the beneficiary) to treat them as nontaxable;
5. legal recognition of contracts between LAT partners; and
6. provision of a registration system for those who want to register their partnerships.

These suggestions are consistent with those in other studies in which LATs have been asked about their legal preferences. One such study was based on interviews with 54 LATs between the ages of 40 and 66 in Belgium.[7] The respondents voiced a desire to have paid leaves of absence to look after their partners, status as next of kin for hospital visitation and medical decisions, and lower inheritance taxes. They were concerned about rights in the event their partner died—whether their status would be recognized in connection with disposition of the body and memorial rites—and rights to a continued relationship with the partner's children if the relationship ended. In the absence of a will, however, they thought a partner's children should inherit instead of the partner, because LATs had not contributed to the accumulation of one another's estates. They also wanted some way to formalize their relationships. Other scholars, similarly, mention LATs' concerns about access to a LAT partner in case of accident, medical care, and the like.[8]

One British study asked 50 LAT interviewees whether LATs should have rights similar to married couples as to inheritance.[9] One-third of the respondents (a group with a median duration of five years in the relationship and most with previous experience of relationship breakdown and no plans to live together in the future) said they did not think so, giving as reasons, for example, that LATs have no joint material project and that children should inherit first anyway. Just under one-third (whose median age was 42 and who planned to cohabit or marry in the future) thought that inheritance rights should be extended to LATs and that one LAT partner's money and property should be available to his or her partner upon death, assuming some length of relationship and mutual commitment. The remainder of the respondents thought that whether LATs received rights to inheritance should depend on the circumstances, with the presence of dependent children being a major justification for establishing legal provisions. In short, these results were inconclusive but generally negative about the idea of extending inheritance rights to typical LATs. The opinions of the group with the longest period of living apart and no plans to live together deserve the most attention, and they thought LATs should not have rights similar to those of married couples with respect to inheritance.

To summarize, the legal rights sought both by the LATs I interviewed and by those on which other studies were based are primarily those that enable mutual caretaking, especially in illness, and (in the United States) those pertaining to health insurance coverage, which also has obvious relevance to caretaking. Some would also like tax preferences with respect to pensions and inheritance comparable to those given to spouses. These would apply, of course, only if the partner were designated as the primary beneficiary of the pension or will. A demand for some sort of registration system also appears repeatedly.

These proposals by various LATs and the general purposes of family law inform my conclusions about what legal reforms are desirable, which I describe in the next section.

## Recommendations for Legal Reforms to Protect LATs

In my book about cohabitation I recommended that cohabitants who had been together for two years or had a child together should be treated as though they were married; that cohabitants be given the ability to opt out of these obligations by contract; and that a system of partnership registration should be provided for those who desired it.[10] This proposal was directed to the US setting as it currently exists, without the social and economic supports available in a social welfare state such as Sweden. Under these circumstances, my goal was primarily to protect vulnerable parties—mostly women and children—at the end of cohabiting relationships, even though it meant privatizing many welfare functions. Remedies against the state and third parties were provided by assimilating cohabitation to marriage, including but not limited to Social Security survivors benefits, unemployment insurance, and damages for wrongful death and various tort remedies. I made this recommendation based on social science data showing that cohabitants belonged to many groups who were socially and economically vulnerable in American society; that the majority pooled their income and were substantially interdependent economically in other ways as well; and that a large number of children lived with these couples. These conditions do not apply to LATs.

I was initially struck by the differences between LATs and cohabitants, especially by LATs' lack of the extensive financial interdependence exhibited by cohabitants. LATs by definition each have their own homes and the protection that entails against extreme vulnerability upon separation from or the death of a partner. LATs also appear to be a relatively well-educated group, so I thought that perhaps we could simply rely on them to enter into other legal arrangements, such as drafting wills and executing contracts to address their own needs. After my extensive research about LATs, however, I realized that they are involved in a great deal of mutual caretaking and, in some instances, are economically intertwined even though they have separate residences. Based on my convictions about the purposes of family law and in response to needs perceived in my qualitative interviews, I therefore concluded that a limited number of legal remedies should be provided for LATs.

As a preliminary matter, a system of registration of their partnerships should be made available to LATs who want to formalize their relationships. These partnerships should provide the legal benefits I describe below at a minimum, as well as others the parties may wish to designate. It is obviously much easier for a court to administer legal remedies without having to decide whether couples qualify for them; registration makes their status clear in advance. Other authorities as well—hospitals, insurance agencies, and funeral directors, for example—have to make decisions quickly, so that a system of certifying who is a LAT and who is not would be valuable. Providing a registration scheme would also allow for the public and social recognition many LATs fear they would lack upon their partner's death.

Because most people fail to ensure that they are protected when it requires them to take affirmative legal action, however, the legal rights I recommend should also be available in the absence of registration upon a showing of a committed relationship. In the absence of registration, I suggest that legal rights should attach only when a LAT relationship has lasted for five years. Moreover, the group I have designated as "young" or "dating" LATs (aged 18 to 24) should be excluded from any legal recognition if they do not register. As discussed above, persons in this group still depend on their families of origin for caretaking—or don't need much of it. The remaining groups of LATs should be entitled to some rights upon a showing of their frequent and intimate interactions, mutual caretaking, and sharing of the activities characteristic of LATs, such as meals, vacations, and holidays. Courts seem to be developing tests in the context of alimony and cohabitation (described in chapter 8) that would work in the case of a major dispute. Most of the rights outlined below would be unlikely to give rise to litigation, however.

The ideal should be to provide legal remedies that support the functions that LAT couples provide for each other. For example, LATs provide extensive physical caretaking in the event of a partner's illness, which is a substantial benefit to society. They should be given the legal tools to facilitate this caretaking, such as medical and family leave to care for a LAT partner, hospital visitation privileges otherwise limited to immediate family members, status as next of kin for medical care decision making and post-death arrangements, and eligibility for coverage under one another's health insurance policies. A number of state law tort remedies would also be appropriate to confer on LATs, such as standing to seek damages for negligent or intentional infliction of emotional distress if they witness the wrongfully caused injury or death of their partner and for loss of consortium in the event of his or her death. This last recommendation is based not on economic loss, which these legal remedies do not compensate, but instead on the emotional interconnection between LAT partners, who are the mainstays of one another's lives.

Another situation in which the law might intervene to protect LATs would be if the couple separated and one party suffered relationship-generated economic disadvantage. Given the financial self-sufficiency of most LATs, this situation should be relatively rare. Any legal remedy should depend on evidence that the parties intended to provide redress in those circumstances. Thus contracts between LATs addressing property and support issues should be recognized and enforced, just as they are in most states for cohabitants. The underlying insight of the *Marvin* case, after all, was that cohabitants are as competent as any other individuals to enter contracts with respect to their earnings and property. The same applies to LATs. As one scholar has noted, it is arbitrary to exclude LATs from judicial enforcement of agreements just because they do not share a residence.[11] This will require courts to examine the parties' relationship to reach conclusions about any express promises to share property and about conduct, such as the commingling of assets, from which such an agreement may be inferred. Division of jointly acquired property, regardless of which partner's name is on the title, should be handled in this way or according to general equitable principles such as unjust enrichment or constructive trust.[12]

The death of one party would impose a considerable blow upon their partner, but it should not be economically disastrous. Because many LATs have children from previous relationships, they should not be one another's heirs under intestacy laws (that is, in the absence of wills). The majority I interviewed did have wills, although one can't count on that.[13] If a LAT's partner is a primary beneficiary of their will or if they have designated their partner as the primary beneficiary of their pension assets, these transfers should be treated as nontaxable events, as they are for spouses. Although tax law should not treat LAT couples as an economic unit while they are alive, designation as the primary beneficiary of a will or pension is in the nature of an intentional provision for postmortem support analogous to a contract and also a form of postmortem caretaking, and thus such treatment appears just.

Apart from the situations described, the law should not intervene with respect to the economic arrangements of LATs upon separation or death. Research shows that LATs value their economic independence highly. Although willing to offer support to one another, they reject the idea of a legal obligation to provide economic support or care. If they separate or a partner dies, the economic effect should not be severe in most instances. The economically weaker party may not be able to engage in the same social activities or holiday travel as before, but each will still have their own residence and the ability to self-support.

Finally, the law should not interfere with or punish LATs by, for example, using their living arrangement as a cause to terminate alimony from a previous spouse. To address problems described in chapter 8, the law of alimony should be revised to clarify that termination of support to a former spouse should rest solely on changed circumstances affecting the recipient's need for it and not upon their future intimate relationships—that is, on economics, not sexual behavior.

Ideally, welfare benefits, health care, and pensions in the United States should be based on one's status as an individual and not on family or marital status and should be universally available, thus making individuals free to choose the living arrangement that is right for them without fearing the economic consequences of doing so. If this were so, some of the problems described above would disappear. In the foreseeable meantime, however, the legal changes I propose would provide some minimum legal protections to persons who choose to live apart, thus allowing them to choose without constraint among the variety of living arrangements now available. This would not only honor their freedom of choice but also support their mutual caretaking and, where appropriate, offer minimal protections against vulnerabilities that may arise as a result of the relationship.

# Conclusion

Whether told in statistics, in the languages of social science and of case law, or in their own words, this has been the story of people who are committed intimate partners but live apart. Despite a deep and intimate connection to one another, they maintain separate residences. These couples make up about 10 percent of the adult population in the United States as a whole but are officially classified as single persons. They fall into different age groups, with differing motivations for living apart yet also some similarities. Some do so because of various constraints on living together, and others do so by choice.

These couples, known as LATs, think of one another as family and take care of one another's physical and emotional needs while remaining largely independent financially. The study of these groups by social scientists has given rise to debates about whether they are a new family form and about the meaning of living apart to different groups among them. Particular attention has been paid in this book to the unique motivations of women, gay males, and persons of more advanced age, all of whom find LAT especially attractive.

LATs are similar to commuting married couples in that they sometimes are responding to constraints of the labor market and a drive for gender equality. They are different, however, in that commuting is almost universally involuntary, temporary, and based out of one primary home, whereas many LATs affirmatively choose their separate residential status, maintain it in the long run, and have two independent primary homes. Because commuters are married, that status addresses any legal problems that may face both cohabitants and LATs. LATs resemble cohabitants in many respects as well, in that they are both typically unmarried (with some exceptions among LATs, especially among gay males), and their lifestyles deviate from the norm. They often share an ideological opposition to marriage and various economic incentives to remain formally single as well. Yet cohabitants are economically interdependent in ways that LATs are not, intertwined by sharing invest-ments in a home, joint finances, and often children. Neither cohabitants nor LATs receive adequate recognition or protection under the law as it now stands.

My conclusion has been that LATs, like cohabitants, deserve more at-tention from the legal system beyond the notice that they have received with respect to palimony and termination of alimony. I have argued that LATs should be given piecemeal recognition, extending to them the privileges of spouses concerning hospital visitation, family leave, health insurance coverage, and the like. That is, they should be recognized le-gally with respect to areas that support their mutual caregiving but not, by and large, those reflecting economic interdependence. If they wish to enter into agreements or partnerships that would offer additional obliga-tions and benefits, they should be able to do so.

Studying LATs has caused me repeatedly to confront the conclusions of scholars such as Anthony Giddens, Zygmunt Bauman, and others to the effect that intimate relationships in the modern world have been reduced to a series of individualistic interactions between two self-interested people who are seeking only what they can get out of a re-lationship and are poised to leave when the balance of benefits shifts.[1] Perhaps this is so of some individuals, primarily those who remain truly single, but this ultimate stance of individualism does not charac-terize the LATs I interviewed, who are devoted and highly loyal to one another; indeed, they are there for their partners "in sickness and in health." At the cost of maintaining two households and addressing nu-merous logistical problems, LATs have developed a new way of living. It is not one that would suit everyone, but it allows many to achieve a relationship that is stable, committed, and intimate but also egalitarian, one that is close while allowing considerable independence, in a world where such relationships may not be easy to construct or maintain.

# ACKNOWLEDGMENTS

There are so many people to thank for their help on this book. I begin with the LATs in New York City, upstate New York, and England who so generously shared their stories with me; I could not have written this without them. I also want to thank my colleagues at Cornell Law School, who encouraged me and gave me numerous suggestions, and the Dorothea S. Clarke Program in Feminist Jurisprudence at Cornell Law School for financial support. I am grateful as well for comments received from participants at the various workshops and classes to which I presented my research in various forms and at various stages; they are, in chronological order: the Washington University Department of Economics Workshop on Work, Family, and Public Policy in 2016; the Family Law and Social Change seminar at the University of Exeter School of Law in 2017; the Network on Family Regulation and Society at the University of Bath in 2017; the 2017 meeting of the Socio-Legal Studies Association in Newcastle-upon-Tyne; the 2017 meeting of the Law and Society Association in Mexico City; the 2017 Conference on Empirical Legal Studies at Cornell Law School; the 2018 meeting of the Association of American Law Schools in San Diego; and the Regulating Family, Sex, and Gender Workshop at the University of Chicago Law School in 2018. I am also thankful for the insights and encouragement offered to me by Susan F. Appleton, Anne Barlow, Mary Anne Case, Simon Duncan, Jo Miles, Robert A. Pollak, Aníbal Rosario-Lebrón, and Robin West. Finally, I thank Amy Emerson, Latia Ward, and Jacob Sayward of the Cornell Law Library, my research assistants David Eichert and Cyril Heron, and my administrative assistants Ernestine DaSilva and Lyndsey Clark, all of whom supplied me with countless materials and aid. A special thanks is owed to David Eichert for the particular insights he brought to this volume by his authorship of chapter 5. Martin T. Wells's help in interpreting data from the 2016 surveys was invaluable. As always, my partner Ben Altman critiques, edits, makes suggestions, encourages, and keeps me sane. No book is the product of just one person, and this one bears the imprint of all these contributions.

Portions of this manuscript have been published in an earlier form. Revised versions of sections of one previously published article appear scattered throughout: How Should the Law Treat Couples Who Live Apart Together?, 29 *Child & Family Law Quarterly* 335 (2018), published by LexisNexis. An earlier version of chapter 4 appeared as Living Apart Together, Women, and Family Law, in 23 *Cardozo Journal of Law & Gender* 47 (2017). Chapter 6 is based on my article Living Apart Together as a "Family Form" Among Persons of Retirement Age: The Appropriate Family Law Response, originally published in the American Bar Association's *Family Law Quarterly*, Vol. 52, Issue No. 1 (2018), at page 1. Use of all this previous work has been approved by their respective publishers.

# NOTES

## INTRODUCTION

1 Jan Trost, *Marriage, Cohabitation and LAT Relationships*, 47 J. COMP. FAM. STUD. 17, 22–23 (2016).

2 *Id.* at 22. *See also* Sofie Ghazanfareeon Karlsson & Klas Borell, *Intimacy and Autonomy, Gender and Ageing: Living Apart Together*, 27 AGEING INT'L 11, 13 (2002).

3 Ingrid Arnet Connidis, Klas Borell & Sofie Ghazanfareeon Karlsson, *Ambivalence and Living Apart Together in Later Life: A Critical Research Proposal*, 79 J. MARRIAGE & FAM. 1404, 1406 (2017) (contrasting with the lack of terminology in the United States, where terms borrowed from teen culture, such as "girlfriend" and "boyfriend," seem inappropriate).

4 *See, e.g.*, Simon Duncan & Miranda Phillips, *People Who Live Apart Together (LATs): New Family Form or Just a Stage?*, 21 INT'L REV. SOC. 513, 515 (2011) (10% of adults in Britain are LATs); Arnaud Régnier-Loilier, Éva Beaujouan & Catherine Villeneuve-Gokalp, *Neither Single, Nor in a Couple: A Study of Living Apart Together in France*, 21 DEMOGRAPHIC RES. 75, 85 (2009) (reporting that 10% of French men and 11% of French women between 18 and 79 were LATs); Anna Reimondos, Ann Evans & Edith Gray, *Living-apart-together (LAT) Relationships in Australia*, 87 FAM. MATTERS 43, 43–44 (2011) (reporting that 7% to 9% of the Australian population aged 18 and older were LAT); STATISTICS CANADA, COUPLES WHO LIVE APART, www150.statcan.gc.ca/ (stating that 9% of Canadians aged 25 to 64 were LATs in 2017); Charles Q. Strohm, Judith Seltzer, Susan Cochran & Vickie Mays, *"Living Apart Together" Relationships in the United States*, 21 DEMOGRAPHIC RES. 177, 190–92 (2009) (finding that 7% of women and 6% of men were LATs, but 12%–13% in California).

5 Features of the Second Demographic Transition include acceptance of premarital sex, divorce and cohabitation, a decline in the importance of marriage and fertility (and the separation of the two), and a general delay in family formation; many associate it with a rise in individualism and egalitarianism. Paul R. Amato & Lydia N. Hayes, *"Alone Together" Marriage and "Living Apart Together" Relationships, in* CONTEMPORARY ISSUES IN FAMILY STUDIES: GLOBAL PERSPECTIVES ON PARTNERSHIPS, PARENTING AND SUPPORT IN A CHANGING WORLD 31, 41 (Anela Abela & Janet Walker, eds. 1st ed. 2014).

6 *See* Abigail Geiger & Gretchen Livingston, *8 Facts about Love and Marriage in America*, PEW RES.: FACT-TANK (Feb. 13, 2019), www.pewresearch.org/fact-tank/2019/02/13/8-facts-about-love-and-marriage.

7 CYNTHIA GRANT BOWMAN, UNMARRIED COUPLES, LAW, AND PUBLIC POLICY 223–28 (2010).

## CHAPTER 1. LATS—WHO ARE THEY?

1 I interviewed only the female partner in this couple, so "Kevin's" responses are based on her description of them.

2 The term "economy of gratitude," denoting a sense of obligation imposed as the result of a gift, is from ARLIE RUSSELL HOCHSCHILD, WITH ANNE MAC-HUNG, THE SECOND SHIFT: WORKING FAMILIES AND THE REVOLUTION AT HOME 18 (1989).

3 I interviewed only the female partner in this couple.

4 Parliament did not initially open civil partnerships in Britain to any but same-sex couples, although the UK Supreme Court had found this to constitute discrimination. R. v. Secretary of State, [2018] UKSC 32. Since December 2, 2019, different-sex couples have been able to enter into civil partnerships in England and Wales. Civil Partnerships, Marriages and Deaths (Registration etc) Act 2019. Similar reforms have been in place in Northern Ireland since January 13, 2020. The Civil Partnership Act 2004 as amended in 2019 enables both same- and different-sex couples to enter into a civil partnership. In Scotland, legislation to allow different-sex civil partnerships is currently pending in the Scottish Parliament and is almost certain to pass.

5 Simon Duncan, *Women's Agency in Living Apart Together: Constraint, Strategy and Vulnerability*, 63 SOC. REV. 589, 599–601 (2015).

## CHAPTER 2. WHAT DOES SOCIAL SCIENCE TELL US ABOUT LATS?

1 CAROLINE SÖRGJERD, RECONSTRUCTING MARRIAGE: THE LEGAL STATUS OF RELATIONSHIPS IN A CHANGING SOCIETY 16 (2012).

2 Irene Levin & Jan Trost, *Living Apart Together*, 2 COMMUNITY, WORK & FAM. 279, 281–83 (1999).

3 Irene Levin, *Living Apart Together: A New Family Form*, 52 CURRENT SOC. 223, 228–29 (2004).

4 *Id.* at 229.

5 Anna Reimondos, Ann Evans & Edith Gray, *Living-apart-together (LAT) Relationships in Australia*, 87 FAM. MATTERS 43, 43–44 (2011); STATISTICS CANADA, COUPLES WHO LIVE APART (2017), www150.statcan.gc.ca.

6 Charles Q. Strohm, Judith Seltzer, Susan Cochran & Vickie Mays, *"Living Apart Together" Relationships in the United States*, 21 DEMOGRAPHIC RES. 177, 190–92 (2009).

7  Arnaud Régnier-Loilier, Éva Beaujouan & Catherine Villeneuve-Gokalp, *Neither Single, Nor in a Couple: A Study of Living Apart Together in France*, 21 DEMO-GRAPHIC RES. 75, 85 (2009).

8  Norbert F. Schneider, *Partnerschaften mit Getrennten Haushalten in den Neuen und Alten Bundesländern* (Couples with separate households in the new and old states of Germany), in FAMILIE AN DER SCHWELLE ZUM NEUEN JAHRTAUSEND: WANDEL UND ENTWICKLUNG FAMILIALER LEBENSFOR-MEN (Family on the threshold of the new century: change and development of family lifestyles) 93 (Walter Bien, ed. 1996).

9  Aart C. Liefbroer, Anne-Rigt Poortman & Judith A. Seltzer, *Why Do Intimate Partners Live Apart? Evidence on LAT Relationships Across Europe*, 32 DEMO-GRAPHIC RES. 251, 265 (2015). *See also* Luis Ayuso, *What Future Awaits Couples Living Apart Together (LAT)?*, 67 SOC. REV. 226 (2019).

10  Jens B. Asendorpf, *Living Apart Together: Alters- und Kohortenabhängigkeit einer heterogenen Lebensform* (Age and age cohort membership of a heterogeneous lifestyle), 4 KÖLNER ZEITSCHRIFT FÜR SOZIOLOGIE UND SOZIALPSY-CHOLOGIE 749, 761 (2008). *See also* Darja Reuschke, *Living Apart Together over Long Distances—Time-Space Patterns and Consequences of a Late-Modern Living Arrangement*, 64 ERDKUNDE 215, 217 (2010) (finding that 6.3% of all adults, amounting to one in nine of all partnered adults, or 4.3 million people, were LAT).

11  *See* STATISTICS NETHERLANDS, MORE THAN ONE FIFTH OF PEOPLE LIVING APART ENGAGED IN LAT RELATIONSHIP, www.cbs.nl/en-gb/news/2015/04/more-than-one-fifth-of-people-living-apart-engaged-in-lat-relationship.

12  Levin, *supra* note 3, at 224–25, 237–38; *see also* Jan Trost, *LAT Relationships Now and in the Future*, in THE FAMILY: CONTEMPORARY PERSPECTIVES AND CHALLENGES 217–19 (Koen Matthijs, ed. 1998).

13  Vicky Lyssens-Danneboom & Dimitri Mortelmans, *Living Apart Together and Money: New Partnerships, Traditional Gender Roles*, 76 J. MARRIAGE & FAM. 949, 950–51 (2014).

14  Jenny de Jong Gierveld, *Remarriage, Unmarried Cohabitation, Living Apart Together: Partner Relationships Following Bereavement or Divorce*, 66 J. MAR-RIAGE & FAM. 236, 238 (2004); see also Jenny de Jong Gierveld, *The Dilemma of Repartnering: Considerations of Older Men and Women Entering New Intimate Relationships in Later Life*, 27 AGEING INT'L 61, 65 (2002).

15  Jenny de Jong Gierveld, *Intra-couple Caregiving of Older Adults Living Apart To-gether: Commitment and Independence*, 34 CANADIAN J. AGING 356, 357 (2015).

16  John Haskey, *Living Arrangements in Contemporary Britain: Having a Partner Who Usually Lives Elsewhere and Living Apart Together (LAT)*, 122 POPULATION TRENDS 35, 42 (2005).

17  John Haskey & Jane Lewis, *Living-apart-together in Britain: Context and Meaning*, 2 INT'L J. L. CONTEXT 37, 39 (2006).

18  *Id.*

19  Simon Duncan & Miranda Phillips, *People Who Live Apart Together (LATs): New Family Form or Just a Stage?*, 21 INT'L REV. SOC. 513, 515 (2011).

20  Reuschke, *supra* note 10. Some couples living in Europe—migrant workers, for example—may live apart across national borders on a semipermanent basis as a result of economic pressures. *See, e.g.*, Cris Beauchemin, Jocelyn Nappa, Paul Baizan, Amparo Gonzalez-Ferrer, Kim Caaris & Valentina Mazzucato, *Reunifying Versus Living Apart Together Across Borders: A Comparative Analysis of Sub-Saharan Migration to Europe*, 49 INT'L MIGRATION REV. 173 (2015). Couples separated by military service or imprisonment would also fall into this group.

21  Martin Turcotte, *Living Apart Together*, STAT. CAN. (Mar. 2013), at 3.

22  Simon Duncan, Miranda Phillips, Julia Carter, Sasha Roseneil & Mariya Stoilova, *Practices and Perceptions of Living Apart Together*, 5 FAM. SCI. 1, 2 (2014) (Table 1). One study of both Germany and the United Kingdom estimated that 60% to 65% of LATs live within five miles of one another. John Ermisch & Thomas Siedler, *Living Apart Together*, *in* CHANGING RELATIONSHIPS 29, 41 (Malcolm Brynin & John Ermisch, eds. 2009).

23  Duncan et al. reported that 44% of those living within one mile apart saw each other in person every day; moreover, 85% to 90% of all LATs overall had contact by phone, text, or email at least once a day, and 55% multiple times a day. Duncan et al., *supra* note 22, at 3. A Swedish study of LATs aged 60 or over also reported frequent contact: 36% had daily contact, 51% a couple of times a week, and only 12% twice a month or less. Sofie Ghazanfareeon Karlsson & Klas Borell, *Intimacy and Autonomy, Gender and Ageing: Living Apart Together*, 27 AGEING INT'L 11, 15 (2002).

24  Karen Upton-Davis, *Living Apart Together Relationships (LAT): Severing Intimacy from Obligation*, 29 GENDER ISSUES 25, 34 (2012).

25  Anne Milan & Alice Peters, *Couples Living Apart*, CANADIAN SOCIAL TRENDS (Summer 2003), at 4.

26  *Id.* at 2 (sample included individuals aged 15 and older).

27  Laura M. Funk & Karen M. Kobayashi, *From Motivations to Accounts: An Interpretive Analysis of "Living Apart Together" Relationships in Mid- to Later-Life Couples*, 37 J. FAM. ISSUES 1101, 1105–06 (2016).

28  *Id.*

29  *See id.* at 1105.

30  Strohm et al., *supra* note 6, at 191.

31  LYNN JAMIESON & ROONA SIMPSON, LIVING ALONE: GLOBALIZATION, IDENTITY AND BELONGING 79 (2013).

32  Liefbroer et al., *supra* note 9, at 280.

33  Different scholars develop different categories. Mine are closest to those used by Coulter and Hu, who divided their subjects into nested young adults, independent adults, and seniors. Rory Coulter & Yang Hu, *Living Apart Together and Cohabitation Intentions in Great Britain*, 38 J. FAM. ISSUES 1701, 1713 (2017).

34  Haskey, *supra* note 16, at 39; Reimondos et al., *supra* note 5 at 49 (Table 1) (report-
    ing that 44% of LATs in Australia were between 18 and 24); Milan & Peters, *supra*
    note 25, at 3 (reporting that 54% of male and 57% of female LATs in Canada were
    between 20 and 29); Régnier-Loilier et al., *supra* note 7, at 87 (Table 3) (reporting
    that 65% of men and 54% of women in France between the ages of 18 and 24 who
    were partnered were LATs).

35  Régnier-Loilier et al., *supra* note 7, at 85.

36  Catherine Villeneuve-Gokalp, *Vivre en Couple Chacun Chez Soi* (Living as a
    couple with each having their own home), 52 POPULATION 1059, 1062 (1997).

37  *Id.* at 1063 (reporting that only 12% of French LATs in this age group stayed
    together for five years).

38  Ermisch & Siedler, *supra* note 22, at 36.

39  Castro-Martin, Marta Dominguez-Folgueras & Teresa Martin-Garcia, *Not Truly
    Partnerless: Non-residential Partnerships and Retreat from Marriage in Spain*, 18
    DEMOGRAPHIC RES. 443, 444, 447 (2008). This is similar to the situation in
    Japan, where both the rate of marriage and the rate of cohabitation are low. Miho
    Iwasawa, *Partnership Transition in Contemporary Japan: Prevalence of Childless
    Non-Cohabiting Couples*, 2 JAP. J. POPULATION 76, 84 (2004).

40  Castro-Martin et al., *supra* note 39, at 448–49, 451.

41  Arnaud Régnier-Lollier & Daniele Vignoli, *The Diverse Nature of Living Apart
    Together Relationships: An Italy-France Comparison*, 35 J. POPULATION RES. 1, 9
    (2018).

42  *Id.* at 19; *see also* Liefbroer et al., *supra* note 9, at 268. Both studies cited rely on
    new statistical information available in the cross-national Generations and Gen-
    der Survey.

43  Coulter & Hu, *supra* note 33, at 1712.

44  Duncan & Phillips, *supra* note 19, at 529.

45  *See, e.g.*, Régnier-Loilier et al., *supra* note 7, at 86; Funk & Kobayashi, *supra* note
    27, at 1106–07. Coulter and Hu break this group down into Single Parents (11% of
    LATs, mostly women) and Independent Adults (32% of LATs), as distinguished
    from Nested Young Adults (44% of LATs), who still live with their parents. Coul-
    ter & Hu, *supra* note 33, at 1713 (2016).

46  Régnier-Loilier et al., *supra* note 7, at 105; Simon Duncan, Julia Carter, Miranda
    Phillips, Sasha Roseneil & Mariya Stoilova, *Why Do People Live Apart Together?*
    2 FAMILIES, RELATIONSHIPS & SOCIETIES 323, 328–29 (2013); Levin, *supra*
    note 3, at 232–33; Levin & Trost, *supra* note 2, at 285–86.

47  *See, e.g.*, Levin, *supra* note 3, at 231.

48  Levin, *supra* note 3, at 230; Funk & Kobayashi, *supra* note 27, at 1113.

49  Lyssens-Danneboom & Mortelmans, *supra* note 13, at 956; Villeneuve-Gokalp,
    *supra* note 36, at 1072; Levin & Trost, *supra* note 2, at 283–84.

50  Jill Brooke, *Home Alone Together*, N.Y. TIMES, May 4, 2006, at F1.

51  Régnier-Loilier et al., *supra* note 7, at 105; Funk & Kobayashi, *supra* note 27, at
    1112.

52 This perspective was gained from interviews the author conducted with LAT couples living in New York City in 2016.

53 Sasha Roseneil, *On Not Living with a Partner: Unpicking Coupledom and Cohabitation*, 11 SOC. RES. ONLINE 10 (2006).

54 Lyssens-Danneboom & Mortelmans, *supra* note 13, at 956; Duncan et al., *supra* note 46, at 328 (Table 2).

55 *See, e.g.*, Funk & Kobayashi, *supra* note 27, at 1108–09; Simon Duncan & Miranda Phillips, *People Who Live Apart Together (LATs)—How Different Are They?*, 58 SOC. REV. 112, 120 (Table 2) (2010).

56 Funk & Kobayashi, *supra* note 27, at 1109. This consideration was raised numerous times by LATs interviewed by the author as well.

57 Brooke, *supra* note 50.

58 Levin & Trost, *supra* note 2, at 286; Haskey & Lewis, *supra* note 17, at 45.

59 Roseneil, *supra* note 53, at 8; Funk & Kobayashi, *supra* note 27, at 1107–09.

60 *See, e.g.*, Levin & Trost, *supra* note 2, at 286–87; Funk & Kobayashi, *supra* note 27, at 1112.

61 *See, e.g.*, Funk & Kobayashi, *supra* note 27, at 1115; Duncan et al., *supra* note 22, at 4; *see also* Ofra Or, *Midlife Women in Second Partnerships Choosing Living Apart Together: An Israeli Case Study*, 28 ISR. STUD. REV. 41, 47 (2013) (describing the effects of previous experiences of "traumatic economic catastrophe" upon divorce).

62 *See, e.g.*, Milan & Peters, *supra* note 25, at 4 (reporting that 34% of LATs in Canada say they live that way in order to retain their independence); Lyssens-Danneboom, *supra* note 13, at 960 (describing how important independence is to female LATs in their management of money); Haskey & Lewis, *supra* note 17, at 43 (emphasizing the importance of independence to LATs in Britain).

63 Roseneil, *supra* note 53, at 8; Funk & Kobayashi, *supra* note 27, at 1111–12.

64 Duncan et al. estimate the percentage of LATs who are "preference LATs" to be 22%. Duncan et al., *supra* note 46, at 329.

65 JAMIESON & SIMPSON, *supra* note 32, at 78–79.

66 de Jong Gierveld, *The Dilemma of Repartnering*, *supra* note 14, at 65.

67 *See* Vincent Caradec, *Les Formes de la Vie Conjugale des Jeunes Couples "Âgés"* (Forms of conjugal living among "aged" young couples), 51 POPULATION 897, 905 (1996) (translation mine).

68 Reimondos et al., *supra* note 5, at 53; de Jong Gierveld, *The Dilemma of Repartnering*, *supra* note 14, at 73–74 (2002); Caradec, *supra* note 67, at 906.

69 Caradec, *supra* note 67, at 906.

70 Jacquelyn J. Benson & Marilyn Coleman, *Older Adults Developing a Preference for Living Apart Together*, 78 J. MARRIAGE & FAM. 797, 804 (2016).

71 Caradec, *supra* note 67, at 911. *But see* de Jong Gierveld, *The Dilemma of Repartnering*, *supra* note 14, at 72 (only private pensions may be lost in the Netherlands upon remarriage, not the state pension to which everyone is entitled).

72 Caradec, *supra* note 67, at 907 (France); Gierveld, *The Dilemma of Repartnering*, *supra* note 14, at 71–72 (Netherlands); Funk & Kobayashi, *supra* note 27, at 1107–10 (Canada).

73 Sofie Ghazanfareeon Karlsson & Klas Borell, *A Home of Their Own: Women's Boundary Work in LAT-Relationships*, 19 J. AGING STUD. 73, 74–75 (2005).

74 Karlsson & Borell, *supra* note 23, at 24.

75 Caradec, *supra* note 67, at 907.

76 Reimondos et al., *supra* note 5, at 48.

77 *Id.* A smaller, qualitative study of LATs in Belgium reported an average duration of 5.7 years. Lyssens-Danneboom & Mortelmans, *supra* note 13, at 953 (the 54 participants, though drawn from a sample aged 18 and over, tended to be older).

78 Régnier-Loilier et al., *supra* note 7, at 97.

79 Sofie Ghazanfareeon Karlsson, Stina Johansson, Anne Gerdner & Klas Borell, *Caring While Living Apart*, 49 J. GERONTOLOGICAL SOC. WORK 3, 16 (2007).

80 Funk & Kobayashi, *supra* note 27, at 1106.

81 Ermisch & Siedler, *supra* note 22, at 30.

82 Julia Carter, Simon Duncan, Mariya Stoilova & Miranda Phillips, *Sex, Love and Security: Accounts of Distance and Commitment in Living Apart Together Relationships*, 50 SOC. 576, 578 (2016).

83 Rosalinde van der Wiel, Clara H. Mulder & Ajay Bailey, *Pathways to Commitment in Living-Apart-Together Relationships in the Netherlands: A Study on Satisfaction, Alternatives, Investments and Social Support*, 36 ADVANCES LIFE COURSE RES. 13, 15 (2018).

84 Karen M. Kobayashi, Laura Funk & Mushira Mohsin Khan, *Constructing a Sense of Commitment in "Living Apart Together" (LAT) Relationships: Interpretive Agency and Individualization*, 65 CURRENT SOC. 991, 993, 1001, 1005 (2016).

85 Brooke, *supra* note 50 ("I am as devoted as any husband to her."). *See also* Carter et al., *supra* note 82, at 582.

86 van der Wiel et al., *supra* note 83, at 19, 21; Haskey & Lewis, *supra* note 17, at 44.

87 Carter et al., *supra* note 82, at 589–90.

88 Karen Upton-Davis, *Subverting Gendered Norms of Cohabitation: Living Apart Together for Women over 45*, 24 J. GENDER STUD. 104, 108 (2015).

89 For information on the income-sharing of married and cohabiting couples, *see* Kristen R. Heimdal & Sharon K. Houseknecht, *Cohabiting and Married Couples' Income Organization: Approaches in Sweden and the United States*, 65 J. MARRIAGE & FAM. 525, 533 (2003) (finding that a majority of both married and cohabiting couples in the United States and Sweden maintain joint finances); Catherine Kenney, *Cohabiting Couples, Filing Jointly? Resource Pooling and US Poverty Policies*, 53 FAM. REL. 237, 243–46 (2004) (finding that cohabiting parents do generally pool resources).

90 Sofie Ghazanfareeon Karlsson & Klas Borell, *Intimacy and Autonomy, Gender and Ageing: Living Apart Together*, 27 AGEING INT'L 11, 18–19 (2002).

91  Or, *supra* note 61, at 47.
92  Lyssens-Danneboom & Mortelmans, *supra* note 13, at 955.
93  de Jong Gierveld, *supra* note 15, at 361–62.
94  Karlsson et al., *supra* note 79, at 17.
95  *Id.* at 21 (Table 6).
96  *See, e.g.,* Duncan et al., *supra* note 22, at 7–8 (respondents were asked who would care for them if ill).
97  *Id.* at 7 (Table 7).
98  Benson & Coleman, *supra* note 70, at 803–04.
99  *Id.* at 808.
100  *Id.* at 809.
101  Levin, *supra* note 3, at 225.
102  *See* Sasha Roseneil & Shelley Budgeon, *Cultures of Intimacy and Care Beyond "the Family": Personal Life and Social Change in the Early 21ˢᵗ Century*, 52 CURRENT SOC. 135, 141–42 (2004).
103  *See* Duncan & Phillips, *supra* note 55, at 116. ANTHONY GIDDENS, THE TRANSFORMATION OF INTIMACY: SEXUALITY, LOVE AND EROTICISM IN MODERN SOCIETIES 152–56 (1992) (seeing pure relationships as a result of the modern insistence upon autonomy and gender equality). *See also* ZYGMUNT BAUMAN, LIQUID LOVE: ON THE FRAILTY OF HUMAN BONDS (2003) (positing that modern men and women are without any fixed or durable bonds at all).
104  Haskey & Lewis, *supra* note 17, at 42.
105  *Id.* at 46.
106  *Id.*
107  *Id.*
108  *Id.* at 45. *See also* Chaya Koren & Zvi Eisikovits, *Life Beyond the Planned Script: Accounts and Secrecy of Older Persons Living in Second Coupledom in Old Age in a Society in Transition*, 28 J. SOC. & PERSONAL RELATIONSHIPS 44 (2011) (suggesting that LAT can provide an acceptable arrangement for older couples in a society where cohabitation is non-normative).
109  Duncan & Phillips, *supra* note 55, at 117.
110  *Id.* at 115.
111  *Id.* at 117–19.
112  *Id.* at 118–19; *see also* Duncan & Phillips, *supra* note 19, at 519.
113  Duncan & Phillips, *supra* note 55, at 123, 132.
114  *Id.* at 123.
115  Mariya Stoilova, Sasha Roseneil, Julia Carter, Simon Duncan & Miranda Phillips, *Constructions, Reconstructions and Deconstructions of "Family" amongst People Who Live Apart Together (LATs)*, 68 BRIT. J. SOC. 78, 93 (2017).
116  *Id.* at 79.
117  Ingrid Arnet Connidis, Klas Borell & Sofie Ghazanfareeon Karlsson, *Ambivalence and Living Apart Together in Later Life: A Critical Research Proposal*, 79 J. MARRIAGE & FAM. 1404, 1405, 1409 (2017).

118 Benson & Coleman, *supra* note 70, at 806, 807; Jacquelyn J. Benson & Marilyn Coleman, *Older Adult Descriptions of Living Apart Together*, 65 FAM. REL. 439, 446 (2016).

119 Denise R. Brothers, "Doing" LAT: Redoing Gender and Redoing Family in Living Apart Together Relationships in Later Life 83 (2013) (unpublished Ph.D. dissertation, Miami University), https://etd.ohiolink.edu/!etd.send_file?accession=miami 1429881367&disposition=inline (emphasis in the original).

## CHAPTER 3. LATS IN THE UNITED STATES

1 *See* NATIONAL OPINION RESEARCH CENTER, GENERAL SOCIAL SURVEYS, 1972–2002: CUMULATIVE CODEBOOK Qs 135 (March 2019); UCLA CENTER FOR HEALTH POLICY RES, CALIFORNIA HEALTH INTERVIEW SURVEY (2005).

2 Data was collected by telephone, both cellular and land line; the ESP data was collected between February 9, 2016, and April 19, 2016, and the CNSS data between September 19, 2016, and December 13, 2016. Datasets from the CNSS are available at CORNELL INSTITUTE FOR SOCIAL AND ECONOMIC RESEARCH, CORNELL NATIONAL SOCIAL SURVEY, https://cisermgmt.cornell.edu. The CNSS sample is nationally representative, and the ESP results are generalizable to New York State.

3 The New York survey asked first "Are you currently in a committed couple relationship with someone with whom you do not live?" and then, as the second question, "Are you married to that person?" and thus included married persons who lived in separate residences with respect to all the questions that followed. As a result, 10 married respondents were included in the New York study. After reviewing the results of the New York survey, I amended the first question on the national survey to ask "Are you currently in a committed but unmarried relationship with someone with whom you do not live?," thus including only unmarried respondents who lived separately in the national data.

4 In this chapter, when reporting percentages in the text, I have rounded off to the next higher or lower whole number.

5 Charles Strohm, Judith Seltzer, Susan Cochran & Vickie Mays, *"Living Apart Together" Relationships in the United States*, 21 DEMOGRAPHIC RES. 177 (2009).

6 More than 15% of all same-sex couples in the United States live in California. Christopher Carpenter & Gary J. Gates, *Gay and Lesbian Partnership: Evidence from California*, 45 DEMOGRAPHY 573, 574 (2008).

7 Strohm et al., *supra* note 5, at 178.

8 U.S. BUREAU OF THE CENSUS, CENSUS QUICK FACTS, www.census.gov /quickfacts/table/PST045216/00 (last visited Apr. 10, 2017).

9 *See* Alisa C. Lewin, *Health and Relationship Quality Later in Life: A Comparison of Living Apart Together (LAT), First Marriages, Remarriages, and Cohabitation*, 38 J. FAM. ISSUES 1754, 1766 (2017) (relying on data from the National Social Life, Health, and Aging Project from 2005 to 2006).

10  *See* Mark Regnerus & Jeremy Uecker, *Premarital Sex in America: How Young Americans Meet, Mate, and Think about Marrying* 26 (2011); *see generally* ORLANDO PATTERSON, RITUALS OF BLOOD: CONSEQUENCES OF SLAVERY IN TWO AMERICAN CENTURIES 1–167 (1998); KATHRYN EDIN & TIMOTHY J. NELSON, DOING THE BEST I CAN: FATHERHOOD IN THE INNER CITY 99, 149 (2013).

11  *See generally* Edin & Nelson, *supra* note 10.

12  Four respondents to the New York survey (out of 103 total LATs) and six respondents to the U.S. survey (out of 93 total LATs) did not answer this question, so this table reports responses from 99 and 87 LATs in each survey respectively.

13  U.S. Bureau of the Census, *American FactFinder: Income in the Past 12 Months*, https://factfinder.census.gov/ (last visited Jan. 29, 2017) (documenting the income in 2015 inflation-adjusted dollars).

14  One respondent to the U.S. survey did not answer this question.

15  On the New York survey, 12 respondents answered "do not know" to this question, and an additional four refused to answer, so this table reports findings for 87 New York LAT respondents; one respondent did not answer this question on the U.S. survey, so the total number responding on that was 92.

16  LYNN JAMIESON & ROONA SIMPSON, LIVING ALONE: GLOBALIZATION, IDENTITY AND BELONGING 84 (2013).

17  *See* Carolyn Vogler, Michaela Brockmann & Richard D. Wiggins, *Managing Money in New Heterosexual Forms of Intimate Relationships*, 37 J. SOCIO-ECONOMICS 552, 567 (2008) (Table 11) (quantifying married respondents and cohabiting parents' use of a joint pooling system); Kristen R. Heimdal & Sharon K. Houseknecht, *Cohabiting and Married Couples' Income Organization: Approaches in Sweden and the United States*, 65 J. MARRIAGE & FAM. 525, 533 (2003) (stating that a majority of both married and cohabiting couples in the United States and Sweden maintain joint finances).

18  Their universal satisfaction with LAT may also reflect the selectivity of my sample. A few individuals I approached turned down my request for an interview, because they didn't want to talk publicly about their relationship or "it wasn't a good time." Some of these may have been more ambivalent about living apart than those who were willing to speak openly about their private life.

19  *See* Rory Coulter & Yang Hu, *Living Apart Together and Cohabitation Intentions in Great Britain*, 38 J. FAM. ISSUES 1701, 1706 (2017).

20  *See, e.g.*, Karen Upton-Davis, *Living Apart Together Relationships (LAT): Severing Intimacy from Obligation*, 29 GENDER ISSUES 25, 34 (2012).

21  One other study reported a similar disparity between expectations and actual experience of care, reporting that all but one LAT did in fact provide care and that the barrier was not so much the offer as the acceptance of care. Jenny de Jong Gierveld, *Intra-couple Caregiving of Older Adults Living Apart Together: Commitment and Independence*, 34 CANADIAN J. AGING 356, 359–62 (2015).

CHAPTER 4. GENDER DIFFERENCE IN LIVING APART TOGETHER

1 *See, e.g.*, Karen Upton-Davis, *Living Apart Together Relationships (LAT): Severing Intimacy from Obligation*, 29 GENDER ISSUES 25 (2012) [hereafter "*Severing Intimacy*"]; Karen Upton-Davis, *Subverting Gendered Norms of Cohabitation: Living Apart Together for Women over 45*, 24 J. GENDER STUD. 104, 108 (2015) [hereafter "*Subverting Gendered Norms*"].

2 Jenny de Jong Gierveld, *The Dilemma of Repartnering: Considerations of Older Men and Women Entering New Intimate Relationships in Later Life*, 27 AGEING INT'L 61, 65–66 (2002).

3 *Id.* at 75 (citing Karen D. Pyke, *Women's Employment as Gift or Burden? Marital Power Across Marriage, Divorce, and Remarriage*, 8 GENDER & SOC'Y 73, 81–85 (1994) (discussing changes in women's marital power across marriage, divorce, and remarriage).

4 CENTRAL BUREAU FOR STATISTICS NETHERLANDS, MORE THAN ONE FIFTH OF PEOPLE LIVING APART ENGAGED IN LAT RELATIONSHIP, www.cbs.nl/en-gb/news/2015/04/more-than-one-fifth-of-people-living-apart-engaged-in-lat-relationship.

5 Sofie Ghazanfareeon Karlsson & Klas Borell, *Intimacy and Autonomy, Gender and Ageing: Living Apart Together*, 27 AGEING INT'L 11, 14 (2002).

6 *Id.* at 17 (Table 1).

7 Sofie Ghazanfareeon Karlsson & Klas Borell, *A Home of Their Own: Women's Boundary Work in LAT-Relationships*, 19 J. AGING STUD. 73, 75, 79–82 (2005).

8 *Id.* at 75.

9 Karlsson & Borell, *supra* note 5, at 18–19.

10 *Id.* at 20–21.

11 Sofie Ghazanfareeon Karlsson, Stina Johansson, Anne Gerdner & Klas Borell, *Caring While Living Apart*, 49 J. GERONTOLOGICAL SOC. WORK 3, 19, 20, 24 (2007).

12 Upton-Davis, *Severing Intimacy, supra* note 1.

13 *Id.* at 32.

14 Upton-Davis, *Subverting Gendered Norms, supra* note 1, at 107.

15 *Id.* at 110.

16 *Id.* at 112.

17 Ofra Or, *Midlife Women in Second Partnerships Choosing Living Apart Together*, 28 ISR. STUD. REV. 41, 45 (2013).

18 *Id.* Snowball sampling is a nonrandom method that involves asking interview subjects if they know, and can refer you to, other individuals in the same target group whom you might interview.

19 Or, *supra* note 17, at 46.

20 *Id.* at 53–54. *See* ANTHONY GIDDENS, THE TRANSFORMATION OF INTIMACY: SEXUALITY, LOVE AND EROTICISM IN MODERN SOCIETIES 58 (1992).

21  *See generally*, Vicky Lyssens-Danneboom & Dimitri Mortelmans, *Living Apart Together and Money: New Partnerships, Traditional Gender Roles*, 76 J. MARRIAGE & FAM. 949, 950–51 (2014).

22  Laura M. Funk & Karen M. Kobayashi, *From Motivations to Accounts: An Interpretive Analysis of "Living Apart Together" Relationships in Mid- to Later-Life Couples*, 37 J. FAM. ISSUES 1101, 1105 (2016).

23  *Id.*

24  *Id.* at 1119.

25  Denise R. Brothers, "Doing" LAT: Redoing Gender and Redoing Family in Living Apart Together Relationships in Later Life 50–52, 73 (2015) (unpublished Ph.D. dissertation, Miami University), https://etd.ohiolink.edu.

26  *Id.* at 76.

27  Simon Duncan, *Women's Agency in Living Apart Together: Constraint, Strategy and Vulnerability*, 63 SOCIOLOGICAL REV. 589 (2015) [hereafter "*Women's Agency*"]. *See also Differential Agency: Living Apart Together, in* JULIA CARTER & SIMON DUNCAN, REINVENTING COUPLES: TRADITION, AGENCY AND BRICOLAGE 133–69 (2018) [hereafter "*Differential Agency*"].

28  Duncan, *Women's Agency, supra* note 27, at 591, 594–95.

29  *Id.* at 595–96 (Figure 1). The only difference was that women more frequently cited prior obligations to others, specifically their children, as a reason not to cohabit. *Id.* at 595.

30  *Id.* at 596–98, 597 (Figure 2).

31  *Id.* at 598–99, 601–03. Some scholars think that the age difference between the subjects in Upton-Davis's and Duncan's studies goes a long way toward explaining their differing conclusions about gender. *See* Alisa C. Lewin, *Intentions to Live Together among Couples Living Apart: Differences by Age and Gender*, 34 EUR. J. POPULATION 721, 725 (2018); Brothers, *supra* note 25, at 76.

32  Duncan, *Women's Agency, supra* note 27, at 602.

33  *Id.* at 605.

34  *Id.* at 600. *See also* Julia Carter, Simon Duncan, Mariya Stoilova & Miranda Phillips, *Sex, Love and Security: Accounts of Distance and Commitment in Living Apart Together Relationships*, 50 SOC. 576, 578 (2016) (discussing how agency is always exercised within relationality).

35  *See, e.g.*, Duncan, *Women's Agency, supra* note 27, at 600. Duncan also notes that "some women who LAT 'redo' gendered norms through their everyday practice." *Id.* at 605.

36  NAT'L OPINION RES. CENTER, GENERAL SOCIAL SURVEYS, 1972–2002: CUMULATIVE CODEBOOK Qs. 545–48 (Feb. 2003); UCLA CENTER FOR HEALTH POL'Y RES., CALIFORNIA HEALTH INTERVIEW SURVEY (2005).

37  Charles Strohm, Judith Seltzer, Susan Cochran & Vickie Mays, *"Living Apart Together" Relationships in the United States*, 21 DEMOGRAPHIC RES. 177 (2009); Jacquelyn J. Benson & Marilyn Coleman, *Older Adults Developing a Preference for Living Apart Together*, 78 J. MARRIAGE & FAM. 797 (2016).

38  Strohm et al., *supra* note 37, at 191.

39  Benson & Coleman, *supra* note 37, at 800.

40  Jill Brooke, *Home Alone Together*, N.Y. TIMES (May 4, 2006), www.nytimes.com. *See also* Manisha Krishnan, *Living Apart, Together*, MACLEANS, Sept. 17, 2013 (discussing older LATs in Canada and women's desire to be free of traditional domestic roles they had experienced in the past).

41  All percentages in the text and tables in this chapter have been rounded to the nearest whole number.

42  In 2016, women's median weekly earnings for full-time work in the United States were $749, while men earned $915 per week. INSTITUTE FOR WOMEN'S POLICY RESEARCH, THE GENDER WAGE GAP: 2016 (March 2017), https:// iwpr.org.

43  "Other reasons" was not included as an option on the New York survey.

44  Strohm et al., *supra* note 37, at 191. The prominence of children in the home as the main reason given by LATs in popular press articles is also striking. *See* Brooke, *supra* note 40.

45  The question breaking down cost-sharing into different methods was asked only on the CNSS, after responses to the ESP suggested its desirability.

46  One of the partners in one couple predicted that that they would eventually live together or break up. Also, both partners in one long-distance couple thought they might eventually live together but were now separated by the needs of both children and jobs in different towns.

47  *See, e.g.*, Robin West, *Jurisprudence and Gender*, 55 U. CHI. L. REV. 1, 14–28 (1989).

48  Duncan referred to those who were reacting to past experiences of cohabitation as "vulnerable," distinguishing them from those labeled "strategic," who were acting purposefully and particularly valued individual autonomy. Duncan, *Women's Agency*, *supra* note 27, at 599–601.

49  Ingrid Arnet Connidis, Klas Borell & Sofie Ghazanfareeon Karlsson, *Ambivalence and Living Apart Together in Later Life: A Critical Research Proposal*, 79 J. MAR-RIAGE & FAM. 1404, 1411 (2017).

50  Brothers, *supra* note 25, at 65–66.

51  Duncan, *Differential Agency*, in Carter & Duncan, eds., *supra* note 27, at 164.

## CHAPTER 5. GAY MALE COUPLES AND LAT

1  *See* David M. Frost & Kelly A. Gola, *Meanings of Intimacy: A Comparison of Members of Heterosexual and Same-Sex Couples*, 15 ANALYSES SOC. ISSUES & PUB. POL'Y 382, 396 (2015).

2  JANE TRAIES, THE LIVES OF OLDER LESBIANS: SEXUALITY, IDENTITY & THE LIFE COURSE 54 (2016); Charles Q. Strohm, Judith A. Seltzer, Susan D. Cochran & Vickie M. Mays, *"Living Apart Together" Relationships in the United States*, 21 DEMOGRAPHIC RES. 177, 200 (2009). Remarkably, a survey of people over the age of 55 in the United Kingdom found that same-sex couples are three

times more likely than different-sex couples to live apart. STONEWALL, LESBIAN, GAY AND BISEXUAL PEOPLE IN LATER LIFE 6 (2011).

3  *See* Strohm et al., *supra* note 2, at 201.

4  *See* PETER ROBINSON, THE CHANGING WORLD OF GAY MEN 37, 61–62, 187 (2008) (discussing how labels like "queer" emerged and were taken up or rejected by a variety of men during the 20th century).

5  JANE WARD, NOT GAY: SEX BETWEEN STRAIGHT WHITE MEN 34–36 (2015).

6  Lisa M. Diamond, *Three Critical Questions for Future Research on Lesbian Relationships*, 21 J. LESBIAN STUD. 106, 107–10 (2017).

7  Eric Swank, Breanne Fahs & David M. Frost, *Region, Social Identities, and Disclosure Practices as Predictors of Heterosexist Discrimination Against Sexual Minorities in the United States*, 83 SOC. INQUIRY 238 (2013). At the same time, participation in urban gay nightlife is only one of many different ways in which lesbian, gay, and bisexual individuals relate to their sexual identities, and many same-sex couples in urban areas choose not to attend these "gay" events at all. ROBINSON, *supra* note 4, at 72–94.

8  WAYNE BREKHUS, PEACOCKS, CHAMELEONS, CENTAURS: GAY SUBURBIA AND THE GRAMMAR OF SOCIAL IDENTITY 5 (2003).

9  HEATHER MURRAY, NOT IN THIS FAMILY: GAYS AND THE MEANING OF KINSHIP IN POSTWAR NORTH AMERICA 193 (2010); Brian de Vries & Gil Herdt, *Aging in the Gay Community*, *in* GAY, LESBIAN, BISEXUAL & TRANSGENDER AGING: CHALLENGES IN RESEARCH, PRACTICE & POLICY 84, 89 (Tarynn M. Witten & A. Evan Eyler, eds. 2012).

10  MURRAY, *supra* note 9 at 194; de Vries & Herdt, *supra* note 9, at 89.

11  TRAIES, *supra* note 2, at 54; Strohm et al., *supra* note 2, at 183.

12  M. V. LEE BADGETT, WHEN GAY PEOPLE GET MARRIED: WHAT HAPPENS WHEN SOCIETIES LEGALIZE SAME-SEX MARRIAGE 16–17 (2010).

13  *Id.* at 34–35.

14  *See* TRAIES, *supra* note 2, at 48–49.

15  BADGETT, *supra* note 12, at 23.

16  *Id.* at 24–29.

17  Liz Montegary, *For the Richer, Not the Poorer: Marriage Equality, Financial Security, and the Promise of Queer Economic Justice*, *in* QUEER FAMILIES AND RELATIONSHIPS AFTER MARRIAGE EQUALITY 31, 32 (Michael W. Yarbrough, Angela Jones & Joseph Nicholas DeFilippis, eds. 2019).

18  BADGETT, *supra* note 12, at 28–29.

19  This corresponds with research that shows that worries about legal status drive same-sex couples to make more substantial end-of-life plans than their different-sex counterparts. Mieke Beth Thomeer, Rachel Donnelly, Corinne Reczek & Debra Umberson, *Planning for Future Care and the End of Life: A Qualitative Analysis of Gay, Lesbian, and Heterosexual Couples*, 58 J. HEALTH & SOC. BEHAV. 473, 482–83 (2017).

20 Strohm et al., *supra* note 2, at 201.

21 Obergefell v. Hodges, 576 U.S. 644, ____, 135 S. Ct. 2584, 2608 (2015).

22 Jes L. Matsick & Terri D. Conley, *Maybe 'I Do,' Maybe I Don't: Respectability Politics in the Same-Sex Marriage Ruling*, 15 ANALYSES SOC. ISSUES & PUB. POL'Y 409, 410–11 (2015).

23 *See, e.g.*, ROBINSON, *supra* note 4, at 128.

24 Colleen C. Hoff & Sean C. Beougher, *Sexual Agreements among Gay Male Couples*, 39 ARCHIVES SEXUAL BEHAV. 774, 778 (2010); Brad van Eeden-Moorefield, Kevin Malloy & Kristen Benson, *Gay Men's (Non)Monogamy Ideals and Lived Experience*, 75 SEX ROLES 43, 51 (2016).

25 Van Eeden-Moorefield et al., *supra* note 24, at 118. While some lesbian couples choose to open up their relationship by engaging in sex with other people, many more choose to remain monogamous. Gina Potârcă, Melinda Mills & Wiebke Neberich, *Relationship Preferences Among Gay and Lesbian Online Daters: Individual and Contextual Influences*, 77 J. MARRIAGE & FAM. 523, 532–33 (2015).

26 Matsick & Conley, *supra* note 22, at 409.

27 *See* Kristoff Bonello & Malcolm C. Cross, *Gay Monogamy: I Love You But I Can't Have Sex With Only You*, 57 J. HOMOSEXUALITY 117, 118 (2009).

28 *Id.* at 123–24.

29 Phillip L. Hammack, Ilan H. Meyer, Evan A. Krueger, Marguerita Lightfoot & David M. Frost, *HIV Testing and Pre-exposure Prophylaxis (PrEP) Use, Familiarity, and Attitudes Among Gay and Bisexual Men in the United States: A National Probability Sample of Three Birth Cohorts*, 13 PLOS ONE 1, 6–8 (2018).

30 JULIA CARTER & SIMON DUNCAN, REINVENTING COUPLES: TRADITION, AGENCY AND BRICOLAGE 149 (2018).

31 *See* Karen I. Fredricksen-Goldsen, *Informal Caregiving in the LGBT Communities*, in GAY, LESBIAN, BISEXUAL & TRANSGENDER AGING: CHALLENGES IN RESEARCH, PRACTICE & POLICY 59, 64 (Tarynn M. Witten & A. Evan Eyler, eds. 2012); Strohm et al., *supra* note 2, at 202.

32 Thomeer et al., *supra* note 19, at 475–79.

33 Fredricksen-Goldsen, *supra* note 31, at 66.

34 *Id.* at 68; Thomeer et al., *supra* note 19, at 477–78.

35 MARJORIE H. CANTOR, MARK BRENNAN & R. ANDREW SHIPPY, CAREGIVING AMONG OLDER LESBIAN, GAY, BISEXUAL, AND TRANSGENDER NEW YORKERS 2–3 (2004); Fredricksen-Goldsen, *supra* note 31, at 61–63.

36 Fredricksen-Goldsen, *supra* note 31, at 64.

37 Sondra E. Solomon, Esther D. Rothblum & Kimberly F. Balsam, *Money, Housework, Sex, and Conflict: Same-Sex Couples in Civil Unions, Those Not in Civil Unions, and Heterosexual Married Siblings*, 52 SEX ROLES 561, 572 (2005); Strohm et al., *supra* note 2, at 202. *See also* Abbie E. Goldberg, *"Doing" and "Undoing" Gender: The Meaning and Division of Housework in Same-Sex Couples*, 5 J. FAM. THEORY & REV. 85, 95–96 (2013) (showing how same-sex couples often struggle with the gendered meanings of household chores); Claire Cain Miller, *How Same-*

*Sex Couples Divide Chores, and What It Reveals about Modern Parenting*, N.Y. TIMES (May 16, 2018), www.nytimes.com/2018/05/16/upshot/same-sex-couples -divide-chores-much-more-evenly-until-they-become-parents.html.

38 "Daddy/boy" refers to a gay subculture in which men engage in sexual roleplay which emphasizes perceived age differences between the two partners. This dichotomy can also extend beyond sex to describe a relationship that replicates a nurturing father/son relationship. Garrett Prestage, Graham Brown, John De Wit, Benjamin Bavinton, Christopher Fairley, Bruce Maycock, Colin Batrouney, Phillip Keen, Ian Down, Mohamed Hammoud & Iryna Zablotska, *Understanding Gay Community Subcultures: Implications for HIV Prevention*, 19 AIDS & BEHAV. 2224, 2226 (2015).

## CHAPTER 6. LATS IN THE THIRD AGE

1 The leading edge of the so-called Baby Boom consists of those born between 1946 and 1955. *See* Margaret Hellie Huyck, *Romantic Relationships in Later Life*, 25 GENERATIONS 9, 13 (2001).

2 *See* CASEY E. COPEN, KIMBERLY DANIELS, JONATHAN VESPA & WILLIAM MOSHER, FIRST MARRIAGES IN THE UNITED STATES: DATA FROM THE 2006–2010 NATIONAL SURVEY OF FAMILY GROWTH 5, 9 (2012).

3 *See, e.g.*, WORLD BANK, LIFE EXPECTANCY AT BIRTH, TOTAL (YEARS), https://data.worldbank.org/indicator/SP.DYN.LE00.IN?contextual=max&end=2 015&locations=US&start=1960&view=chart (increasing longevity); Renee Stepler, *Led by Baby Boomers, Divorce Rates Climb for America's 50+ Population*, PEW RESEARCH CENTER, www.pewresearch.org.

4 U.S. Bureau of the Census, *Living Arrangements of Adults 18 Years and Over in the United States* (2015), https://factfinder.census.gov/faces/tableservices/jsf/pages /productview.xhtml?pid=ACS_15_5YR_B09021&prodType=table.

5 *Id.*; Sharon Sassler, *Partnering Across the Life Course: Sex, Relationships, and Mate Selection*, 72 J. MARRIAGE & FAM. 557, 566 (2010); Toni Calasanti & K. Jill Kiecolt, *Diversity among Late-Life Couples*, 31 GENERATIONS 10, 11 (2007). *See also* Matthew R. Wright & Susan L. Brown, *Psychological Well-being among Older Adults: The Role of Partnership Status*, 79 J. MARRIAGE & FAM. 833, 834 (2017) (reporting that 30% of men older than 65 were unmarried versus 60% of women).

6 *See, e.g.*, Alinde J. Moore & Dorothy C. Stratton, *The "Current Woman" in an Older Widower's Life*, in INTIMACY IN LATER LIFE 122 (Kate Davidson & Graham Fennell, eds. 2004).

7 *See, e.g.*, Jaroslava Hasmanová Marhánková, *Women's Attitudes Toward Forming New Partnerships in Widowhood: The Search for "Your Own Someone" and for Freedom*, 28 J. WOMEN & AGING 34, 35 (2016).

8 *See* HUIJING WU, AGE VARIATION IN THE REMARRIAGE RATE, 1990 & 2015, https://create.piktochart.com/output/24418004-wu-age-variation-remarriage-rate-1990-2015-fp-17-21 (2017); The Share of Americans Living without

a Partner Has Increased, Especially among Young Adults, PEW RESEARCH CENTER (Oct. 11, 2017), www.pewresearch.org.

9   Huyck, *supra* note 1, at 13. *See also* Torbjörn Bildtgård & Peter Öberg, *Time as a Structuring Condition Behind New Intimate Relationships in Later Life*, 35 AGEING & SOC'Y 1505, 1509 (2014) (emphasizing importance of life course theory).

10  Susan L. Brown & Matthew R. Wright, *Marriage, Cohabitation, and Divorce in Later Life*, 1 INNOVATION IN AGING (Sept. 1, 2017), igx015, https://doi.org (Table 1).

11  BERNARD D. STARR & MARCELLA BAKUR WEINER, THE STARR-WEINER REPORT ON SEX & SEXUALITY IN THE MATURE YEARS (1981). *See* TONI M. CALASANTI & KATHLEEN F. SLEVIN, GENDER, SOCIAL INEQUALITIES, AND AGING 80 (2001) (regarding disregard of sex among the elderly by Kinsey and other sex researchers). Indeed, a major sex survey in the United Kingdom as late as 2000 included no one above the age of 44 in the sample. Kate Davidson & Graham Fennell, *Introduction: New Intimate Relationships in Later Life, in* INTIMACY IN LATER LIFE viii, 4 (Kate Davidson & Graham Fennell, eds. 2004).

12  STARR & WEINER, *supra* note 11, at 35.

13  Stacy Tessler Lindau, L. Philip Schumm, Edward O. Laumann, Wendy Levinson, Colm A. O'Muircheartaigh & Linda J. Waite, *A Study of Sexuality and Health Among Older Adults in the United States*, 357 N. ENG. J. MED. 762, 766, 772 (2007). Even among those in the group from 75 to 84, 39% of men and 17% of women were sexually active. *Id.* at 766. A 1999 AARP poll confirmed the importance of sex to quality of life among older adults. CALASANTI & SLEVIN, *supra* note 11, at 81.

14  *See, e.g.*, Jacquelyn J. Benson & Marilyn Coleman, *Older Adults Developing a Preference for Living Apart Together*, 78 J. MARRIAGE & FAM. 797, 797 (2016).

15  *See, e.g.*, Donna J. Rankin, *Intimacy and the Elderly: Nursing Homes and Senior Citizen Care*, BUSINESS INSIGHTS (Nov. 1989), http://go.galegroup.com; Winnie Hu, *Too Old for Sex? A Nursing Home in the Bronx Says No Such Thing*, N.Y. TIMES, July 13, 2016, at A15.

16  *See, e.g.*, CALASANTI & SLEVIN, *supra* note 11, at 89–91. Postmenopausal women experience vaginal changes, including both less lubrication and a thinning of the vaginal wall, that make intercourse painful for many, while older men have difficulty achieving and maintaining an erection. *Id.* at 82–83.

17  *See* CALASANTI & SLEVIN, *supra* note 11, at 85–91. *See also* Ingrid Arnet Connidis, *Intimate Relationships: Learning from Later Life Experience, in* AGE MATTERS: REALIGNING FEMINIST THINKING 141–43 (Toni M. Calasanti & Kathleen F. Slevin, eds. 2006).

18  Bildtgård & Öberg, *supra* note 9, at 1514–15, 1522 (2014). *See also id.* at 1521; Connidis, *supra* note 17, at 129 (pointing out that individuals today spend longer in a life stage not dominated by work, allowing them to redefine gender relations).

19  Bildtgård & Öberg, *supra* note 9, at 1516–18.

20 Huyck, *supra* note 1, at 9. *Cf.* Connidis, *supra* note 17, at 126 (defining intimate relationship as including "commitment, deep feelings and expressions of caring and compassion, thinking about one another and sharing values and goals, physical intimacy ranging from close proximity to sexuality, and interdependence").

21 *See, e.g.,* Teresa M. Cooney & Kathleen Dunne, *Intimate Relationships in Later Life: Current Realities, Future Prospects,* 22 J. FAM. ISSUES 838, 853 (2001); Wendy K. Watson & Charlie Stelle, *Dating for Older Women: Experiences and Meanings of Dating in Later Life,* 23 J. WOMEN & AGING 263, 265 (2011).

22 Wright & Brown, *supra* note 5, at 833 (reporting that older adult cohabitation increased almost threefold between 2000 and 2013); Calasanti & Kiecolt, *supra* note 5, at 15 (reporting that cohabitants constituted only 3.7% of unmarried men and 0.9% of unmarried women aged 65 or older). Both remarriage and cohabitation are uncommon among women who are widows. Sara M. Moorman, Alan Booth & Karen L. Fingerman, *Women's Romantic Relationships After Widowhood,* 27 J. FAM. ISSUES 1281, 1285 (2006)

23 Richard A. Bulcroft & Kris A. Bulcroft, *The Nature and Functions of Dating in Later Life,* 13 RES. ON AGING 244, 246 (1991); *see also* Kris Bulcroft & Margaret O'Connor, *The Importance of Dating Relationships on Quality of Life for Older Persons,* 35 FAM. REL. 397, 399 (1986) (describing dating as a monogamous relationship).

24 Susan L. Brown & Sayaka K. Shinohara, *Dating Relationships in Older Adulthood: A National Portrait,* 75 J. MARRIAGE & FAM. 1194, 1196–97 (2013).

25 *See* Deborah Carr, *The Desire to Date and Remarry Among Older Widows and Widowers,* 66 J. MARRIAGE & FAM. 1051, 1053–54 (2004).

26 Calasanti & Kiecolt, *supra* note 5, at 14; Marhánková, *supra* note 7, at 36.

27 One study showed a stark gender difference in reasons given for not remarrying, with more than half the widows in the study, and none of the widowers, saying that they enjoyed their freedom. (Virtually all the widows and none of the widowers cited not wanting to look after another person.) Kate Davidson, *Gender Differences in New Partnership Choices and Constraints for Older Widows and Widowers,* in DAVIDSON & FENNELL, *supra* note 6, at 76 (Table 4.3).

28 Wright & Brown, *supra* note 5, at 845–46.

29 Carr, *supra* note 25, at 1053; *see also* Cooney & Dunne, *supra* note 21, at 848. Many states follow the UMDA provision that automatically terminates alimony upon remarriage. NAT'L CONF. OF COMM'ERS ON UNIFORM STATE LAWS, UNIFORM MARRIAGE AND DIVORCE ACT § 316 (b) ("Unless otherwise agreed in writing or expressly provided in the decree, the obligation to pay future maintenance is terminated upon the death of either party or the remarriage of the party receiving maintenance."). In some states, alimony is terminated upon cohabitation as well. Emily M. May, *Should Moving In Mean Losing Out? Making a Case to Clarify the Legal Effect of Cohabitation on Alimony,* 62 DUKE L.J. 403 (2012). *See also* www.ssa.gov/planners/retire/divspouse.html (concerning possible loss of social security benefits on a previous spouse's account in case of remarriage).

30 *See, e.g.*, Carr, *supra* note 25, at 1064–65; Connidis, *supra* note 17, at 138.

31 *See, e.g.*, Marhánková, *supra* note 7, at 39.

32 *See* Brown & Shinohara, *supra* note 24, at 1201 (seeing LAT as a next step for older daters).

33 Jacquelyn J. Benson & Marilyn Coleman, *Older Adult Descriptions of Living Apart Together*, 65 FAM. REL. 439, 445 (2016).

34 *See, e.g.*, Marhánková, *supra* note 7, at 43; Carr, *supra* note 25, at 1065; Sassler, *supra* note 5, at 566; Moorman et al., *supra* note 22, at 1301; Connidis, *supra* note 17, at 137–38.

35 Jenny de Jong Gierveld, *Remarriage, Unmarried Cohabitation, Living Apart Together: Partner Relationships Following Bereavement or Divorce*, 66 J. MARRIAGE & FAM. 236, 238, 240 (2004).

36 Jenny de Jong Gierveld, *The Dilemma of Repartnering: Considerations of Older Men and Women Entering New Intimate Relationships in Later Life*, 27 AGEING INT'L 61, 65 (2002).

37 Jenny de Jong Gierveld, *Intra-couple Caregiving of Older Adults Living Apart Together: Commitment and Independence*, 34 CANADIAN J. ON AGING 356, 357 (2015).

38 Bildtgård & öberg, *supra* note 9, at 1507, 1511.

39 John Haskey & Jane Lewis, *Living-apart-together in Britain: Context and Meaning*, 2 INT'L J. L. CONTEXT 37, 39 (2006).

40 Simon Duncan & Miranda Phillips, *People Who Live Apart Together (LATs)—How Different Are They?*, 58 SOC. REV. 112, 122 (2010) (Table 3).

41 Martin Turcotte, *Living Apart Together*, STAT. CAN. 4 (2013) (Table 2).

42 Arnaud Régnier-Loilier, Éva Beaujouan & Catherine Villeneuve-Gokalp, *Neither Single, Nor in a Couple: A Study of Living Apart Together in France*, 21 DEMOGRAPHIC RES. 75, 87 (2009) (Table 3).

43 Arnaud Régnier-Lollier & Daniele Vignoli, *The Diverse Nature of Living Apart Together Relationships: An Italy-France Comparison*, 35 J. POPULATION RES. 1, 14 (2018).

44 Sofie Ghazanfareeon Karlsson & Klas Borell, *Intimacy and Autonomy, Gender and Ageing: Living Apart Together*, 27 AGEING INT'L 11 (2002).

45 Alisa C. Lewin, *Intentions to Live Together among Couples Living Apart: Differences by Age and Gender*, 34 EUR. J. POPULATION 721, 731 (2018).

46 NATIONAL SOCIAL LIFE, HEALTH, AND AGING PROJECT (NSHAP), www.norc.org (last visited May 29, 2019).

47 Denise R. Brothers, "Doing" LAT: Redoing Gender and Redoing Family in Living Apart Together Relationships in Later Life 14 (2015) (unpublished Ph.D. dissertation, Miami University), https://etd.ohiolink.edu.

48 Paula Ganzi Licata, *Unwedded Bliss: For Some Loving Couples, Happiness Is Keeping Their Homes, Finances and Routines Separate*, NEWSDAY, June 22, 2013, sec. ACT II, at B04. A similar article appeared in a Canadian magazine at about the same time. Manisha Krishnan, *Living Apart, Together: 1.9 Million Canadians,*

*Many 60-plus, Are Saying No to Cohabitation and Marriage*, MACLEAN'S (Sept. 17, 2013), www.macleans.ca/society/life/living-apart-together/ (describing lifestyle of older Canadian LATs, including one couple of 16 years' duration who were 91 and 94 years old). In Canada, maintaining separate residences is also important because cohabitation gives rise to rights to support for the so-called common-law partner. *Id. See also* CYNTHIA GRANT BOWMAN, UNMARRIED COUPLES, LAW, AND PUBLIC POLICY 188–91 (2010).

49  Licata, *supra* note 48.

50  *Id.*

51  de Jong Gierveld, *supra* note 36, at 74–76.

52  Karlsson & Borell, *supra* note 44, at 17, 23.

53  *See* Benson & Coleman, *supra* note 14.

54  *Id.* at 805.

55  Vincent Caradec, *Les Formes de la Vie Conjugale des Jeunes Couples "Âgés"* (Forms of conjugal living among "aged" young couples), 51 POPULATION 897, 907 (1996).

56  *See, e.g.*, Benson & Coleman, *supra* note 14. The other scholarly article on this subject does not focus on Third Age LAT couples. Charles Strohm, Judith Seltzer, Susan Cochran & Vickie Mays, *"Living Apart Together" Relationships in the United States*, 21 DEMOGRAPHIC RES. 177 (2009).

57  Benson & Coleman, *supra* note 14, at 800.

58  According to one French scholar, "[L]a maison est le lieu des souvenirs" [home is the place of memories]. Caradec, *supra* note 55, at 905, 906 (translation mine).

59  Anna Reimondos, Ann Evans & Edith Gray, *Living-apart-together (LAT) Relationships in Australia*, 87 FAM. MATTERS 43, 53 (2011); de Jong Gierveld, *supra* note 36, at 73–74; Caradec, *supra* note 55, at 906.

60  Caradec, *supra* note 55, at 906.

61  Constance Rosenblum, *Living Apart Together*, N.Y. TIMES (Sept. 15, 2013), www.nytimes.com.

62  *Id.* This couple had in fact been LATs for 42 years and married for six years.

63  Caradec, *supra* note 55, at 911. *But see* de Jong Gierveld, *supra* note 36, at 72 (stating that only private pensions may be lost in the Netherlands upon remarriage, but not the state pension to which everyone is entitled).

64  Caradec, *supra* note 55, at 907 (France); Gierveld, *supra* note 36, at 71–72 (Netherlands); Laura M. Funk & Karen M. Kobayashi, *From Motivations to Accounts: An Interpretive Analysis of "Living Apart Together" Relationships in Mid- to Later-Life Couples*, 37 J. FAM. ISSUES 1101, 1107–10 (2016) (Canada).

65  Sofie Ghazanfareeon Karlsson & Klas Borell, *A Home of Their Own: Women's Boundary Work in LAT Relationships*, 19 J. AGING STUD. 73, 74–75 (2005).

66  Karlsson & Borell, *supra* note 44, at 24.

67  Funk & Kobayashi, *supra* note 64, at 1116.

68  Karlsson & Borell, *supra* note 44, at 23–24.

69  Funk & Kobayashi, *supra* note 64, at 1113–14.

70 Kate Davidson, *Late Life Widowhood, Selfishness and New Partnership Choices: A Gendered Perspective*, 21 AGEING & SOC'Y 297, 305–08 (2001).

71 Jacquelyn Benson, Steffany Kerr & Ashley Ermer, *Living Apart Together Relationships in Later Life: Constructing an Account of Relational Maintenance, in* 11 CONTEMPORARY PERSPECTIVES FAM. RES. 202–03 (2017).

72 Brothers, *supra* note 47, at 41.

73 Benson et al., *supra* note 71, at 206.

74 Sofie Ghazanfareeon Karlsson & Majen Espvall, *Intimacy and Obligations in LAT Relationships in Later Life, in* COUPLE RELATIONSHIPS IN THE MIDDLE AND LATER YEARS: THEIR NATURE, COMPLEXITY, AND ROLE IN HEALTH AND ILLNESS 85 (Jamila Bookwala, ed. 2016).

75 de Jong Gierveld, *supra* note 37, at 357.

76 *Id.*

77 Karlsson & Borell, *supra* note 44, at 14, 20.

78 Sofie Ghazanfareeon Karlsson, Stina Johansson, Anne Gerdner & Klas Borell, *Caring While Living Apart*, 49 J. GERONTOLOGICAL SOC. WORK 3, 17–24 (2007).

79 de Jong Gierveld, *supra* note 37, at 359–62.

80 *Id.* at 361, 363.

81 Benson & Coleman, *supra* note 14, at 803–04.

82 Benson & Coleman, *supra* note 33, at 446.

83 Benson & Coleman, *supra* note 14, at 810.

84 Jenny de Jong Gierveld, *Remarriage, Unmarried Cohabitation, Living Apart Together: Partner Relationships Following Bereavement or Divorce*, 66 J. MARRIAGE & FAM. 236, 241 (2004).

85 Caradec, supra note 55, at 911 .

86 *See* CODE FED. REG. § 404.331 (entitling divorced persons who were married for at least 10 years prior to divorce and have been divorced at least two years to claim Social Security on the former spouse's account so long as they are not remarried and are not entitled to an equal or greater benefit on their own account).

87 Brothers, *supra* note 47, at 15–16; Rosalinde van der Wiel, Clara H. Mulder & Ajay Bailey, *Pathways to Commitment in Living-Apart-Together Relationships in the Netherlands: A Study on Satisfaction, Alternatives, Investments and Social Support*, 36 ADVANCES IN LIFE COURSE RES. 17, 20 (2018).

88 Alisa C. Lewin, *Health and Relationship Quality Later in Life: A Comparison of Living Apart Together (LAT), First Marriages, Remarriages, and Cohabitation*, 38 J. FAM. ISSUES 1754, 1755 (2017).

89 The unfolding of a preference for LAT over time appears to be common. *See* Benson & Coleman, *supra* note 14, at 807.

## CHAPTER 7. COMMUTER MARRIAGE AND COHABITATION

1 U.S. Bureau of the Census, Sex by Marital Status for the Population 15 Years and Over (2018), https://data.census.gov/cedsci/table?q=sex%20by%20martial%20

status%20for%20the%20population%20&hidePreview=false&tid=ACSDT1Y2018.
B12001&t=Marital%20Status%20and%20Marital%20History%3AAge%20and%20
Sex&vintage=2018 (2018: ACS 1-Year Estimates Detailed Tables).

2  Betty Frankle Kirschner & Laurel Richardson Walum, *Two-Location Families: Married Singles*, 1 ALTERNATIVE LIFESTYLES 513, 516 (1978); Elaine A. Anderson & Jane W. Spruill, *The Dual-Career Commuter Family: A Lifestyle on the Move*, 19 MARRIAGE & FAM. REV. 131, 132 (1993).

3  Agnes Farris, *Commuting*, in WORKING COUPLES 100 (Rhona Rapoport & Robert N. Rapoport with Janice M. Bumstead, eds. 1978); NAOMI GERSTEL & HARRIET GROSS, COMMUTER MARRIAGE: A STUDY OF WORK AND FAMILY 27 (1984).

4  Karla Mason Bergen, *Accounting for Difference: Commuter Wives and the Master Narrative of Marriage*, 38 J. APPLIED COMM. RES. 47, 48 (2010).

5  GERSTEL & GROSS, *supra* note 3, at 7.

6  Sue Shellenbarger, *Marriage from a Distance*, WALL ST. J., Aug. 15, 2018, at A11 (reporting that the number of married couples living apart increased 44% between 2000 and 2017).

7  *Id.* at 39–43. *See also* Richard Glotzer, *Miles That Bind: Commuter Marriage and Family Strengths*, 12 MICH. FAM. REV. 7, 11 (2007) (describing the emergence of a global economy impervious to time and distance).

8  Danielle J. Lindemann, *Going the Distance: Individualism and Interdependence in the Commuter Marriage*, 79 J. MARRIAGE & FAM. 1419, 1419 (2017); Bergen, *supra* note 4, at 48–49.

9  Cybele Weisser, *Two Cities, Two Careers, Too Much?*, CNN MONEY (Jan. 1, 2006), https://money.cnn.com.

10  GERSTEL & GROSS, *supra* note 3, at 9.

11  *Id.* at 2.

12  Kathrijn Govaerts & David N. Dixon, . . . *Until Careers Do Us Part: Vocational and Marital Satisfaction in the Dual-Career Commuter Marriage*, 11 INT'L J. ADVANCEMENT COUNSELLING 265, 265–67 (1988); Bergen, *supra* note 4, at 48.

13  LAURA STAFFORD, MAINTAINING LONG-DISTANCE AND CROSS-RESIDENTIAL RELATIONSHIPS 70 (2005).

14  *See generally* Glotzer, *supra* note 7; Roxanne Greitz Miller, *Wither* [sic] *Thou Goest: The Trailing Spouse or Commuter Marriage Dilemma*, in WOMEN'S EXPERIENCES IN LEADERSHIP IN K-16 SCIENCE EDUCATION COMMUNITIES, BECOMING AND BEING (Katherine C. Wieseman & Molly H. Weinburgh, eds. 2009).

15  Barbara B. Bunker et al., *Quality of Life in Dual-Career Families: Commuting Versus Single-Residence Couples*, 54 J. MARRIAGE & FAM. 399, 406 (1992).

16  Bergen, *supra* note 4, at 56–57.

17  John Orton & Sharyn M. Crossman, *Long Distance Marriage (LDM): Cause of Marital Disruption or a Solution to Unequal Dual-Career Development?*, in FAMILY, SELF, AND SOCIETY: EMERGING ISSUES, ALTERNATIVES, AND IN-

TERVENTIONS 327, 339 (Douglas B. Gutknecht, Edgar W. Butler, Larry Criswell & Jerry Meints, eds. 1983).

18 GERSTEL & GROSS, *supra* note 3, at 150–51.

19 Farris, *supra* note 3, at 101–02.

20 GERSTEL & GROSS, *supra* note 3, at 115–16.

21 Farris, *supra* note 3, at 104; GERSTEL & GROSS, *supra* note 3, at 115.

22 Barbara B. Bunker et al., *supra* note 15, at 405.

23 GERSTEL & GROSS, *supra* note 3, at 14–18.

24 Karla Mason Bergen et al., *"How Do You Get Two Houses Cleaned?": Accomplishing Family Caregiving in Commuter Marriages*, 7 J. FAM. COMM. 287, 300–01 (2007)

25 Govaerts & Dixon, *supra* note 12, at 267.

26 GERSTEL & GROSS, *supra* note 3, at 104–07; FAIRLEE E. WINFIELD, COMMUTER MARRIAGE: LIVING TOGETHER, APART 47–49 (1985).

27 Farris, *supra* note 3, at 102–03.

28 GERSTEL & GROSS, *supra* note 3, at 144–45; Glotzer, *supra* note 7, at 14.

29 GERSTEL & GROSS, *supra* note 3, at 146–47.

30 Govaerts & Dixon, *supra* note 12, at 267; Farris, *supra* note 3, at 104.

31 STAFFORD, *supra* note 12, at 73; GERSTEL & GROSS, *supra* note 3, at 147–48.

32 Jane W. Spruill, The Sharing of Family Tasks and Role Strain in the Commuter Marriage (1984) (Master's Thesis, University of Maryland). *See also* Anderson & Spruill, *supra* note 2, at 144.

33 STAFFORD, *supra* note 13, at 73.

34 GERSTEL & GROSS, *supra* note 3, at 36–37; Farris, *supra* note 3, at 104.

35 Govaerts & Dixon, *supra* note 12, at 275.

36 Spruill, *supra* note 32, at 16–17.

37 GERSTEL & GROSS, *supra* note 3, at 82–84.

38 Spruill, *supra* note 32, at 48.

39 Anderson & Spruill, *supra* note 2, at 140, 143.

40 GERSTEL & GROSS, *supra* note 3, at 131; Orton & Crossman, *supra* note 17, at 340.

41 Bergen et al., *supra* note 24, at 295–97 (2007); Karla Mason Bergen, *supra* note 4, at 50–59.

42 Anderson & Spruill, *supra* note 2, at 143.

43 Govaerts & Dixon, *supra* note 12, at 275–77.

44 Lindemann, *supra* note 8, at 1429.

45 GERSTEL & GROSS, *supra* note 3, at 1, 199–201.

46 *Id.* 72.

47 WINFIELD, *supra* note 26, at 40.

48 *See* Lindemann, *supra* note 8, at 1419–21; GERSTEL & GROSS, *supra* note 3, at 48, 201.

49 Renee Stepler, *Number of U.S. Adults Cohabiting with a Partner Continues to Rise, Especially Among Those 50 and Older*, PEW RES. CTR. (Apr. 6, 2017), www.pewre

search.org. *See also* U.S. Bureau of the Census, Historical Living Arrangements of Adults (Nov. 2019), Table AD-3. Living Arrangements of Adults 18 and Over, 1967 to the Present, www.census.gov/data/tables/time-series/demo/families/adults .html. The census statistics on cohabitation have been substantially improved since 2007 by the inclusion of more sensitive questions about possible cohabitants present in a household (who may not be the household head) to make up for previous underestimation of the numbers. Sheela Kennedy & Catherine A. Fitch, *Measuring Cohabitation and Family Structure in the United States: Assessing the Impact of New Data from the Current Population Survey*, 49 DEMOGRAPHY 1479, 1481–96 (2012).

50  Shelly Lundberg, Robert A. Pollak & Jenna Stearns, *Family Inequality: Diverging Patterns in Marriage, Cohabitation, and Childbearing*, 30 J. ECON. PERSPEC-TIVES 79, 84 (2016).

51  *Id.* at 84; CYNTHIA GRANT BOWMAN, UNMARRIED COUPLES, LAW, AND PUBLIC POLICY 99–102 (2010).

52  *See, e.g.*, Arland Thornton & Linda Young-DeMarco, *Four Decades of Trends in Attitudes Toward Family Issues in the United States: The 1960s through the 1990s*, 63 J. MARRIAGE & FAM. 1009, 1024 (2001) (Table 5).

53  *See generally* Pamela J. Smock, Wendy D. Manning & Meredith Porter, *"Everything's There Except Money": How Money Shapes Decisions to Marry among Cohabitors*, 67 J. MARRIAGE & FAM. 680 (2005). *See also* Patrick Ishizuka, *The Economic Foundations of Cohabiting Couples' Union Transitions*, 53 DEMOGRA-PHY 535, 547 (2018) (providing quantitative empirical support for the "marriage bar" theory).

54  June Carbone, *Out of the Channel and into the Swamp: How Family Law Fails in a New Era of Class Division*, 39 HOFSTRA L. REV. 861–66 (2011); Lundberg et al., *supra* note 50; *see generally* JUNE CARBONE & NAOMI CAHN, MARRIAGE MARKETS: HOW INEQUALITY IS REMAKING THE AMERICAN FAM-ILY (2014).

55  *See* BOWMAN, *supra* note 51, at 111–17.

56  Timothy A. Ortyl, *Long-Term Heterosexual Cohabiters and Attitudes Toward Marriage*, 54 SOC. Q. 584, 594–98 (2013).

57  Sharon Sassler & Amanda J. Miller, *Class Differences in Cohabitation Processes*, 60 FAM. REL. 163, 175 (2011); Nicole Hiekel & Renske Keizer, *Risk-avoidance or Utmost Commitments? Dutch Focus Group Research on Cohabitation and Marriage*, 32 DEMOGRAPHIC RES. 311, 328 (2015).

58  Larry L. Bumpass, James A. Sweet & Andrew Cherlin, *The Role of Cohabitation in Declining Rates of Marriage*, 53 J. MARRIAGE & FAM. 913, 918 (1991); Sharon Sassler & James McNally, *Cohabiting Couples' Economic Circumstances and Union Transitions: A Re-examination Using Multiple Imputation Techniques*, 32 SOC. SCI. RES. 553, 575 (2003).

59  Paula Span, *More Older Couples Are 'Shacking Up': The New Old Age*, N.Y. TIMES (May 8, 2017), https://nyti.ms/2pmirQ9.

60 Stepler, *supra* note 49.

61 Larry L. Bumpass, *What's Happening to the Family? Interactions Between Demographic and Institutional Change*, 27 DEMOGRAPHY 483, 487 (1990) (describing median as 1.5 years); Allan V. Horwitz & Helen Raskin White, *The Relationship of Cohabitation and Mental Health: A Study of a Young Adult Cohort*, 60 J. MARRIAGE & FAM. 505, 509 (1998) (describing average as 1.75 years); U.S. DEP'T OF HEALTH AND HUMAN SERVICES, CENTERS FOR DISEASE CONTROL AND PREVENTION, NAT'L CENTER FOR HEALTH STATISTICS, COHABITATION, MARRIAGE, DIVORCE, AND REMARRIAGE IN THE UNITED STATES: DATA FROM THE NATIONAL SURVEY OF FAMILY GROWTH 4, 49 (2002), www.cdc.gov (Table 15) (estimating the probability that a woman's first cohabitation will end within 10 years at 62%).

62 *See* Sara E. Mernitz, *A Cohort Comparison of Trends in First Cohabitation Duration in the United States*, 38 DEMOGRAPHIC RES. 2073–82 (2018); Anne Barlow, Carole Burgoyne, Elizabeth Clery & Janet Smithson, *Cohabitation and the Law: Myths, Money and the Media, in* BRITISH SOCIAL ATTITUDES: THE 24TH REPORT 29, 33 (Alison Park, John Curtice, Katarina Thomson, Miranda Phillips, Mark C. Johnson & Elizabeth Clery, eds. 2008). Cohabitation lasts for much longer periods in countries, such as Sweden, where it is long well-established, accepted, and legally protected. Kajsa Walleng, *The Swedish Cohabitees Act in Today's Society, in* FAMILY LAW AND CULTURE IN EUROPE: DEVELOPMENTS, CHALLENGES AND OPPORTUNITIES 95, 100 (Katharina Boele-Woelki, Nina Dethloff & Werner Gephart, eds. 2014) (reporting that 13% of cohabiting unions last more than 20 years in Sweden).

63 Susan L. Brown, Jennifer Roebuch Bulanda & Gary R. Lee, *Transitions Into and Out of Cohabitation in Later Life*, 74 J. MARRIAGE & FAM. 774, 788–90 (2012).

64 Hiekel & Keizer, *supra* note 57, at 313, 317.

65 Compare, *e.g.*, Anne-Right Poortman & Melinda Mills, *Investments in Marriage and Cohabitation: The Role of Legal and Interpersonal Commitment*, 74 J. MARRIAGE & FAM. 357, 357 (2012), with Simone Wong, *Shared Commitment, Interdependency and Property Relations: A Socio-Legal Project for Cohabitation*, 24 CHILD & FAM. L.Q. 60, 70 (2012).

66 *See, e.g.*, Nicole Hiekel, Aart C. Liefbroer & Anne-Right Poortman, *Income Pooling Strategies Among Cohabiting and Married Couples: A Comparative Perspective*, 30 DEMOGRAPHIC RES. 1527, 1528–29, 1548 (2014).

67 Carolyn Vogler, Michaela Brockmann & Richard D. Wiggins, *Managing Money in New Heterosexual Forms of Intimate Relationships*, 37 J. SOCIO-ECONOMICS 552, 567 (2008) (Table 11) (reporting that married respondents and cohabiting parents use a joint pooling system); Kristen R. Heimdal & Sharon K. Houseknecht, *Cohabiting and Married Couples' Income Organization: Approaches in Sweden and the United States*, 65 J. MARRIAGE & FAM. 525, 533 (2003) (finding that a majority of both married and cohabiting couples in the United States and Sweden maintain joint finances); Catherine Kenney, *Cohabiting Couples, Filing Jointly? Resource*

*Pooling and U.S. Poverty Policies*, 53 FAM. REL. 237, 243–46 (2004) (finding that cohabiting parents do generally pool resources).

68 Heimdal & Houseknecht, *supra* note 67, at 533; Carolyn Vogler, *Cohabiting Couples: Rethinking Money in the Household at the Beginning of the Twenty First Century*, 53 SOC. REV. 1, 13 (2005).

69 Katherine J. Ashby & Carole B. Burgoyne, *Separate Financial Entities? Beyond Categories of Money Management*, 37 J. SOCIO-ECONOMICS 458 (2008).

70 *Id.* at 477; Barlow et al., *supra* note 62, at 47–48.

71 FAMILY STRUCTURE AND CHILDREN'S LIVING ARRANGEMENTS, www .childstats.gov (last visited May 31, 2019).

72 PEW RES. CTR., PARENTING IN AMERICA: 1. THE AMERICAN FAMILY TODAY (Dec. 17, 2015), www.pewsocialtrends.org.

73 *See, e.g.*, Steven Stack & J. Ross Eshleman, *Marital Status and Happiness: A 17-Nation Study*, 60 J. MARRIAGE & FAM. 527 (1998); Claire M. Kamp Dush & Paul R. Amato, *Consequences of Relationship Status and Quality for Subjective Well-Being*, 22 J. SOC. & PERSONAL RELATIONSHIPS 607 (2005); Anke C. Zimmermann & Richard A. Easterlin, *Happily Ever After? Cohabitation, Marriage, Divorce, and Happiness in Germany*, 32 POPULATION & DEV. REV. 511 (2006).

74 Compare Allan V. Horwitz & Helen Raskin White, *The Relationship of Cohabitation and Mental Health: A Study of a Young Adult Cohort*, 60 J. MARRIAGE & FAM. 505, 510–11 (1998) (reporting no significant difference in depression between cohabitants and married persons) with Susan L. Brown, *The Effect of Union Type on Psychological Well-Being: Depression among Cohabitors Versus Marrieds*, 41 J. HEALTH & SOC. BEHAV. 241, 247, 253 (2000) (finding that cohabitants report substantially higher levels of depression than their married counterparts).

75 *See* BOWMAN, *supra* note 51, at 46–51.

76 *See* Anne Barlow, *Legislating for Cohabitation in Common Law Jurisdictions in Europe: Two Steps Forward and One Step Back?*, *in* FAMILY LAW AND CULTURE IN EUROPE: DEVELOPMENTS, CHALLENGES AND OPPORTUNITIES 77, 80 (Katharina Boele-Woelki, Nina Dethloff & Werner Gephart, eds. 2014).

77 *See* BOWMAN, *supra* note 51, at 28–38.

78 Blumenthal v. Brewer, 69 N.E.3d 834 (Ill. 2016). *See also* Hewitt v Hewitt, 394 N.E.2d 1204 (Ill. 1979).

79 Marvin v. Marvin, 557 P.2d 106 (Cal. 1976).

80 Lawrence W. Waggoner, *With Marriage on the Decline and Cohabitation on the Rise, What About Marital Rights for Unmarried Partners?*, 41 ACTEC L. J. 49, 68 (2015).

81 Connell v. Francisco, 898 P.2d 831 (Wash. 1995); Vasquez v. Hawthorne, 33 P.3d 735 (Wash. 2001).

82 For more detail about domestic partnership arrangements prior to same-sex marriage, *see* BOWMAN, *supra* note 51, at 59–69.

83 *See, e.g.*, Melissa Murray, Obergefell v. Hodges *and Nonmarriage Inequality*, 104 CALIF. L. REV. 1207, 1242–49 (2016).

84 Barlow et al., *supra* note 62, at 40–43; JULIA CARTER & SIMON DUNCAN, REINVENTING COUPLES: TRADITION, AGENCY AND BRICOLAGE 87 (2018).

85 Jennifer K. Robbennolt & Monica Kirkpatrick Johnson, *Legal Planning for Unmarried Committed Partners: Empirical Lessons for a Preventive and Therapeutic Approach*, 41 ARIZ. L. REV. 417, 435–36, 438, 441 (1999) (describing a study that found that only 29% of committed unmarried couples had written agreements).

86 *See, e.g.*, Dunphy v. Gregor, 642 A.2d 372 (N.J. 1994) (allowing suit for negligent infliction of emotional distress by cohabitant).

87 *See* Courtney Joslin, *Discrimination In and Out of Marriage*, 98 B.U. L. REV. 1, 7, 16–17 (2018) (housing discrimination); Cynthia Grant Bowman, *Legal Treatment of Cohabitation in the United States*, 26 L. & POL'Y 119, 142–43 (2004) (health care decision-making).

88 Barlow et al., *supra* note 62, at 35.

89 June Carbone & Naomi Cahn, *Nonmarriage*, 76 MD. L. REV. 55, 102 (2016).

90 *See, e.g.*, Marsha Garrison, *Is Consent Necessary? An Evaluation of the Emerging Law of Cohabitant Obligation*, 52 UCLA L. Rev. 815, 840, 845–46 (2005).

91 *See, e.g.*, Shahar Lifshitz, *Married Against Their Will? Toward a Pluralist Regulation of Spousal Relationships*, 66 WASH. & LEE L. REV. 1565 (2009); William N. Eskridge, Jr., *Family Law Pluralism: The Guided-Choice Regime of Menus, Default Rules, and Override Rules*, 100 GEO. L.J. 1881 (2013).

92 *See* Lifshitz, *supra* note 91, at 1604–06.

93 *See* ALI Principles of the Law of Family Dissolution §§ 4.09–.10, 5.04, 6.04–.06 (2002).

94 *Id.* at § 6.03.

95 Waggoner, *supra* note 80, at 88.

96 BOWMAN, *supra* note 51, at 223–28. *See also* Grace Ganz Blumberg, *Cohabitation Without Marriage: A Different Perspective*, 28 UCLA L. REV. 1125, 1166 (1981) (proposing property distribution and support remedies after two years or birth of a child).

97 For a more detailed description of the Canadian law on cohabitation and how it got that way, *see* BOWMAN, *supra* note 51, at 186–94.

98 *See id.* at 194–200.

99 *See id.* at 206–14.

100 *See id.* at 201–06.

101 *See id.* at 214–20.

102 Scotland had common law marriage until 2006; when it was abolished, Scottish family law was revised so as to add protections for cohabitants who had suffered economic disadvantage from a relationship. Barlow, *supra* note 76, at 82–83.

103 BOWMAN, *supra* note 51, at 176–77; Barlow, *supra* note 76, at 88.

104 Barlow, *supra* note 76 at 89–91.

105 CARTER & DUNCAN, *supra* note 84, at 87–88.

106 Barlow et al., *supra* note 62, at 44–46.

CHAPTER 8. LATS AND THE LAW AS IT NOW STANDS

1 The Supreme Court case that struck down the "substitute father" rule in fact involved a LAT. King v. Smith, 392 U.S. 309, 315 (1968) (Mr. Williams came to the welfare recipient's house on weekends but was not the father of her children; he was in fact married with children of his own.). Even now, some states take the income of a male cohabitant into account in calculating the assistance due to a mother. *See, e.g.*, CAL. WELFARE AND INSTITUTIONS CODE § 11351.5 (West 2019). My investigation of the case law, however, does not show that this has caused problems for LATs.

2 Taylor v. Fields, 224 Cal. Rptr. 186 (Cal. App. 1986).

3 Bergen v. Wood, 14 Cal. App. 4th 854, 18 Cal. Rptr. 2d (Cal. App. 1993).

4 *Id.* at 858.

5 Cochran v. Cochran, 106 Cal. Rptr. 2d 899 (Cal. App. 2001).

6 *Id.* at 906.

7 *See* Stasia Rudiman, *Alimony and Cohabitation from Then to Now*, 22 J. CON-TEMP. LEGAL ISSUES 568 (2015).

8 *See* Levine v. Konvitz, 890 A.2d 354 (N.J. Super. 2006).

9 Devaney v. L'Esperance, 949 A.2d 743 (N.J. 2008). *See also* Steven K. Berenson, *Should Cohabitation Matter in Family Law?*, 13 J. L. & FAM. STUD. 289 (2011) (discussing this and other cases about alimony and cohabitants in New Jersey).

10 *Devaney*, 949 A.2d at 749, *quoting* In re Estate of Roccamonte, 808 A.2d 838, 844–45 (N.J. 2002).

11 *Devaney*, 949 A.2d at 752–53 (Long, J., concurring).

12 *Id.* at 749–50.

13 Wessel v. Burritt, 2008 N.J. Super. Unpub. LEXIS 2125 (N.J. Sup. Ct., App. Div. Oct. 14, 2008).

14 N.J. REV. STAT. Tit. 25, sec. 25:1–5 (h) (West 2010).

15 Jennifer K. Robbennolt & Monica Kirkpatrick Johnson, *Legal Planning for Un-married Committed Partners: Empirical Lessons for a Preventive and Therapeutic Approach*, 41 ARIZ. L. REV. 417, 436, 438, 441 (1999) (describing a study that found that only 29% of committed unmarried couples had written agreements).

16 Twila L. Perry, *The "Essentials of Marriage": Reconsidering the Duty of Support and Services*, 15 YALE J. L. & FEMINISM 1, 24 (2003).

17 *See, e.g.*, Ira Mark Ellman, *The Theory of Alimony*, 77 CAL. L. REV. 1 (1989).

18 *See, e.g.*, Washburn v. Washburn, 677 P.2d 152 (Wash. 1084) (en banc); Mahoney v. Mahoney, 453 A.2d 527 (N.J. 1982).

19 *See, e.g.*, Cynthia Lee Starnes, *Divorce and the Displaced Homemaker: A Discourse on Playing with Dolls, Partnership Buyouts and Dissociation under No-Fault*, 60 U. CHI. L. REV. 67, 130–38 (1993); Martha M. Ertman, *Commercializing Marriage: A Proposal for Valuing Women's Work through Premarital Security Agreements*, 77 TEX. L. REV. 17 (1998).

20 N.Y. DOM. REL. LAW, § 236 (B)(6) (McKinney 2016); MASS. GEN. LAWS ch. 208, § 49 (West 2012).

21  *See, e.g.,* MASS. GEN. LAWS ch. 208, § 50 (West 2012).

22  *See* Perry, *supra* note 16, at 26.

23  Cynthia Lee Starnes, *I'll Be Watching You: Alimony and the Cohabitation Rule,* 50 FAM. L.Q. 261, 300 (2016).

24  *Id.* at 264.

25  Lang v. Superior Ct, 126 Cal. Rptr. 122 n.1 (Cal. App. 1975).

26  In re Marriage of Steiding, 2014 Cal. App. Unpub. LEXIS 5718 (Cal. Ct. App. Aug. 13, 2014)

27  *Id.* at *4–6.

28  Woillard v. Woillard, 2014 Cal. App. Unpub. LEXIS 208 (Cal. Ct. App. Jan. 14, 2014).

29  *See* Adessa v. Adessa, 2009 N.J. Super. Unpub. LEXIS 1316, *7 (Super. Ct. NJ, App. Div. May 29, 2009).

30  *Id.* at *6 (quoting Konzelman v. Konzelman, 729 A.2d 7 (N.J. 1999)).

31  *Id.* at *7 (quoting Konzelman v. Konzelman, 729 A.2d 7 (N.J. 1999)).

32  *See* CYNTHIA GRANT BOWMAN, UNMARRIED COUPLES, LAW, AND PUBLIC POLICY 32–33 (2010) (discussing Illinois's treatment of cohabitation as a condition for terminating alimony).

33  *Id.* at 32; *see also* 750 ILL. COMP. STAT. ANN. 5/510(c) (2011).

34  Schoenhard v. Schoenhard, 392 N.E.2d 764, 768 (Ill. App. Ct. 1979).

35  In re Marriage of Roofe, 460 N.E.2d 784, 785 (Ill. App. Ct. 1984).

36  In re Marriage of Sappington, 462 N.E.2d 881, 882–83 (Ill. App. Ct. 1984) (not terminating alimony because sexual intercourse was a necessary element and new partner was impotent). *Cf.* In re Marriage of Frasco, 638 N.E. 2d 655 (Ill. App. 1994) (terminating alimony even though cohabiting couple did not have a sexual relationship because they lived together like a married couple otherwise).

37  In re Marriage of Herrin, 634 N.E.2d 1168 (Ill. App. 1994). *See also* Allan L. Karnes, *Terminating Maintenance Payments When an Ex-Spouse Cohabitates in Illinois: When Is Enough Enough?,* 41 J. MARSHALL L. REV. 435 (2008) (discussing the Illinois case law on this subject).

38  *Herrin,* 634 N.E.2d at 1171.

39  *Id. But see* In re Marriage of Bates, 819 N.E.2d 714, 733 (Ill. 2004) (upholding trial and appellate court decision that couple were simply dating, not in a resident, continuing, conjugal relationship because they did not live in the same residence, did not commingle funds, and did not vacation together). The Illinois Supreme Court decided *Bates* five months after *Herrin* was decided but with no reference to it, although it considered some of the same factors.

40  In re Marriage of Susan, 856 N.E. 2d 1167, 1169–70 (Ill. App. Ct. 2006).

41  *Id.* at 1171–73.

42  In re Marriage of Cook, 2014 Ill. App. Unpub. LEXIS 459, *37 (Ill. App. Ct., 2d Dist. Mar. 13, 2014). *See also* In re Marriage of Kunowski, 2012 Ill. App. Unpub. LEXIS 2007, *24–26 (Ill. App. Ct., 2d Dist. Aug. 17, 2012) (determining that it was not a cohabiting relationship because couple did not commingle finances or

spend vacations together); In re Marriage of Wheat, 2013 Ill. App. Unpub. LEXIS 1492, *13–15 (Ill. App. Ct., 4th Dist. July 1, 2013) (affirming trial court holding that it was not a marriage-like relationship where couple kept belongings and finances separate and only saw each other two to four times a week, rarely spending the night).

43  In re Marriage of Miller, 40 N.E.3d 206 (Ill. App. 2015).

44  George v. George, 2016 Ill. App. Unpub. LEXIS 815, *4–5 (Ill. App. Ct., 1st Dist. Apr. 26, 2016).

45  North Carolina courts have also found that LATs were cohabitants and terminated alimony. *See, e.g.*, Rehm v. Rehm, 409 S.E.2d 723 (N.C. App. 1991). A Missouri court terminated alimony in a case where LATs spent weekends together and were financially independent but had purchased a house jointly and had plans to marry in the future. Adamson v. Adamson, 958 S.W.2d 598 (Mo. Ct. App. 1998).

46  Paul v. Paul, 60 A.3d 1080 (Del. 2012).

47  Honeycutt v. Honeycutt, 152 S.W.3d 556 (Tenn. Ct. App. 2003).

48  Albertina Antognini, *Against Nonmarital Exceptionalism*, 51 U.C. Davis L. Rev. 1891, 1941, 1957 (2018).

49  Perry, *supra* note 16, at 28.

50  *Id.* at 27.

## CHAPTER 9. HOW SHOULD THE LAW TREAT LATS?

1  Cynthia Grant Bowman, Unmarried Couples, Law, and Public Policy 2 (2010).

2  *See, e.g.*, Marsha Garrison, *Is Consent Necessary? An Evaluation of the Emerging Law of Cohabitant Obligation*, 52 UCLA L. Rev. 815, 840, 845–46 (2005); June Carbone & Naomi Cahn, *Nonmarriage*, 76 Md. L. Rev. 55, 102 (2016).

3  Elizabeth S. Scott & Robert E. Scott, *From Contract to Status: Collaboration and the Evolution of Novel Family Relationships*, 115 Colum. L. Rev. 293, 314 (2015).

4  William N. Eskridge, Jr., *Family Law Pluralism: The Guided-Choice Regime of Menus, Default Rules, and Override Rules*, 100 Geo. L.J. 1881 (2013).

5  Jessica R. Feinberg, *The Survival of Nonmarital Relationship Statuses in the Same-Sex Marriage Era: A Proposal*, 87 Temple L. Rev. 47 (2014).

6  *See, e.g.*, Maxine Eichner, *Marriage and the Elephant: The Liberal Democratic State's Regulation of Intimate Relationships Between Adults*, 30 Harv. J. L. & Gender 25, 53–55 (2007); Courtney G. Joslin, *Family Support and Supporting Families*, 68 Vand. L. Rev. En Banc 153, 156 (2015).

7  Vicky Lyssens-Danneboom, Sven Eggermont & Dimitri Mortelmans, *Living Apart Together (LAT) and Law: Exploring Legal Expectations among LAT Individuals in Belgium*, 22 Soc. & Legal Stud. 357 (2013).

8  Ingrid Arnet Connidis, Klas Borell & Sofie Ghazanfareeon Karlsson, *Ambivalence and Living Apart Together in Later Life: A Critical Research Proposal*, 79 J. Marriage & Fam. 1404, 1414 (2017).

9 Simon Duncan, Julia Carter, Miranda Phillips, Sasha Roseneil & Mariya Stoilova, *Legal Rights for People Who "Live Apart Together"?*, 34 J. SOC. WELFARE & FAM. L. 443, 451 (2012).

10 BOWMAN, *supra* note 6, at 223–30.

11 Steven K. Berenson, *Should Cohabitation Matter in Family Law?*, 13 J. L. & FAM. STUD. 289, 319 (2011).

12 Unjust enrichment is an equitable doctrine that imposes an obligation to make restitution when one person is enriched at the expense of another under circumstances the law deems unjust. A constructive trust is an equitable remedy a court may impose where one person holds property that, for example, was intended to benefit another.

13 According to the Gallup poll, only 44% of Americans reported having wills in 2016. Jeffrey M. Jones, *Majority in US Do Not Have a Will*, GALLUP NEWS (May 18, 2016), www.gallup.com.

## CONCLUSION

1 ANTHONY GIDDENS, THE TRANSFORMATION OF INTIMACY: SEXUALITY, LOVE AND EROTICISM IN MODERN SOCIETIES 152–56 (1992) (seeing pure relationships as a result of the modern insistence upon autonomy and gender equality); ZYGMUNT BAUMAN, LIQUID LOVE: ON THE FRAILTY OF HUMAN BONDS (2003) (positing that modern men and women are without any fixed or durable bonds at all).

# BIBLIOGRAPHY

## BOOKS AND ARTICLES

Aloni, Erez. "Deprivative Recognition." *University of California Los Angeles Law Review* 61 (2014): 1276–1345.

Amato, Paul R., and Lydia N. Hayes. "'Alone Together' Marriage and 'Living Apart Together' Relationships." In *Contemporary Issues in Family Studies: Global Perspectives on Partnerships, Parenting and Support in a Changing World*, edited by Angela Abela and Janet Walker. Chichester, UK: John Wiley and Sons, 2014.

American Law Institute. *ALI Principles of the Law of Family Dissolution.* St. Paul: American Law Institute Publishers, 2002.

Anderson, Elaine A., and Jane W. Spruill. "The Dual-Career Commuter Family: A Lifestyle on the Move." *Marriage and Family Review* 19 (1993): 131–47.

Antognini, Albertina. "Against Nonmarital Exceptionalism." *University of California Davis Law Review* 51: 1891–1972.

———. "The Law of Nonmarriage." *Boston College Law Review* 58 (2017): 2–63.

Asendorpf, Jens B. "Living Apart Together: Alters- und Kohortenabhängigkeit einer heterogenen Lebensform" (Age and cohort dependence of a heterogeneous lifestyle). In *Kölner Zeitschrift für Soziologie und Sozialpsychologie* 60 (2008): 749–64.

Ashby, Katherine J., and Carole B. Burgoyne. "Separate Financial Entities? Beyond Categories of Money Management." *Journal of Socio-Economics* 37 (2008): 458–80.

Ayuso, Luis. "What Future Awaits Couples Living Apart Together (LAT)?" *Sociological Review* 67 (2019): 226–44.

Badgett, M. V. Lee. *When Gay People Get Married: What Happens When Societies Legalize Same-Sex Marriage.* New York: New York University Press, 2009.

Barlow, Anne. "Legislating for Cohabitation in Common Law Jurisdictions in Europe: Two Steps Forward and One Step Back?" In *Family Law and Culture in Europe: Developments, Challenges and Opportunities*, edited by Katharina Boele-Woelki, Nina Dethloff, and Werner Gephart. Cambridge, UK: Intersentia, 2014.

Barlow, Anne, Carole Burgoyne, Elizabeth Clery, and Janet Smithson. "Cohabitation and the Law: Myths, Money and the Media." In *British Social Attitudes: The 24th Report*, edited by Alison Park, John Curtice, Katarina Thomson, Miranda Phillips, Mark C. Johnson, and Elizabeth Clery. London: Sage Publishing, 2008.

Bauman, Zygmunt. *Liquid Love: On the Frailty of Human Bonds.* Cambridge, UK: Polity Press, 2003.

Beauchemin, Cris, Jocelyn Nappa, Paul Baizan, Amparo Gonzalez-Ferrer, Kim Caaris, and Valentina Mazzucato. "Reunifying Versus Living Apart Together across Borders: A Comparative Analysis of Sub-Saharan Migration to Europe." *International Migration Review* 49 (2015): 173–99.

Benson, Jacquelyn J., and Marilyn Coleman. "Older Adult Descriptions of Living Apart Together." *Family Relations* 65 (2016): 439–49.

———. "Older Adults Developing a Preference for Living Apart Together." *Journal of Marriage and Family* 78 (2016): 797–812.

Benson, Jacquelyn, Steffany Kerr, and Ashley Ermer. "Living Apart Together Relationships in Later Life: Constructing an Account of Relational Maintenance." *Contemporary Perspectives in Family Research* 11 (2017): 193–215.

Berenson, Steven K. "Should Cohabitation Matter in Family Law?" *Journal of Law and Family Studies* 13 (2011): 289–328.

Bergen, Karla Mason. "Accounting for Difference: Commuter Wives and the Master Narrative of Marriage." *Journal of Applied Communication Research* 38 (2010): 47–64.

Bergen, Karla Mason, Erika Kirby, and M. Chad McBride. "'How Do You Get Two Houses Cleaned?' Accomplishing Family Caregiving in Commuter Marriages." *Journal of Family Communications* 7 (2007): 287–307.

Bildtgård, Torbjörn, and Peter Öberg. "Time as a Structuring Condition behind New Intimate Relationships in Later Life." *Ageing and Society* 35 (2015): 1505–28.

Blumberg, Grace Ganz. "Cohabitation without Marriage: A Different Perspective." *University of California Los Angeles Law Review* 28 (1981): 1125–80.

Bonello, Kristoff, and Malcolm C. Cross. "*Gay Monogamy: I Love You But I Can't Have Sex with Only You.*" JOURNAL OF HOMOSEXUALITY 57 (2009): 117–39.

Bowman, Cynthia Grant. "A Feminist Proposal to Bring Back Common Law Marriage." *Oregon Law Review* 75 (1997): 709–80.

———. "Legal Treatment of Cohabitation in the United States." *Law and Policy* 26 (2004): 119–51.

———. *Unmarried Couples, Law, and Public Policy.* New York: Oxford University Press, 2010.

Brekhus, Wayne. *Peacocks, Chameleons, Centaurs: Gay Suburbia and the Grammar of Social Identity.* Chicago: University of Chicago Press, 2003.

Brooke, Jill. "Home Alone Together." *New York Times*, May 4, 2006.

Brothers, Denise R. "'Doing' LAT: Redoing Gender and Redoing Family in Living Apart Together Relationships in Later Life." PhD diss., Miami University, 2015.

Brown, Susan L. "The Effect of Union Type on Psychological Well-Being: Depression among Cohabitors Versus Marrieds." *Journal of Health and Social Behavior* 41 (2000): 241–55.

Brown, Susan L., and Matthew R. Wright. "Marriage, Cohabitation, and Divorce in Later Life." *Innovation in Aging* 1 (2017): 1–11.

Brown, Susan L., Jennifer Roebuch Bulanda, and Gary R. Lee. "Transitions Into and Out of Cohabitation in Later Life." *Journal of Marriage and Family* 74 (2012): 774–93.

Brown, Susan L., and Sayaka K. Shinohara. "Dating Relationships in Older Adulthood: A National Portrait." *Journal of Marriage and Family* 75 (2013): 1194–1202.

Bulcroft, Kris, and Margaret O'Connor. "The Importance of Dating Relationships on Quality of Life for Older Persons." *Family Relations* 35 (1986): 397–401.

Bulcroft, Richard A., and Kris A. Bulcroft. "The Nature and Functions of Dating in Later Life." *Research on Aging* 13 (1991): 244–60.

Bumpass, Larry L. "What's Happening to the Family? Interactions between Demographic and Institutional Change." *Demography* 27 (1990): 483–98.

Bumpass, Larry L., and Hsien-Hen Lu. "Trends in Cohabitation and Implications for Children's Family Contexts in the United States." *Population Studies* 54 (2000): 29–41.

Bumpass, Larry L., James A. Sweet, and Andrew Cherlin. "The Role of Cohabitation in Declining Rates of Marriage." *Journal of Marriage and Family* 53 (1991): 913–27.

Bunker, Barbara B., Josephine M. Zubek, Virginia J. Vanderslice, and Robert W. Rice. "Quality of Life in Dual-Career Families: Commuting versus Single-Residence Couples." *Journal of Marriage and Family* 54 (1992): 399–407.

Calasanti, Toni, and K. Jill Kiecolt. "Diversity among Late-Life Couples." *Generations* 31 (2007): 10–17.

Calasanti, Toni, and Kathleen F. Slevin. *Gender, Social Inequalities, and Aging*. Walnut Creek, CA: AltaMira Press, 2001.

Caradec, Vincent. "Les Formes de la Vie Conjugale des Jeunes Couples 'Âgés'" (Forms of conjugal living among "aged" young couples). *Population* 51 (1996): 897–927.

Carbone, June. "Out of the Channel and into the Swamp: How Family Law Fails in a New Era of Class Division." *Hofstra Law Review* 39 (2011): 859–98.

Carbone, June, and Naomi Cahn. *Marriage Markets: How Inequality Is Remaking the American Family*. New York: Oxford University Press, 2014.

———. "Nonmarriage." *Maryland Law Review* 76 (2016): 55–121.

Carpenter, Christopher, and Gary J. Gates. "Gay and Lesbian Partnership: Evidence from California." *Demography* 45 (2008): 573–90.

Carr, Deborah. "The Desire to Date and Remarry among Older Widows and Widowers." *Journal of Marriage and Family* 66 (2004): 1051–68.

Carter, Julia, and Simon Duncan. "Differential Agency: Living Apart Together." In *Reinventing Couples: Tradition, Agency and Bricolage*, edited by Julia Carter and Simon Duncan. London: Palgrave MacMillan, 2018.

———. *Reinventing Couples: Tradition, Agency and Bricolage*. London: Palgrave MacMillan, 2018.

Carter, Julia, Simon Duncan, Mariya Stoilova, and Miranda Phillips. "Sex, Love and Security: Accounts of Distance and Commitment in Living Apart Together Relationships." *Sociology* 50 (2016): 576–93.

Castro-Martin, Marta Dominguez-Folgueras, and Teresa Martin-Garcia. "Not Truly Partnerless: Non-residential Partnerships and Retreat from Marriage in Spain." *Demographic Research* 18 (2008): 443–68.

Connidis, Ingrid Arnet. "Intimate Relationships: Learning from Later Life Experience." In *Age Matters: Realigning Feminist Thinking*, edited by Toni M. Calasanti and Kathleen F. Slevin. New York: W. W. Norton and Company, 2006.

Connidis, Ingrid Arnet, Klas Borell, and Sofie Ghazanfareeon Karlsson. "Ambivalence and Living Apart Together in Later Life: A Critical Research Proposal." *Journal of Marriage and Family* 79 (2017): 1404–18.

Cooney, Teresa M., and Kathleen Dunne. "Intimate Relationships in Later Life: Current Realities, Future Prospects." *Journal of Family Issues* 22 (2001): 838–58.

Copen, Casey E., Kimberly Daniels, Jonathan Vespa, and William Mosher. *First Marriages in the United States: Data from the 2006-2010 National Survey of Family Growth*. Centers for Disease Control and Prevention. Hyattsville, MD: National Center for Health Statistics, 2012.

Coulter, Rory, and Yang Hu. "Living Apart Together and Cohabitation Intentions in Great Britain." *Journal of Family Issues* 38 (2015): 1701–29.

Davidson, Kate. "Gender Differences in New Partnership Choices and Constraints for Older Widows and Widowers." In *Intimacy in Later Life*, edited by Kate Davidson and Graham Fennell. New York: Routledge, 2004.

———. "Late Life Widowhood, Selfishness and New Partnership Choices: A Gendered Perspective." *Ageing and Society* 21 (2001): 297–317.

Davidson, Kate, and Graham Fennell. "Introduction: New Intimate Relationships in Later Life." In *Intimacy in Later Life*, edited by Kate Davidson and Graham Fennell. New York: Routledge, 2004.

de Jong Gierveld, Jenny. "The Dilemma of Repartnering: Considerations of Older Men and Women Entering New Intimate Relationships in Later Life." *Ageing International* 27 (2002): 61–78.

———. "Intra-couple Caregiving of Older Adults Living Apart Together: Commitment and Independence." *Canadian Journal on Aging* 34 (2015): 356–64.

———. "Remarriage, Unmarried Cohabitation, Living Apart Together: Partner Relationships Following Bereavement or Divorce." *Journal of Marriage and Family* 66 (2004): 236–43.

de Vries, Brian, and Gil Herdt. "Aging in the Gay Community." In *Gay, Lesbian, Bisexual and Transgender Aging: Challenges in Research, Practice and Policy*, edited by Tarynn M. Witten and A. Evan Eyler. Baltimore: Johns Hopkins University Press, 2012.

Diamond, Lisa M. "Three Critical Questions for Future Research on Lesbian Relationships." *Journal of Lesbian Studies* 21 (2017):106–19.

Duncan, Simon. "Women's Agency in Living Apart Together: Constraint, Strategy and Vulnerability." *Sociological Review* 63 (2014): 589–607.

Duncan, Simon, Julia Carter, Miranda Phillips, Sasha Roseneil, and Mariya Stoilova. "Legal Rights for People Who 'Live Apart Together'?" *Journal of Social Welfare and Family Law* 34 (2012): 443–58.

———. "Why Do People Live Apart Together?" *Families, Relationships and Societies* 2 (2013): 323–38.

Duncan, Simon, and Miranda Phillips. "People Who Live Apart Together (LATs)—How Different Are They?" *Sociological Review* 58 (2010): 112–34.

———. "People Who Live Apart Together (LATs): New Family Form or Just a Stage?" *International Review of Sociology* 21 (2011): 513–32.

Duncan, Simon, Miranda Phillips, Julia Carter, Sasha Roseneil, and Mariya Stoilova. "Practices and Perceptions of Living Apart Together." *Family Science* 5 (2014): 1–10.

Edin, Kathryn. "What Do Low-Income Single Mothers Say about Marriage?" *Social Problems* 47 (2000): 112–33.

Edin, Kathryn, and Timothy J. Nelson. *Doing the Best I Can: Fatherhood in the Inner City.* Berkeley: University of California Press, 2013.

Eichner, Maxine. "Marriage and the Elephant: The Liberal Democratic State's Regulation of Intimate Relationships between Adults." *Harvard Journal of Law and Gender* 30 (2007): 25–67.

Ellman, Ira Mark. "The Theory of Alimony." *California Law Review* 77 (1989): 1–81.

Ermisch, John, and Thomas Siedler. "Living Apart Together." In *Changing Relationships,* edited by Malcolm Brynin and John Ermisch. New York: Routledge, 2009.

Ertman, Martha M. "Commercializing Marriage: A Proposal for Valuing Women's Work through Premarital Security Agreements." *Texas Law Review* 77 (1998): 17–112.

Eskridge, William N., Jr. "Family Law Pluralism: The Guided-Choice Regime of Menus, Default Rules, and Override Rules." *Georgetown Law Journal* 100 (2012): 1881–1988.

Farris, Agnes. "Commuting." In *Working Couples,* edited by Rhona Rapoport, Robert N. Rapoport, and Janice M. Bumstead. London: Routledge and Kegan Paul, 1978.

Feinberg, Jessica R. "The Survival of Nonmarital Relationship Statuses in the Same-Sex Marriage Era: A Proposal." *Temple Law Review* 87 (2014): 45–98.

Fredricksen-Goldsen, Karen I. "*Informal Caregiving in the LGBT Communities.*" In *Gay, Lesbian, Bisexual & Transgender Aging: Challenges in Research, Practice & Policy,* edited by Tarynn M. Witten and A. Evan Eyler. Baltimore: Johns Hopkins University Press, 2012.

Frost, David M., and Kelly A. Gola. "Meanings of Intimacy: A Comparison of Members of Heterosexual and Same-Sex Couples." *Analyses of Social Issues and Public Policy* 15 (2015): 382–400.

Funk, Laura M., and Karen M. Kobayashi. "From Motivations to Accounts: An Interpretive Analysis of 'Living Apart Together' Relationships in Mid- to Later-Life Couples." *Journal of Family Issues* 37 (2016): 1101–22.

Garrison, Marsha. "Is Consent Necessary? An Evaluation of the Emerging Law of Cohabitant Obligation." *University of California Los Angeles Law Review* 52 (2005): 815–98.

Geiger, Abigail, and Gretchen Livingston. "8 Facts about Love and Marriage in America." Pew Research Center, February 13, 2019. www.pewresearch.org/fact-tank/2019/02/13/8-facts-about-love-and-marriage.

Gerstel, Naomi, and Harriet Gross. *Commuter Marriage: A Study of Work and Family.* New York: Guilford Press, 1984.

Ghazanfareeon Karlsson, Sofie, and Klas Borell. "A Home of Their Own: Women's Boundary Work in LAT Relationships." *Journal of Aging Studies* 19 (2005): 73–84.

———. "Intimacy and Autonomy, Gender and Ageing: Living Apart Together." *Ageing International* 27 (2002): 11–26.

Ghazanfareeon Karlsson, Sofie, and Majen Espvall. "Intimacy and Obligations in LAT Relationships in Later Life." In *Couple Relationships in the Middle and Later Years: Their Nature, Complexity, and Role in Health and Illness*, edited by Jamila Bookwala. Washington, DC: American Psychological Association, 2016.

Ghazanfareeon Karlsson, Sofie, Stina Johansson, Anne Gerdner, and Klas Borell. "Caring While Living Apart." *Journal of Gerontological Social Work* 49 (2007): 3–27.

Giddens, Anthony. *The Transformation of Intimacy: Sexuality, Love and Eroticism in Modern Societies.* Cambridge, UK: Polity Press, 1992.

Glotzer, Richard. "Miles That Bind: Commuter Marriage and Family Strengths." *Michigan Family Review* 12 (2007): 7–31.

Govaerts, Kathrijn, and David N. Dixon. ". . . Until Careers Do Us Part: Vocational and Marital Satisfaction in the Dual-Career Commuter Marriage." *International Journal for the Advancement of Counselling* 11 (1988): 265–81.

Hammack, Phillip L., Ilan H. Meyer, Evan A. Krueger, Marguerita Lightfoot, and David M. Frost. "HIV Testing and Pre-exposure Prophylaxis (PrEP) Use, Familiarity, and Attitudes among Gay and Bisexual Men in the United States: A National Probability Sample of Three Birth Cohorts." *PLOS ONE* 13 (2018): 1–11.

Haskey, John. "Living Arrangements in Contemporary Britain: Having a Partner Who Usually Lives Elsewhere and Living Apart Together (LAT)." *Population Trends* 122 (2005): 35–45.

Haskey, John, and Jane Lewis. "Living-apart-together in Britain: Context and Meaning." *International Journal of Law in Context* 2 (2006): 37–48.

Heimdal, Kristen R., and Sharon K. Houseknecht. "Cohabiting and Married Couples' Income Organization: Approaches in Sweden and the United States." *Journal of Marriage and Family* 65 (2003): 525–38.

Hiekel, Nicole, and Renske Keizer. "Risk-avoidance or Utmost Commitments? Dutch Focus Group Research on Cohabitation and Marriage." *Demographic Research* 32 (2015): 311–40.

Hiekel, Nicole, Aart C. Liefbroer, and Anne-Right Poortman. "Income Pooling Strategies among Cohabiting and Married Couples: A Comparative Perspective." *Demographic Research* 30 (2014): 1527–60.

Hochschild, Arlie Russell, with Anne Machung. *The Second Shift: Working Families and the Revolution at Home.* New York: Avon Books, 1997.

Hoff, Colleen C., and Sean C. Beougher. "Sexual Agreements among Gay Male Couples." 39 *Archives of Sexual Behavior* 39 (2010): 774–87.

Horwitz, Allan V., and Helen Raskin White. "The Relationship of Cohabitation and Mental Health: A Study of a Young Adult Cohort." *Journal of Marriage and Family* 60 (1998): 505–14.

Hu, Winnie. "Too Old for Sex? A Nursing Home in the Bronx Says No Such Thing." *New York Times*, July 13, 2016.

Huyck, Margaret Hellie. "Romantic Relationships in Later Life." *Generations* 25 (2001): 9–17.

Institute for Women's Policy Research. "The Gender Wage Gap: 2016." iwpr.org /wp-content/uploads/2017/03/C454.pdf.

Ishizuka, Patrick. "The Economic Foundations of Cohabiting Couples' Union Transitions." *Demography* 53 (2018): 535–57.

Iwasawa, Miho. "Partnership Transition in Contemporary Japan: Prevalence of Childless Non-Cohabiting Couples." *Japanese Journal of Population* 2 (2004): 76–92.

Jackson, Nicky Ali. "Observational Experiences of Intrapersonal Conflict and Teenage Victimization: A Comparative Study among Spouses and Cohabitors." *Journal of Family Violence* 11 (1996): 191–203.

Jamieson, Lynn, and Roona Simpson. *Living Alone: Globalization, Identity and Belonging.* Houndmills, Basingstoke, Hampshire, UK: Palgrave MacMillan, 2013.

Jones, Jeffrey M. "Majority in U.S. Do Not Have a Will." *Gallup News*, May 18, 2016. www.gallup.com/poll/191651/majority-not.aspx.

Joslin, Courtney. "Discrimination In and Out of Marriage." *Boston University Law Review* 98 (2018): 1–54.

——. "Family Support and Supporting Families." *Vanderbilt Law Review En Banc* 68 (2015): 153–81.

Kamp Dush, Claire M., and Paul R. Amato. "Consequences of Relationship Status and Quality for Subjective Well-Being." *Journal of Social and Personal Relationships* 22 (2005): 607–27.

Karnes, Allan L. "Terminating Maintenance Payments When an Ex-Spouse Cohabitates in Illinois: When Is Enough Enough?" *John Marshall Law Review* 41 (2008): 435–72.

Kennedy, Sheela, and Catherine A. Fitch. "Measuring Cohabitation and Family Structure in the United States: Assessing the Impact of New Data from the Current Population Survey." *Demography* 49 (2012): 1479–98.

Kenney, Catherine. "Cohabiting Couples, Filing Jointly? Resource Pooling and U.S. Poverty Policies." *Family Relations* 53 (2004): 237–47.

Kirschner, Betty Frankle, and Laurel Richardson Walum. "Two-Location Families: Married Singles." *Alternative Lifestyles* 1 (1978): 513–25.

Kobayashi, Karen M., Laura Funk, and Mushira Mohsin Khan. "Constructing a Sense of Commitment in 'Living Apart Together' (LAT) Relationships: Interpretive Agency and Individualization." *Current Sociology* 65 (2016): 991–1009.

Koren, Chaya, and Zvi Eisikovits. "Life Beyond the Planned Script: Accounts and Secrecy of Older Persons Living in Second Couplehood in Old Age in a Society in Transition." *Journal of Social and Personal Relationships* 28 (2011): 44–63.

Krishnan, Manisha. "Living Apart, Together." *Maclean's*, September 17, 2013.

Landale, Nancy S., and Katherine Fennelly. "Informal Unions among Mainland Puerto Ricans: Cohabitation or an Alternative to Legal Marriage?" *Journal of Marriage and Family* 54 (1992): 269–80.

Levin, Irene. "Living Apart Together: A New Family Form." *Current Sociology* 52 (2004): 223–40.

Levin, Irene, and Jan Trost. "Living Apart Together." *Community, Work and Family* 2 (1999): 279–94.

Lewin, Alisa C. "Health and Relationship Quality Later in Life: A Comparison of Living Apart Together (LAT), First Marriages, Remarriages, and Cohabitation." *Journal of Family Issues* 38 (2017): 1754–74.

———. "Intentions to Live Together Among Couples Living Apart: Differences by Age and Gender." *European Journal of Population* 34 (2018): 721–43.

Licata, Paula Ganzi. "Unwedded Bliss: For Some Loving Couples, Happiness Is Keeping Their Homes, Finances, and Routines Separate." *Newsday*, June 22, 2013.

Lichter, Daniel T., Sharon Sassler, and Richard N. Turner. "Cohabitation, Postconception Unions, and the Rise in Nonmarital Fertility." *Social Sciences Research* 47 (2014): 134–47.

Liefbroer, Aart C., Anne-Rigt Poortman, and Judith A. Seltzer. "Why Do Intimate Partners Live Apart? Evidence on LAT Relationships Across Europe." *Demographic Research* 32 (2015): 251–86.

Lifshitz, Shahar. "Married Against Their Will? Toward a Pluralist Regulation of Spousal Relationships." *Washington and Lee Law Review* 66 (2009): 1565–1634.

Lindau, Stacy Tessler, L. Philip Schumm, Edward O. Laumann, Wendy Levinson, Colm A. O'Muircheartaigh, and Linda J. Waite. "A Study of Sexuality and Health among Older Adults in the United States." *New England Journal of Medicine* 357 (2007): 762–74.

Lindemann, Danielle J. "Going the Distance: Individualism and Interdependence in the Commuter Marriage." *Journal of Marriage and Family* 79 (2017): 1419–34.

Lundberg, Shelly, Robert A. Pollak, and Jenna Stearns. "Family Inequality: Diverging Patterns in Marriage, Cohabitation, and Childbearing." *Journal of Economic Perspectives* 30 (2016): 79–101.

Lyssens-Danneboom, Vicky, Sven Eggermont, and Dimitri Mortelmans. "Living Apart Together (LAT) and Law: Exploring Legal Expectations Among LAT Individuals in Belgium." *Social and Legal Studies* 22 (2013): 357–76.

Lyssens-Danneboom, Vicky, and Dimitri Mortelmans. "Living Apart Together and Money: New Partnerships, Traditional Gender Roles." *Journal of Marriage and Family* 76 (2014): 949–66.

Magdol, Lynn, Terrie E. Moffit, Avshalom Caspi, and Phil A. Silva. "Hitting without a License: Testing Explanations for Differences in Partner Abuse Between Young Adult Daters and Cohabitors." *Journal of Marriage and Family* 60 (1998): 41–55.

Manning, Wendy D. "Cohabitation and Child Wellbeing." *The Future of Children* 25 (2015): 51–66.

Marhánková, Jaroslava Hasmanová. "Women's Attitudes Toward Forming New Partnerships in Widowhood: The Search for 'Your Own Someone' and for Freedom." *Journal of Women and Aging* 28 (2016): 34–45.

Matsick, Jes L., and Terri D. Conley. "Maybe 'I Do,' Maybe I Don't: Respectability Politics in the Same-Sex Marriage Ruling." *Analyses of Social Issues and Public Policy* 15 (2015): 409–13.

May, Emily M. "Should Moving In Mean Losing Out? Making a Case to Clarify the Legal Effect of Cohabitation on Alimony." *Duke Law Journal* 62 (2012): 403–43.

Mernitz, Sara E. "A Cohort Comparison of Trends in First Cohabitation Duration in the United States." *Demographic Research* 38 (2018): 2073–86.

Milan, Anne, and Alice Peters. "Couples Living Apart." *Canadian Social Trends* 6 (2003): 2–9.

Miller, Roxanne Greitz. "Wither [sic] Thou Goest: The Trailing Spouse or Commuter Marriage Dilemma." In *Women's Experiences in Leadership in K-16 Science Education Communities, Becoming and Being*, edited by Katherine C. Wieseman and Molly H. Weinburgh. Dordrecht, NL: Springer, 2009.

Montegary, Liz. "For the Richer, Not the Poorer: Marriage Equality, Financial Security, and the Promise of Queer Economic Justice." In *Queer Families and Relationships After Marriage Equality, edited by* Michael W. Yarbrough, Angela Jones, and Joseph Nicholas DeFilippis. New York: Routledge, 2019.

Moore, Alinde J., and Dorothy C. Stratton. "The 'Current Woman' in an Older Widower's Life." In *Intimacy in Later Life*, edited by Kate Davidson and Graham Fennell. Piscataway, NJ: Transaction Publishers, 2004.

Moorman, Sara M., Alan Booth, and Karen L. Fingerman, "Women's Romantic Relationships after Widowhood." *Journal of Family Issues* 27 (2006): 1281–1304.

Murray, Heather. *Not in this Family: Gays and the Meaning of Kinship in Postwar North America*. Philadelphia: University of Pennsylvania Press, 2010.

Murray, Melissa. "*Obergefell v. Hodges* and Nonmarriage Inequality." *California Law Review* 104 (2016): 1207–58.

National Conference of Commissioners on Uniform State Laws, *Uniform Marriage and Divorce Act*. Chicago: Uniform Law Commission, 1970.

National Opinion Research Center. "General Social Surveys, 1972–2002: Cumulative Codebook Qs." Chicago: National Opinion Research Center, 2003.

Or, Ofra. "Midlife Women in Second Partnerships Choosing Living Apart Together: An Israeli Case Study." *Israel Studies Review* 28 (2013): 41–60.

Orton, John, and Sharyn M. Crossman. "Long Distance Marriage (LDM): Cause of Marital Disruption or a Solution to Unequal Dual-Career Development?" In *Family, Self, and Society: Emerging Issues, Alternatives, and Interventions*, edited by Douglas B. Gutknecht, Edgar W. Butler, Larry Criswell, and Jerry Meints. Lanham, MD: University Press of America, 1983.

Ortyl, Timothy A. "Long-Term Heterosexual Cohabiters and Attitudes Toward Marriage." *Sociological Quarterly* 54 (2013): 584–609.

Patterson, Orlando. *Rituals of Blood: Consequences of Slavery in Two Centuries*. New York: Basic Civitas Books, 1998.

Perry, Twila L. "The 'Essentials of Marriage': Reconsidering the Duty of Support and Services." *Yale Journal of Law and Feminism* 15 (2003): 1–50.

Pew Research Center. "The Share of Americans Living without a Partner Has Increased, Especially among Young Adults." October 11, 2017. www.pewresearch.org/fact-tank/2017/10/11/the-share-of-americans-living-without-a-partner-has-increased-especially-among-young-adults.

Poortman, Anne-Right, and Melinda Mills. "Investments in Marriage and Cohabitation: The Role of Legal and Interpersonal Commitment." *Journal of Marriage and Family* 74 (2012): 357–76.

Potârcă, Gina, Melinda Mills, and Wiebke Neberich. "Relationship Preferences among Gay and Lesbian Online Daters: Individual and Contextual Influences." *Journal of Marriage and Family* 77 (2015): 523–41.

Prestage, Garrett, Graham Brown, John De Wit, Benjamin Bavinton, Christopher Fairley, Bruce Maycock, Colin Batrouney, Phillip Keen, Ian Down, Mohamed Hammoud, and Iryna Zablotska. "Understanding Gay Community Subcultures: Implications for HIV Prevention." *AIDS and Behavior* 19 (2015): 2224–33.

Pyke, Karen D. "Women's Employment as Gift or Burden? Marital Power across Marriage, Divorce, and Remarriage." *Gender and Society* 8 (1994): 73–91.

Rankin, Donna J. "Intimacy and the Elderly: Nursing Homes and Senior Citizen Care." *Business Insights*, November 1989. go.galegroup.com/ps/i.do?p=AONE&u=nysl_sc_cornl&id=GALE|A8833347&v=2.1&it=r&sid=summon&authCount=1.

Regnerus, Mark, and Jeremy Uecker. *Premarital Sex in America: How Young Americans Meet, Mate and Think about Marrying*. Oxford: Oxford University Press, 2011.

Régnier-Loilier, Arnaud, Éva Beaujouan, and Catherine Villeneuve-Gokalp. "Neither Single, Nor in a Couple: A Study of Living Apart Together in France." *Demographic Research* 21 (2009): 75–108.

Régnier-Loilier, Arnaud, and Daniele Vignoli. "The Diverse Nature of Living Apart Together Relationships: An Italy-France Comparison." *Journal of Population Research* 35 (2018): 1–22.

Reimondos, Anna, Ann Evans, and Edith Gray. "Living-apart-together (LAT) Relationships in Australia." *Family Matters* 87 (2011): 43–55.

Reuschke, Darja. "Living Apart Together over Long Distances—Time-Space Patterns and Consequences of a Late-Modern Living Arrangement." *Erdkunde* 64 (2010): 215–26.

Robbennolt, Jennifer K., and Monica Kirkpatrick Johnson. "Legal Planning for Unmarried Committed Partners: Empirical Lessons for a Preventive and Therapeutic Approach." *Arizona Law Review* 41 (1999): 417–58.

Robinson, Peter. *The Changing World of Gay Men*. New York: Palgrave Macmillan, 2008.

Rosenblum, Constance. "Living Apart Together." *New York Times*, September 15, 2013.

Roseneil, Sasha. "On Not Living with a Partner: Unpicking Coupledom and Cohabitation." *Sociological Research Online* 11 (2006): 1–14.

Roseneil, Sasha, and Shelley Budgeon. "Cultures of Intimacy and Care Beyond 'the Family': Personal Life and Social Change in the Early 21st Century." *Current Sociology* 52 (2004): 135–59.

Rudiman, Stasia. "Alimony and Cohabitation from Then to Now." *Journal of Contemporary Legal Issues* 22 (2015): 568–604.

Sassler, Sharon. "Partnering Across the Life Course: Sex, Relationships, and Mate Selection." *Journal of Marriage and Family* 72 (2010): 557–75.

Sassler, Sharon, and James McNally. "Cohabiting Couples' Economic Circumstances and Union Transitions: A Re-examination Using Multiple Imputation Techniques." *Social Science Research* 32 (2003): 553–78.

Sassler, Sharon, and Amanda J. Miller. "Class Differences in Cohabitation Processes." *Family Relations* 60 (2011): 163–77.

Schmeer, Kammi K. "The Child Health Disadvantage of Parental Cohabitation." *Journal of Marriage and Family* 73 (2011): 181–93.

Schneider, Norbert F. "Partnerschaften mit Getrennten Haushalten in den Neuen und Alten Bundesländern" (Couples with separate households in the new and old states of Germany). In *Familie an der Schwelle zum neuen Jahrtausend: Wandel und Entwicklung familialer Lebensformen* (Family on the threshold of the new century: change and development of family lifestyles), edited by Walter Bien. Wiesbaden, DE: VS Verlag für Sozialwissenschaften, 1996.

Scott, Elizabeth S., and Robert E. Scott. "From Contract to Status: Collaboration and the Evolution of Novel Family Relationships." *Columbia Law Review* 115 (2015): 293–374.

Shellenbarger, Sue. "Marriage from a Distance." *Wall Street Journal*, August 15, 2018, A11.

Smock, Pamela J., Wendy D. Manning, and Meredith Porter. "'Everything's There Except Money': How Money Shapes Decisions to Marry among Cohabitors." *Journal of Marriage and Family* 67 (2005): 680–96.

Sörgjerd, Caroline. *Reconstructing Marriage: The Legal Status of Relationships in a Changing Society*. Portland, OR: International Specialized Book Services, 2012.

Span, Paula. "More Older Couples Are 'Shacking Up': The New Old Age." *New York Times*, May 8, 2017.

Spruill, Jane W. "The Sharing of Family Tasks and Role Strain in the Commuter Marriage." Master's thesis, University of Maryland, 1984.

Stack, Steven, and J. Ross Eshleman. "Marital Status and Happiness: A 17-Nation Study." *Journal of Marriage and Family* 60 (1998): 527–36.

Stafford, Laura. *Maintaining Long-Distance and Cross-Residential Relationships*. New York: Routledge, 2005.

Starnes, Cynthia Lee. "Divorce and the Displaced Homemaker: A Discourse on Playing with Dolls, Partnership Buyouts and Dissociation Under No-Fault." *University of Chicago Law Review* 60 (1993): 67–139.

———. "I'll Be Watching You: Alimony and the Cohabitation Rule." *Family Law Quarterly* 50 (2016): 261–301.

Starr, Bernard D., and Marcella Bakur Weiner. *The Starr-Weiner Report on Sex and Sexuality in the Mature Years.* New York: Stein and Day, 1981.

Statistics Canada. "Couples Who Live Apart." www150.statcan.gc.ca/n1/pub/11-627 -m/11-627-m2019014-eng.htm.

Statistics Netherlands. "More Than One Fifth of People Living Apart Engaged in LAT Relationship." www.cbs.nl/en-gb/news/2015/04/more-than-one-fifth-of-people -living-apart-engaged-in-lat-relationship.

Stepler, Renee. "Led by Baby Boomers, Divorce Rates Climb for America's 50+ Population." Pew Research Center, March 9, 2017. www.pewresearch.org/fact-tank/2017/03/09/led-by-baby-boomers-divorce-rates-climb-for-americas-50 -population.

———. "Number of U.S. Adults Cohabiting with a Partner Continues to Rise, Especially among Those 50 and Older." Pew Research Center, April 6, 2017. www. pewresearch.org/fact-tank/2017/04/06/number-of-u-s-adults-cohabiting-with -a-partner-continues-to-rise-especially-among-those-50-and-older.

Stets, Jan E., and Murray A. Straus. "The Marriage License as a Hitting License: A Comparison of Assaults in Dating, Cohabiting, and Married Couples." In *Violence in Dating Relationships: Emerging Social Issues*, edited by Maureen A. Pirog-Good and Jan E. Stets. New York: Praeger, 1989.

Stoilova, Mariya, Sasha Roseneil, Julia Carter, Simon Duncan, and Miranda Phillips. "Constructions, Reconstructions and Deconstructions of 'Family' amongst People Who Live Apart Together (LATs)." *British Journal of Sociology* 68 (2017): 78–96.

Stolzenberg, Emily J. "The New Family Freedom." *Boston College Law Review* 59 (2018): 1983–2054.

Stonewall. *Lesbian, Gay and Bisexual People in Later Life.* London: Stonewall, 2015.

Strohm, Charles Q., Judith Seltzer, Susan Cochran, and Vickie Mays. "'Living Apart Together' Relationships in the United States." *Demographic Research* 21 (2009): 177–214.

Swank, Eric, Breanne Fahs, and David M. Frost. "Region, Social Identities, and Disclosure Practices as Predictors of Heterosexist Discrimination against Sexual Minorities in the United States." *Social Inquiry* 83 (2013): 238–58.

Thomeer, Mieke Beth, Rachel Donnelly, Corinne Reczek, and Debra Umberson. "Planning for Future Care and the End of Life: A Qualitative Analysis of Gay, Lesbian, and Heterosexual Couples." 58 *Journal of Health and Social Behavior* 58 (2017): 473–87.

Thornton, Arland, and Linda Young-DeMarco. "Four Decades of Trends in Attitudes Toward Family Issues in the United States: The 1960s Through the 1990s." *Journal of Marriage and Family* 63 (2001): 1009–37.

Traies, Jane. *The Lives of Older Lesbians: Sexuality, Identity and the Life Course.* London: Palgrave MacMillan, 2016.

Trost, Jan. "LAT Relationships Now and in the Future." In *The Family: Contemporary Perspectives and Challenges*, edited by Koen Matthijs. Leuven, BE: Leuven University Press, 1998.

———. "Marriage, Cohabitation and LAT Relationships." *Journal of Comparative Family Studies* 47 (2016): 17–26.

Turcotte, Martin. "Living Apart Together." *Statistics Canada* (online), March 2013. www150.statcan.gc.ca/n1/pub/75-006-x/2013001/article/11771-eng.htm.

UCLA Center for Health Policy Research. "California Health Interview Survey." 2005. http://healthpolicy.ucla.edu/chis/Pages/default.aspx.

Upton-Davis, Karen. "Living Apart Together Relationships (LAT): Severing Intimacy from Obligation." *Gender Issues* 29 (2012): 25–38.

———. "Subverting Gendered Norms of Cohabitation: Living Apart Together for Women over 45." *Journal of Gender Studies* 24 (2015): 104–16.

U.S. Bureau of the Census. *American FactFinder: Income in the Past 12 Months (in 2015 Inflation-Adjusted Dollars)*. https://factfinder.census.gov/bkmk/table/1.0/en /ACS/15_1YR/S1901/0100000US.

———. *Census Quick Facts*. www.census.gov/quickfacts/table/PST045216/00.

———. *Family Structure and Children's Living Arrangements*. www.childstats.gov /americaschildren/tables/fam1b.asp.

———. *Historical Living Arrangements of Adults*. Table AD-3. www.census.gov/data /tables/time-serie/demo/families/adults.html.

———. *Living Arrangements of Adults 18 Years and Over in the United States*. https:// factfinder.census.gov/faces/tableservices/jsf/pages/productview.xhtml?src=bkmk.

———. *Sex by Marital Status for the Population 15 Years and Over (2018)*. https:// data.census.gov/cedsci/table?q=sex%20by%20martial%20status%20for%20the%20 population%20&hidePreview=false&tid=ACSDT1Y2018.B12001&t=Marital%20 Status%20and%20Marital%20History%3AAge%20and%20Sex&vintage=2018.

U.S. Department of Health and Human Services. Centers for Disease Control and Prevention. *Cohabitation, Marriage, Divorce, and Remarriage in the United States: Data from the National Survey of Family Growth*. Table 15. Hyattsville, MD: National Center for Health Statistics 2002. www.cdc.gov/nchs/data/series /sr_23_022.pdf.

van der Wiel, Rosalinde, Clara H. Mulder, and Ajay Bailey. "Pathways to Commitment in Living-Apart-Together Relationships in the Netherlands: A Study on Satisfaction, Alternatives, Investments and Social Support." *Advances in Life Course Research* 36 (2018): 13–22.

van Eeden-Moorefield, Brad, Kevin Malloy, and Kristen Benson. "Gay Men's (Non)Monogamy Ideals and Lived Experience." *Sex Roles* 75 (2016): 43.

Villeneuve-Gokalp, Catherine. "Vivre en Couple Chacun Chez Soi" (Living as a couple with each having their own home). *Population* 52 (1997): 1059–81.

Vogler, Carolyn. "Cohabiting Couples: Rethinking Money in the Household at the Beginning of the Twenty First Century." *Sociological Review* 53 (2005): 1–29.

Vogler, Carolyn, Michaela Brockmann, and Richard D. Wiggins. "Managing Money in New Heterosexual Forms of Intimate Relationships." *Journal of Socio-Economics* 37 (2008): 552–76.

Waggoner, Lawrence W. "With Marriage on the Decline and Cohabitation on the Rise, What about Marital Rights for Unmarried Partners?" *ACTEC Law Journal* 41 (2015): 49–93.

Walleng, Kajsa. "The Swedish Cohabitees Act in Today's Society." In *Family Law and Culture in Europe: Developments, Challenges and Opportunities*, edited by Katharina Boele-Woelki, Nina Dethloff, and Werner Gephart. Cambridge, UK: Intersentia, 2014.

Ward, Jane. *Not Gay: Sex Between Straight White Men*. New York: New York University Press, 2015.

Watson, Wendy K., and Charlie Stelle. "Dating for Older Women: Experiences and Meanings of Dating in Later Life." *Journal of Women and Aging* 23 (2011): 263–75.

Weisser, Cybele. "Two Cities, Two Careers, Too Much?" *CNN Money*, January 1, 2006. https://money.cnn.com/magazines/moneymag/moneymag_archive/2006/01/01/8365210/index.htm.

West, Robin. "Jurisprudence and Gender." *University of Chicago Law Review* 55 (1988): 1–72.

Winfield, Fairlee E. *Commuter Marriage: Living Together, Apart*. New York: Columbia University Press, 1985.

Wong, Simone. "Shared Commitment, Interdependency and Property Relations: A Socio-Legal Project for Cohabitation." *Child and Family Law Quarterly* 24 (2012): 60–76.

World Bank. *Life Expectancy at Birth, Total (Years)*. https://data.worldbank.org/indicator/SP.DYN.LE00.IN?contextual=max&end=2015&locations=US&start=1960&view=chart.

Wright, Matthew R., and Susan L. Brown. "Psychological Well-being Among Older Adults: The Role of Partnership Status." *Journal of Marriage and Family* 79 (2017): 833–49.

Wu, Huijing. "Age Variation in the Remarriage Rate, 1990 and 2015." https://create.piktochart.com/output/24418004-wu-age-variation-remarriage-rate-1990-2015-fp-17-21.

Zimmermann, Anke C., and Richard A. Easterlin. "Happily Ever After? Cohabitation, Marriage, Divorce, and Happiness in Germany." *Population and Development Review* 32 (2006): 511–28.

## CASES AND STATUTES

Adamson v. Adamson, 958 S.W.2d 598 (Mo. Ct. App. 1998).

Adessa v. Adessa, 2009 N.J. Super. Unpub. LEXIS 1316, *7 (Super. Ct. N.J., App. Div. May 29, 2009).

Bergen v. Wood, 18 Cal. Rptr. 2d (Cal. App. 1993).

Blumenthal v. Brewer, 69 N.E.3d 834 (Ill. 2016).

California Welfare and Institutions Code § 11351.5 (West 2019).

Cochran v. Cochran, 106 Cal. Rptr. 2d 899 (Cal. App. 2001).

Connell v. Francisco, 898 P.2d 831 (Wash. 1995).

Devaney v. L'Esperance, 949 A.2d 743 (N.J. 2008).

Dunphy v. Gregor, 642 A.2d 372 (N.J. 1994).

George v. George, 2016 Ill. App. Unpub. LEXIS 815 (Ill. App. Ct., 1st Dist. April 26, 2016).

Hewitt v. Hewitt, 394 N.E.2d 1204 (Ill. 1979).

Honeycutt v. Honeycutt, 152 S.W.3d 556 (Tenn. Ct. App. 2003).

Illinois Religious Freedom Protection and Civil Union Act. 750 Ill. Comp. Stat. Ann. 75/5 (2011).

In re Marriage of Bates, 819 N.E.2d 714 (Ill. 2004).

In re Marriage of Cook, 2014 Ill. App. Unpub. LEXIS 459 (Ill. App. Ct., 2d Dist. March 13, 2014).

In re Marriage of Frasco, 638 N.E. 2d 655 (Ill. App. 1994).

In re Marriage of Herrin, 634 N.E.2d 1168 (Ill. App. 1994).

In re Marriage of Kunowski, 2012 Ill. App. Unpub. LEXIS 2007 (Ill. App. Ct., 2d Dist. August 17, 2012).

In re Marriage of Miller, 40 N.E.3d 206 (Ill. App. 2015).

In re Marriage of Roofe, 460 N.E.2d 784 (Ill. App. Ct. 1984).

In re Marriage of Sappington, 462 N.E.2d 881 (Ill. App. Ct. 1984).

In re Marriage of Steiding, 2014 Cal. App. Unpub. LEXIS 5718 (Cal. Ct. App. August 13, 2014).

In re Marriage of Susan, 856 N.E. 2d 1167 (Ill. App. Ct. 2006).

In re Marriage of Wheat, 2013 Ill. App. Unpub. LEXIS 1492 (Ill. App. Ct., 4th Dist. July 1, 2013).

King v. Smith, 392 U.S. 309 (1968).

Lang v. Superior Ct, 53 Cal. App. 3d 852 (1975).

Levine v. Konvitz, 890 A.2d 354 (N.J. Super. 2006).

Mahoney v. Mahoney, 453 A.2d 527 (N.J. 1982).

Marvin v. Marvin, 557 P.2d 106 (Cal. 1976).

Mass. Gen. Laws ch. 208, § 49 (West 2012).

Miron v. Trudel, [1995] 2 S.C.R. 418 (Can.).

N.J. Rev. Stat. Tit. 25, sec. 25:1–5 (West 2010).

N.Y. Dom. Rel. Law, sec. 236(B)(6) (McKinney 2016).

Obergefell v. Hodges, 576 U.S. 644 (2015).

Paul v. Paul, 60 A.3d 1080 (Del. 2012).

R. v. Secretary of State, [2018] UKSC 32.

Rehm v. Rehm, 409 S.E.2d 723 (N.C. App. 1991).

Schoenhard v. Schoenhard, 392 N.E.2d 764 (Ill. App. Ct. 1979).

Taylor v. Fields, 224 Cal. Rptr. 186 (Cal. App. 1986).

Vasquez v. Hawthorne, 33 P.3d 735 (Wash. 2001).

Washburn v. Washburn, 677 P.2d 152 (Wash. 1084) (en banc).

Wessel v. Burritt, 2008 N.J. Super. Unpub. LEXIS 2125 (N.J. Sup. Ct. App. Div. October 14, 2008).

Woillard v. Woillard, Cal. Ct. App., January 14, 2014, 2d Civil No. B242536.

# INDEX

Page numbers in *italics* indicate tables

age, 3; age groups and reasons to live apart, 25–29, 44–46; commitment and, 30; gender and, 60–61, *61*; of interviewed LATs, 67; of midlife LATs, 27; in New York and US national survey, *44*, 44–46, 60–61, *61*; of Third Age LATs, 29, 98; of younger LATs, 25
ALI. *See* American Law Institute
alimony: in California, 146–47, 151; cohabitation and, 146–52, 197n42, 198n45; family law and, 28, 134–35, 144–52, 186n29, 197n36, 197n39, 197n42, 198n45; in Illinois, 148–51, 197n39; in New Jersey, 147–48, 151; no-fault divorce and, 98, 144; termination based on LAT, 144–52; theories and types of, 144–45
American Law Institute (ALI), 135
autonomy, family law and, 154.
    *See also* financial independence; independence and LAT

Baby Boomers, 97, 98; defining, 184n1; independence for, 106–7; sexuality of, 97–101. *See also* Third Age LATs
Belgian LATs, 22, 157–58, 175n77; finances in, 32, 55–56; gender difference in, 55–56
birth rates, 107
Black LATs, *40*, 41, 61–62
blended family, 9, 27
Borell, Klas, 53–54, 74–75
British Social Attitudes Survey, 46

Brothers, Denise, 57
Budgeon, Shelley, 33–34

California alimony cases, 146–47, 151
California Quality of Life Survey, 37
Canada, 21, 174n62; cohabitation in, 136; common-law partners in, 136; duration and commitment of LATs in, 30, 31; education of LATs in, 24–25; elder caregiving between LATs in, 107–8; family law in, 136; gender difference and LATs in, 56–57; income of LATs in, 24; Third Age LATs in, 102, 106, 107–8, 187n48
caregiving, 1–2, 8, 13, 14, 16–17; for elderly, 12, 63–64, 88, 107–9, 116; by gay male LATs, 87–89, 90; gender and, 29, 53–54, *64*, 64–65, 72; by interviewed LATs, 50, 72, 178n21; by LATs in Sweden, 53–54; by LATs in UK, 32–33; in New York and US national survey, 46–48, *64*, 64–65; for older LATs, 32–33; social science on, 31–33; Third Age LATs and, 107–9, 119
children, 9; cohabitation and, 131, 135; commuter marriage and, 123, 126; as reason to live apart, 27, 45–46, 63, 180n29, 181n44
Civil Partnership Act, 2004, 170n4
class, 129–30, 132
CNSS. *See* Cornell National Social Survey
Cochran, Johnnie, 140

cohabitation: alimony and, 146–52, 197n42, 198n45; in Canada, 136; census data on, 129, 191n49; children and, 131; class relating to, 129–30, 132; commitment and, 130; demographics of, 129–30; description of, 128–29; divorce and, 130; domestic labor and, 130–31; duration of, 130, 193n62; in Europe, 26; family law and legal treatment of, 132–43; finances relating to, 129–30, 131, 132; in France, 136; gender and, 130–31; housing and, 136–37; LATs compared to, 131–32; law and, 120, 132–38; legal reform, 134–38; in *Marvin v. Marvin*, 132, 139–41; in Netherlands, 136; palimony and, 139–43; rates, 98; in Scotland, 195n102; social ideology and, 129–30; social science on, 129–31; Third Age LATs and, 105; in UK, 137; in US, 48, 132–38
commitment, 7, 8–9; age and, 30; cohabitation and, 130; and duration of LAT, 30–31, 39; family and, 35; finances and, 30–31; individualism and, 34; in New York and US national survey, 38–39, 47–48; of Third Age LATs, 117–18
common law myth, 137
common-law partners, 136
commuter marriage: census data on, 120–21; children and, 123, 126; daily living activities in, 122; description of, 120–21, 138; domestic labor in, 122, 123–24; economics and, 121; feminism and, 121; gender and, 123–24; interviewed spouses, 125–27; jobs and, 120–21, 123–27; LATs compared to, 127–28; law and, 120, 127–28; scholarship and social science on, 121–23; success in, 126–27; technology in, 125, 128; typical pattern of, 122
commuting, in long-distance relationships, 9, 22–23
conservatism, *43*, 43–44
contracts, 133, 159–60, 194n85, 196n15

Cornell National Social Survey (CNSS), 37. *See also* New York and US national survey

"daddy/boy" gay subculture, 92, 184n38
daily living activities, 28, 70; in commuter marriage, 122; for gay male LATs, 89; for Third Age LATs, 104
dating Third Age LATs, 100–101
demographics: age groups and reasons to live apart, 25–29, 44–46; of cohabitation, 129–30; education and LAT, 24–25; income and LAT, 23–24; of LATs, 2–3, 23–29, 169nn4–5; in New York and US national survey, 38–44; Second Demographic Transition and, 3, 169n5
*Devaney v. L'Esperance* (2008), 141–43
division of domestic labor, 9; cohabitation and, 130–31; in commuter marriage, 122, 123–24; for gay male LATs, 89; gender and, 4, 8, 10, 13, 18, 28, 29, 53–55, 65, 69, 75–76, 105–6, 118, 123–24; for Third Age LATs, 105–6, 118
divorce, 48–49; cohabitation and, 130; devastation after, 28; finances and, 49; and LATs interviewed, 48–49; no-fault, 98, 144; rates, 22, 98; as reasons to live apart, 52–53, 74–75; Social Security and, 151, 189n86; in Sweden, 53; Third Age LATs and, 98
Duncan, Simon, 23, 26, 34–35; on cohabitation, 181n48; on gender, 57–58, 180n31, 180n35
duration of cohabitation, 130, 193n62
duration of LAT relationships, 30–31, 48.60–61, 67, 117; in New York and US national survey, 39

economics, 23–24; commuter marriage and, 121. *See also* finances
education of LATs: college degrees, 24–25; demographics and, 24–25; in New York and US national survey, *42*, 42–43

elder caregiving, 12, 63–64, 88; in Canada, 107–8; in Netherlands, 107; in Sweden, 107; Third Age LATs in US and, 107–9, 116; in United States, 108

Empire State Poll (ESP), 37, 177n2. *See also* New York and US national survey

employment. *See* jobs

England. *See* United Kingdom

Eskridge, William, 155–56

ESP. *See* Empire State Poll

ethnicity. *See* race and ethnicity

Europe: cohabitation in, 26; education of LATs in, 24–25; housing in, 26; LATs in, 2, 3–4, 21. *See also specific countries*

family: blended, 9, 27; commitment and, 35; defining, 35; dependence for care on, in UK, 33–34; dependence for care on in Sweden, 33; for gay male LATs, 87–89; LATs as new family form, 33–36; perceptions of, 9–10, 11, 14–15, 18, 35, 88–89, 110; sexual orientation and, 80–81

Family and Medical Leave Act, 156

family law, 5, 8; alimony and, 28, 134–35, 144–52, 186n29, 197n36, 197n39, 197n42, 198n45; autonomy and, 154; in Canada, 136; children and, 135; on cohabitation, 132–43; different approaches to, 154–57; finances and, 13, 14, 16, 161–62; in France, 136; gay LATs, same-sex marriage, and, 82–84, 85–86, 91, 93–94, 96, 133, 182n19; hospital visitation privileges and, 104, 114, 161; inheritance and, 133–34; legal rights proposed by LATs, 157–59; marriage and, 3, 85–86; in Netherlands, 107, 136; nuclear family and, 3; palimony claims and, 139–43; partnership registrations and, 159–62; property, assets, and, 133, 135–36, 161; purposes of, 153–57; recommendations for LAT protection, 159–63; in Scotland, 195n102; in Sweden, 154; taxes and, 133–34, 162; Third Age LATs and, 104, 114; in UK, 137, 158; in US, 85–86, 132, 133, 139–52, 153–63; wills and, 133–34

Feinberg, Jessica, 156–57

feminism, 54, 76, 98–99, 106, 121

finances, 1–2, 12–13; in Belgium, 32, 55–56; cohabitation relating to, 129, 131, 132; commitment and, 30–31; divorce and, 49; family law and, 13, 14, 16, 161–62; for gay male LATs, 84–85, 91–92, 94–95; gender and, 55–56, 65–66, 70–72, 73, 75–76; housing and, 27–28, 29, 91–92, 105–6; income and, 23–24; income-sharing of couples and, 31–32, 46–47, 175n89; of interviewed LATs, 49–50, 70–72; joint expenses and cost-sharing, 32, 46–47, 47, 66, 66, 71, 111–12, 113; jointly-owned assets and, 49, 115–16, 161; marriage and, 49, 91–92, 108; in New York and US national survey, 46–48, 47, 65–66; palimony claims and, 139–43; prenuptial agreements and, 85; social science on couples' financial arrangements, 31–33; taxes and, 13; Third Age LATs and, 101, 108, 111–14, 116; wills and, 72, 85, 95, 112, 113, 133–34. *See also* income and LAT

financial independence, 8, 32, 118; gender and, 75–76; income and, 24, 49–50; in Israel and LAT, 55; in New York and US national survey, 47

France, 21; cohabitation in, 136; duration and commitment of LATs in, 30; family law in, 136; Third Age LATs in, 102

Funk, Laura, 74, 77

gay and lesbian LATs, 4, 11–13, 78; in interviews, 67; on marriage, 82; in New York and US national survey, 40; same-sex marriage and, 82–84, 85–86, 91, 93–94, 96, 133, 182n19; Third Age, 114–17 gay male LATs: caregiving by, 87–89, 90; Carl and Daniel, 92–95; choosing to live apart, 81–82; coming out, 79–81; "daddy/boy" gay subculture and, 92, 184n38; daily living activities, 89; domestic labor and, 89; family for, 87–89; finances for, 84–85, 91–92, 94–95; gay liberation and, 82–83, 91; housing, 81, 82, 90–91, 93; independence, 82; interviews with, 78–96; marriage for, 82–84, 91, 93–94; non-monogamy, 85–87, 90–91, 95, 183n25; politics and, 93–94; reasons to live apart, 81–82, 92–93; sexual identity, 79–81, 96; wills, 85, 95

gender, cohabitation and, 130–31; commuter marriage and, 123–24

gender and LAT, 4, 52–57; age and, 60–61, 61; in Australia, 54–55; in Belgium, 55–56; in Canada, 56–57; caregiving and, 29, 53–54, 64, 64–65, 72; conclusions with respect to debate about, 74–77, 177n2; domestic labor and, 8, 13, 28, 29, 69, 75, 106, 123–24; Duncan on, 57–58, 180n31, 180n35; equality, 3, 22, 77; finances and, 55–56, 65–66, 70–72, 73, 75–76; financial independence and, 75–76; housing and, 53; income and, 62, 62–63; in interviewed LATs, 67–73; in Israel, 54–55; labor and, 11, 22; marriage and, 16, 35, 54, 57, 77, 186n27; in Netherlands, 52–53; in New York and US national survey, 40, 60–68; patriarchy and, 54; race and, 61–62; reasons to live apart by, 62–64, 63, 68–70, 73; "redoing gender," 57; sexuality and, 99–100; social expectations and, 68–69, 76; social science and popular press articles on, in US, 59–60; in Sweden, 53; Third Age LATs and, 97–98, 106–7, 186n27; in UK, 57–58; in US, 57–67; wills and, 72; women and LAT debate in social science literature abroad and, 52–58

Germany and LAT, 21, 172n22; duration and commitment in, 30; younger LATs in, 26

Ghazanfareeon Karlsson, Sofie, 53–54, 74–75

Giddens, Anthony, 34, 57, 74, 199n1

globalization, 22

government benefits, 33, 130, 136, 139, 154–55, 162

Haskey, John, 34

health insurance, 13, 91, 94, 113–14, 117

Herrin case, 148–50

Hispanic LATs, 40, 41

hospital visitation privileges, 104, 114, 161

housing, 7–8, 11, 13–14; cohabitation and, 136–37; in Europe, 26; finances and, 27–28, 29, 91–92, 105–6; for gay male LATs, 81, 82, 90–91, 93; gender and, 53; independence and, 29, 53, 68, 106; taxes and, 28; for Third Age LATs, 104, 105–6, 109–11, 115

identity: gay male LATs, 79–81, 96; sexual orientation and, 79–80; for women, 28, 68

Illinois alimony termination cases, 148–51, 197n39

income and LAT: in Canada, 24; demographics and, 23–24; finances and, 23–24; financial independence and, 24, 49–50; gender and, 62, 62–63; in New York and US national survey, 42, 42–43, 62, 62–63; from Social Security, 101, 151, 189n86; for Third Age LATs, 101

income-sharing among LATs, 31–32, 46, 175n89

independence and LAT, 13, 14, 174n62; autonomy and, 58, 68, 104; for Baby Boomers, 106–7; for gay male LATs, 82; housing and, 29, 53, 68, 106; from social expectations, 68–69; for Third Age LATs, 104, 106–7; for women, 7–8,

18–19, 28, 53–58, 68–69, 104, 106–7. *See also* financial independence

individualism, 34

inheritance, 133–34

interdependence, 68, 159–60

interviewed commuter spouses, 125–27

interviewed LATs: age of, 67; caregiving by, 50, 72, 178n21; in England, 37–38; on family law and legal desires, 157–59; finances of, 49–50, 70–72; gay male LATs, 78–96; gender in, 67–73; reasons to live apart for, 68–70, 73; snowball sampling and, 54, 179n18; Third Age, 109–19; in US, 37–38, 48–51, 178n18; with wills, 72

intimacy, 97–101, 185n20

involuntary LATs, 10–11

Ireland, 170n4

Israel, 54–55

Italy: Third Age LATs in, 102; younger LATs in, 26


Japan, 173n39

jobs: commuter marriage and, 120–21, 123–27; employment in New York and US national survey, 41–42; gender and labor, 11, 22; as reason to live apart, 10–11, 27

joint expenses and cost-sharing by LATs, 32, 71, 111–12, 113; methods of, 46–47, 47, 66, 66

jointly-owned assets of LATs, 49, 115–16, 161


Kobayashi, Karen, 74, 77


late marriage, 26

LATs. *See* living apart together couples; *specific topics*

law: cohabitation and, 120, 132–38; commuter marriage and, 120, 127–28; contracts and, 133, 159–60, 194n85, 196n15; LATs and, 139–52; tort, 161. *See also* family law

legal reform: cohabitation, 134–38; legal rights proposed by LATs, 157–59; partnership registrations, 159–62; recommendations for LAT protection, 159–63

lesbians. *See* gay and lesbian LATs

*Levine v. Konvitz* (2006), 141

Lewis, Jane, 34

liberalism, *43*, 43–44

Lifshitz, Shahar, 134

living apart together couples (LATs): common themes of, 17–19; defining, 1–3; duration of relationships, 30–31, 39; introduction to, 7–17; numbers of, 20–23; origins of term, 2. *See also specific topics*

long-distance relationships, 9, 22–23. *See also* commuter marriage


marriage: average age of, 22; cohabitation and, 4–5; family law and, 3, 85–86; finances and, 49, 91–92, 108; gay and lesbian LATs on, 82; for gay male LATs, 82–84, 91, 93–94; gender and, 16, 35, 54, 57, 77, 186n27; late, 26; in New York and US national survey, 177n3; patriarchy and, 16, 54; prenuptial agreements and, 85; previous marriages and LATs, 10, 11, 18, 48–49, 52–53, 68–69; same-sex, 82–84, 85–86, 91, 93–94, 96, 133, 182n19; Third Age LATs and, 97–98, 100–101, 104–6, 108–9, 112–13, 117, 186n22, 186n27; in US, 35. *See also* commuter marriage; divorce

*Marvin v. Marvin* (1976), 132, 139–41

messiness, as reason for LAT, 14, 15–16, 18, 69–70, 110

midlife LATs, 9–11; age range of, 27; overview of, 27–29; reasons to live apart for, 27–29; in Scotland, 28–29

migration, in Europe, 172n20

*Miller* case, 149–50

Mitchelson, Marvin, 139–40
mortality rates, 22

National Social Life, Health, and Aging
    Project (NSHAP), 100–101, 103
Native American LATs, 40
neatness, as reason for LAT, 14, 15–16, 18,
    69–70, 110
Netherlands, 22, 171n11; cohabitation in,
    136; duration and commitment of LAT
    in, 30–31; elder caregiving of LATs,
    107; family law in, 107, 136; finances
    of LATs, 174n71; gender difference in
    LATs, 52–53; Third Age LATs in, 29,
    102, 107
New Jersey alimony termination cases,
    147–48, 151
New York and US national survey (CNSS
    and ESP), 37; age distribution in, 44,
    44–46, 60–61, 61; caregiving in, 46–48,
    64, 64–65; commitment in, 38  39,
    47–48; duration of LAT relationships
    in, 39; education in, 42, 43; employ-
    ment in, 41–42; finances in, 46–48,
    47, 65–66; gay and lesbian LATs in,
    40; gender in, 40, 60–68; income in,
    42, 42–43, 62, 62–63; marriage in,
    177n3; numbers and demographics in,
    38–44; race and ethnicity in, 40, 40–41,
    61–62; reasons to live apart in, 44–46,
    45, 62–64, 63; results of, 38–48; social
    ideology in, 43, 43–44
New York LATs, 4, 37–47, 61–65. See also
    gay male LATs
no-fault divorce, 98, 144
NSHAP. See National Social Life, Health,
    and Aging Project

Obergefell v. Hodges (2015), 85–86, 133
older adult sex surveys, 99, 185n11, 185n13
older LATs, 97–119; caregiving between,
    32–33, 107–8; interviews with, 13–17,
    90–92; previous studies of, 101–9;
    sexuality, older adults, and, 98–99,
    185n11, 185n13. See also Third Age LATs
Omnibus Survey, 22–23, 34, 172n22
open relationships, 85–87, 90–91, 95,
    183n25
Or, Ofra, 74–75

Pacte Civile de Solidarité (PACS), 136
palimony claims, 139–43
partnership registration, 157, 159–60
patriarchy, 16, 54
pensions, 18, 33, 108, 130, 136, 162, 188n63
Phillips, Miranda, 23, 26, 34–35
politics: gay male LATs and, 93–94; Third
    Age LATs and, 98, 112
popular press articles, on LAT and gender,
    59–60; on LAT among elderly, 103–4
postmenopausal women, 99, 185n16
postmodern living arrangements, 33–34
property and assets of LATs: family law
    and, 133, 135–36, 161; inheritance of,
    133–34; jointly-owned, 49, 115–16, 161;
    unjust enrichment and, 132–33, 161,
    199n12; wills for, 72, 85, 95, 112, 113,
    133–34, 199n13
"pure relationships," 34, 57, 74, 199n1

race and ethnicity of LATs: gender and,
    61–62; in New York and US national
    survey, 40, 40–41, 61–62
reasons to live apart: age groups and,
    25–29, 44–46; children as, 27, 45–46, 63,
    180n29, 181n44; daily living activities,
    28, 70; divorce as, 52–53, 74–75; fuels
    romance, 70; for gay male LATs, 81–82,
    92–93; by gender, 62–64, 63, 68–70, 73;
    for interviewed LATs, 68–70, 73; jobs
    as, 10–11, 27; for midlife LATs, 27–29;
    neatness and messiness as, 14, 15–16,
    18, 69–70, 110; in New York and US
    national survey, 44–46, 45, 62–64, 63;
    for Third Age LATs, 29, 104–7, 118; for
    younger LATs, 25–26

"redoing gender" concept, 57
Régnier-Loilier, Arnaud, 21
Roseneil, Sasha, 33–34

same-sex marriage, 82–84, 85–86, 91, 93–94, 96, 133, 182n19
Scandinavia, 21; family in, 33
Scotland, 24–25, 170n4; cohabitation in, 195n102; family law in, 195n102; midlife LATs in, 28–29
Scott, Elizabeth, 155
Scott, Robert, 155
Second Demographic Transition, 3, 169n5
selfishness, 106–7
sexual exclusivity, 85–87, 90–91, 95, 183n25
sexuality: alimony and, 152, 197n37; gender and, 99–100; intimate relationships, in later life, 97–101, 185n20; older adult sex surveys, 99, 185n11, 185n13; for postmenopausal women, 99, 185n16; romance and, 70
sexual orientation, 4; family and, 80–81; identity and, 79–80; social expectations and, 80. See also gay and lesbian LATs
sexual revolution, 98
snowball sampling, 54, 179n18
social expectations: gender and, 68–69, 76; sexual orientation and, 80; Third Age LATs and, 98, 108–9
social ideology: cohabitation and, 129–30; in New York and US national survey, 43, 43–44; politics and, 93–94, 98, 112
social recognition of LATs, 8, 160
social science: on age groups and reasons to live apart, 25–29; on caregiving and LATs, 31–33; on cohabitation, 129–31; on commuter marriage, 121–23; on duration and commitment of LATs, 30–31; on economic and financial arrangements of couples, 31–33; evidence about LATs in social science literature, 20–25; on gender, in US, 57

59–60; on LATs as new family form, 33–36; on numbers of LATs, 20–23; women and LAT debate, 52–58, 74–77
Social Security income, 101, 151, 189n86
Spain, 26
SRI. See Survey Research Institute at Cornell University
Starr, Bernard D., 99
Stoilova, Mariya, 35
Strohm et al., 39, 76, 181n84
Survey Research Institute (SRI) at Cornell University, 37
Sweden, 32, 172n23; caregiving by LATs in, 53–54; division of domestic labor in, 53; elder caregiving in, 107; family law in, 154; gender difference among LATs in, 53; Third Age LATs in, 102–3, 104, 107

taxes: family law and, 133–34, 162; finances and, 13; housing and, 28
technology: in commuter marriage, 125, 128; long-distance relationships and, 22
Third Age LATs, 4; age range of, 29, 98; Baby Boomers and, 97, 98, 106–7, 111–12; in Canada, 102, 106, 107–8, 187n48; caregiving and, 107–9, 116, 119; cohabitation and, 105; commitment of, 117–18; common themes about, 117–19; daily living activities for, 104; dating and, 100–101; division domestic labor, 106; divorce and, 98; family law and, 104, 114; finances and, 101, 108, 111–14, 116; in France, 102; gay and lesbian, 114–17; gender and, 97–98, 106–7, 186n27; housing for, 104, 105–6, 109–11, 115; income for, 101; independence for, 104, 106–7; interviewed, 15–17, 109–19; intimacy for, 100–101; in Italy, 102; marriage and, 97–98, 100–101, 104–6, 108–9, 112–13, 117, 186n22, 186n27; in Netherlands, 29, 102, 107; NSHAP on, 100–101, 103; overview of, 29;

Third Age LATs (*cont.*)
politics and, 98, 112; previous studies
of older adults and, 101–9; reasons to
live apart for, 29, 104–7, 118; sexuality
and intimate relationships, 97–101,
185n20; statistics on, 102–4; in Sweden,
102–3, 104, 107; in UK, 102, 185n11; in
US, 103–7, 108; wills for, 112, 113, 116;
women and, 106
tort law, 161

United Kingdom (UK): British Social
Attitudes Survey in, 46; caregiving and
LATs in, 32–33; civil partnerships in,
170n4; cohabitation in, 137; Duncan
and Philips survey in, 34–35; family
in, 33–34; family law in, 137, 158; gay
and lesbian LATs in, 181n8; gender
and LAT in, 57–58; interviews in,
37–38; Omnibus Survey in, 22–23, 34,
172n22; Third Age LATs in, 102, 185n11;
younger LATs in, 25–26
United States (US): caregiving in, 33;
cohabitation in, 48, 132–38; education
of LATs in, 24–25; elder caregiving in,
108; family law in, 85–86, 132, 133, 139–
52, 153–63; gay male LATs in, 78–96;
gender and LATs in, 57–67; interviewed LATs in, 37–38, 48–51, 178n18;

marriage in, 35; palimony claims in,
139–43; social surveys in, 37, 38–48,
60–67; Third Age LATs in, 103–7, 108
unjust enrichment, 132–33, 161, 199n12
Upton-Davis, Karen, 54, 76, 180n31

Viagra, 99

Weiner, Marcella Bakur, 99
widowers, 100–101, 103
wills: family law and, 133–34; gay male
LATs and, 85, 95; gender and, 72; LAT
finances and, 72, 85, 95, 112, 113, 133–34,
199n13; Third Age LATs and, 112, 113,
116
women, 4, 52–77; alimony and sexuality of, 152, 197n37; identity for, 28,
68; independence for, 7–8, 18–19, 28,
53–58, 68–69, 104, 106–7; postmenopausal, 99, 185n16; Third Age LATs
and, 106; women and LAT debate,
52–58, 74–77
women's movement, 57, 98, 121

younger LATs: age range of, 25; in
Germany, 26; interview with, 7–8; in
Italy, 26; overview of, 25–26; reasons
to live apart for, 25–26; in Spain, 26; in
UK, 25–26

# ABOUT THE AUTHORS

Cynthia Grant Bowman is the Dorothea S. Clarke Professor of Feminist Jurisprudence at Cornell Law School. A graduate of Swarthmore College, she has a PhD in political science from Columbia University and a JD from Northwestern University School of Law. She has published widely in diverse areas of family law and on other topics concerning law and gender.

David Eichert, author of chapter 5, is a PhD candidate in International Relations at the London School of Economics. He earned his JD from Cornell Law School and his MA in European and Mediterranean Studies from New York University.